SEVERED
STATES

SEVERED STATES

Dilemmas of Democracy in a Divided World

Robert K. Schaeffer

ROWMAN & LITTLEFIELD PUBLISHERS, INC.
Lanham • Boulder • New York • Oxford

ROWMAN & LITTLEFIELD PUBLISHERS, INC.

Published in the United States of America
by Rowman & Littlefield Publishers, Inc.
4720 Boston Way, Lanham, Maryland 20706

12 Hid's Copse Road
Cumnor Hill, Oxford OX2 9JJ, England

British Library Cataloguing in Publication Information Available

Library of Congress Cataloging-in-Publication Data

Schaeffer, Robert K.
    Severed states : dilemmas of democracy in a divided world / Robert
K. Schaeffer.
        p.   cm.
    Rev. ed. of: Warpaths : the politics of partition. 1990.
    Includes bibliographical references (p.   ) and index.
    ISBN 0-8476-9334-1 (cloth : alk. paper).—ISBN 0-8476-9335-X
(pbk. : alk. paper)
    1. World politics—1945– 2. Partition, Territorial. 3. Military
history, Modern—20th century. I. Schaeffer, Robert K. Warpaths.
II. Title.
    D842.S32   1999
    320.1′2′0904—dc21   98-55390
                                                                  CIP

Printed in the United States of America

⊗ ™ The paper used in this publication meets the minimum requirements of
American National Standard for Information Sciences—Permanence of Paper for
Printed Library Materials, ANSI/NISO Z39.48–1992.

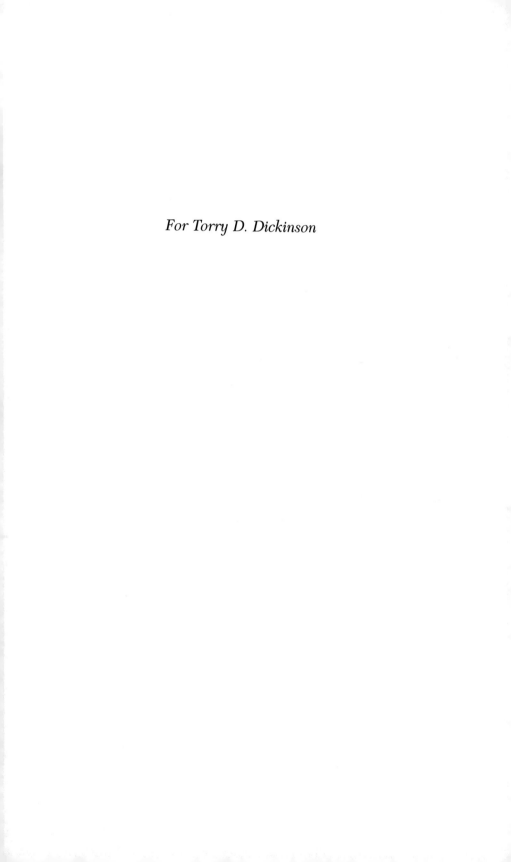

For Torry D. Dickinson

CONTENTS

ACKNOWLEDGMENTS

I became interested in partition while working as a journalist for Friends of the Earth in 1984. Tom Turner encouraged me to research and write an article on the problems associated with partition. This essay became the basis for *Warpaths: The Politics of Partition* (1990). Steve Wasserman and Paul Golob deserve credit for publishing and editing its first incarnation. Soon after it appeared, a number of other countries were partitioned. In 1996, Dean Birkenkamp asked me to revise the book to include contemporary partitions. He deserves credit for imagining its second incarnation.

This work benefited enormously from the contributions of others. Benedict Anderson reviewed my original outline and shared his ideas on nationalism in thoughtful correspondence and conversation. Omar Dahbour invited me to join him for a panel on nationalism in New York City. His work on self-determination gave me insights into the philosophical literature. Metta Spencer introduced me to Pugwash Conferences on Science and World Affairs, which in 1995 won the Nobel Peace Prize. The meetings of its working group on ethnic conflict gave me an opportunity to explore issues related to partition with scholars from around the world. Joseph Rotblat, Giovanni Brenciaglia, Francesco Colagero, and Metta Spencer have my thanks for sharing with me their passion for peace. Metta's invitation to a conference on the "Lessons of Yugoslavia" prompted me to undertake a detailed study of partition there. I am particularly grateful to Metta for her enthusiastic and determined support.

This work was based on research at libraries at the University of California at Berkeley, the University of Maine, the Catholic University of America, San Jose State University, and Kansas State University. The librarians at these institutions generously allowed me to mine their resources and secured innumerable books through interlibrary loan. My research was also assisted by travel and research grants from San Jose State.

Bob Gliner and Mike Otten have my thanks for their support and friendship at San Jose State. Joan Block deserves my thanks for her timely and pragmatic assistance.

From the outset, Torry Dickinson helped develop my ideas and think through difficult problems. She has my respect, admiration, and love.

INTRODUCTION

Partition is a common political practice. Since 1920, thirteen countries have been divided, resulting in the creation of thirty-seven successor states. Partition was supposed to solve difficult social and political problems. But it has regularly led to conflict and violence. War between successor states in Korea, Vietnam, India, Palestine, Yugoslavia, and the Soviet Union and continuing violence in Ireland and Cyprus show that partition has failed to create durable political solutions. Yet despite its sorry history, partition will no doubt be used to divide other countries in the near future. By examining the causes and consequences of partition around the world, this book will explain why partition is, in the words of Irish diplomat Conor Cruise O'Brien, "the expedient of the tired statesman."[1]

The history of partition in thirteen different countries is complicated. But it can be readily understood if their stories are told in groups. After World Wars I and II, Great Britain partitioned Ireland, India, and Palestine along ethnic lines, largely to solve problems associated with "decolonization," the withdrawal of British colonial rule and the transfer of power to competing independence movements in these colonies. Between 1945 and 1954, the United States and Soviet Union (together with some other "great powers") divided Korea, China, Vietnam, and Germany along secular ideological lines, principally to solve problems associated with the cold war. Partition enabled the superpowers to settle their disputes over the boundaries of emerging spheres of influence and secure states for their ideological allies along cold war frontiers. Pakistan was partitioned in 1971 and Cyprus in 1974. Both were partitioned along ethnic lines, with domestic groups and regional powers (India in Pakistan; Greece and Turkey in Cyprus) playing important roles. Then in 1991–1992, Yugoslavia, Ethiopia, the Soviet Union, and Czechoslovakia were divided along ethnic lines. The great powers played little if any role in the partition of these countries. Instead, they were divided by domestic forces, who saw partition as a way to solve problems associated with "democratization." Between 1920 and 1992, foreign powers and domestic forces have divided countries, along ethnic-religious and secular-ideological lines, for different reasons. But wherever partition occurred, political power was transferred and divided among competing social groups.

The argument here is that partition has been the by-product of different developments: decolonization, cold war, and democratization. But they should not be understood separately because each of these developments was associated with the emergence of a new interstate system during World War II.

During the war, Franklin D. Roosevelt and Joseph Stalin joined together, first to fight fascism and then to build a new interstate system. They wanted a "new world order" to replace the old "imperial" system because they both believed that the old order was responsible for the Great Depression and successive world wars. Roosevelt and Stalin used the principle of "self-determination," an idea derived from Woodrow Wilson and Vladimir Lenin, to justify their insistence on widespread decolonization after the war. By breaking up the empires of their enemies and then their allies, U.S. and Soviet leaders hoped to create independent nation-states that would become the building blocks, the constituent political units, of the new interstate system. And at a series of superpower summits during the war, they created the United Nations and World Bank as the institutional foundations of this new system. In the years that followed, empires disappeared and the number of independent states grew rapidly, from about fifty in 1945 to nearly two hundred today.

But while U.S. and Soviet leaders succeeded in creating a new world order, several problems attended its growth. First, decolonization was a difficult and protracted process, leading in some British, French, and Japanese colonies to decolonization and partition. Second, U.S.–Soviet cooperation was based on an agreement to create separate superpower spheres of influence. Although both agreed to recognize each other's spheres, disputes over the boundaries of emerging spheres led to a series of disagreements known collectively as the cold war. Efforts to define these spheres led to the partition of some countries along superpower frontiers. Third, the superpowers both moved to defend countries within their spheres from external threat and prevent countries from leaving their assigned sphere. So they installed or supported dictators in many states within their spheres, particularly in divided states along cold war frontiers. When dictators in both U.S. and Soviet spheres fell, a process that began in 1974 and ended twenty years later in 1994, "democratization" was also accompanied by division in Yugoslavia, Ethiopia, the Soviet Union, and Czecho-slovakia.

It is beyond the scope of this book to make a detailed examination of decolo-nization, the cold war, or democratization as global political developments. These are enormous subjects, each with vast literatures.[2] Instead, this book will concentrate on the partitions that accompanied these wider developments.

Partition occurred for various reasons in different countries. But a collective treatment of diverse partitions is warranted because partition everywhere led to three common problems, which frequently triggered violence and war.

First, partition prompted massive migrations across newly created borders, dividing families and disrupting economies. Tens of thousands fled across fron-tiers in Ireland and Cyprus; hundreds of thousands crossed changing borders in Palestine, Yugoslavia and the former Soviet Union; and millions surged across frontiers in Korea, China, Vietnam, Germany, and Bangladesh. In 1948, as many as seventeen million crossed Indo-Pakistani borders in the six months after partition, probably the largest, fastest migration in human history. Fear, violence, or, more recently, "ethnic cleansing" persuaded or forced people to emigrate en masse.

Yet despite threats, coercion, and violence, many people refused to leave, staying put on the "wrong" side of the border. The great postpartition migra-tions did not empty India of Moslems; as many Moslems remained in India as called Pakistan their new home. Of course, those who did not move to their assigned states became "minorities" in their homeland, a difficult transition be-cause many had previously belonged to a "majority" in undivided states. At the same time, people who had long been members of a "minority" became, after partition, part of the ruling majority in successor states. Not surprisingly, new majorities moved quickly to consolidate their power, which led to a second problem: discrimination.

After partition, government officials quickly created political institutions that discriminated against residual minorities, restricting their ability to estab-lish political parties or vote, observe their religions, practice their customs, speak their languages, or pursue their economic livelihoods. Governments fre-quently subjected minorities to arbitrary military rule or paramilitary disci-pline. Multiple discriminations disenfranchised residential minorities and compromised the meaning of citizenship in divided states. Understandably, disenfranchised groups resisted these developments. But their efforts to re-claim lost rights frequently triggered conflict and uncivil wars within divided states.

Third, partition created border disputes between successor states and joined them in conflicts over their sovereign rights. Government officials regularly contested the boundaries set by partition and challenged their legitimacy, particularly when lines were drawn by foreign powers. Many adopted constitutions that asserted sovereignty over territories held by their neighbors or tried to deny their claim to sovereignty as a state. Disputes and denials made it difficult for successor states to exercise their authority or obtain international recognition. Naturally, the governments of divided states resented and resisted efforts that compromised their sovereignty, and they frequently asserted their rights by force, leading to war between divided states. These interstate wars often prompted foreign intervention, particularly by great power partitioners. When foreign powers intervened, they sometimes deployed conventional armies or threatened to use nuclear weapons against their adversaries. This latter practice contributed to the proliferation of nuclear weapons because the governments of countries threatened with nuclear destruction often decided that the only way to deter such threats would be to obtain nuclear arms of their own, an alarming development given their ongoing conflicts with their neighbors.

Of course, partition did not create identical problems everywhere or always and inevitably lead to war. Conflicts between the two Germanys and the two Chinas never led to war, though partition contributed to "crises" over Berlin and to crises over Quemoy and Matsu, the islands between China and Taiwan. Relations between Bangladesh and Pakistan were normalized a few years after partition, though these successor states were also separated from each other by India. Parts of Yugoslavia and the Soviet Union separated without violence and have established relatively amicable relations with neighboring states, though some successor states of Yugoslavia and the Soviet Union have been consumed by violence. Partition in Czechoslovakia has frequently been described as a "velvet divorce," a peaceful separation. But it is the exception to the general rule. And although violence has been absent in some instances, for reasons that will be explored, conflict within and between divided states has not been routinely avoided.

The conflicts associated with partition make it a highly charged subject matter. For people in divided states, partition evokes strong emotions and deep sympathies. This makes it difficult to perform even routine tasks, such as naming the places involved. Officials from the People's Republic of China object violently whenever the "Republic of China" is used to refer to the offshore island of Taiwan because they regard it as an illegitimate regime. The government in

Taiwan takes the same view. In the Middle East, a war of words is waged over the names used to describe the lands originally assigned to British Palestine: Israel, Greater Israel, the occupied territories, and Palestine.

The problem of names is complicated by the fact that the names of some divided states have changed over time or the meaning of an assumed name has changed. For example, the post-partition state in southern Ireland has had three names: the Irish Free State (1920), Eire (1937), and the Republic of Ireland (1956). Pakistan has had two names: Pakistan (1948) and the Islamic Republic of Pakistan (1956). But while the latter name has remained the same since then, its *meaning* changed in 1972, when the country was partitioned and a new state—Bangladesh—was created in western Pakistan. So the Islamic Republic of Pakistan today refers to a place that is fundamentally different from what it once was. Names are a problem because partition makes an issue of "nation" and "state." At stake is the meaning of citizenship and sovereignty.

To simplify matters for readers who may be unfamiliar with the political baggage names may carry, this book adopts a generic approach to naming. Throughout the text, reference will be made to the geographic location of divided states—North and South Korea, North and South Vietnam, East and West Germany, Northern Ireland and Ireland—or to their commonplace English names: China and Taiwan, India and Pakistan, Ethiopia and Eritrea. In Yugoslavia, the Soviet Union and Czechoslovakia, individual successor states will be identified by their common names—Slovenia, Russia, Slovakia—and they will be described collectively as states of the former Yugoslavia or the former Soviet Union. Palestine presents a particular problem. Before partition it will be referred to as Palestine. After 1948 it will be called either Israel, which refers to the territory of the Jewish state, or Israeli-occupied Palestine, which describes areas controlled but not annexed by Israel (the West Bank and Gaza). Jerusalem will be called just that. Although these choices may not be wholly satisfactory, they are designed to recognize that names, and the definition of citizenship and sovereignty that are implicit in them, are contentious issues and then to provide a way to move on.

Another important choice made in this book is the decision to restrict the study of partition to thirteen countries in this century. Other scholars have suggested that the separation of Sweden and Norway or the breakup of the Austro-Hungarian and Ottoman Empires be included in the study of partition.[3] But I have not done so because an examination of Sweden and Austria-Hungary would require a discussion of dynastic states and dual monarchies, which have frequently been subject to consolidation and disintegration as a matter of routine diplomacy. I think that the division and dissolution of monarchies (and their constituent parts) belongs elsewhere, though the partition of successor states in Austria, Czechoslovakia, and Yugoslavia is treated here. Likewise, when the Ottoman Empire broke up, most of its territories were absorbed as colonies or mandates by other imperial powers: Great Britain and France. This practice, too, was routine among imperial powers, and it deserves treatment elsewhere, though the partition of British-mandated Palestine is examined here. In all three cases, the causes and consequences of division and dissolution differ substantially from the partition of states covered here. This book examines places where political power was not merely redistributed between great powers but transferred to and divided between indigenous successors. The simultaneous devolution and division of power is what defines my use of the term *partition*.

In most cases, partition resulted in the creation of two or more successor states. But in Ireland, Palestine, and Cyprus, only one successor state emerged. In Ireland, partition created a state in the south that slowly became independent of Great Britain. The northern region remained part of Britain, though for many years its parliament was largely responsible for managing the province. In both north and south, the meanings of *independence* and of *state* have changed over time, and these meanings are on the verge of changing again. But partition remains a central political reality for each.

In Palestine, the 1947 UN partition plan provided for two successor states. But the war that followed the British withdrawal in 1948 resulted in the creation of a single, Jewish state in much of Palestine, without a counterpart Arab state. Some of the residual lands were claimed, for a time, by neighboring Jordan and Egypt. After the 1967 war, Israel occupied these residual territories and annexed some of them (Jerusalem), though the status of these lands remains the subject of intense local and international debate. The fact that partition did not produce two successor states and that the status of territories in the region is still indeterminate should not preclude it from a discussion of partition.

In Cyprus, a coup supported by Greece and directed at the Makarios government in 1974 triggered invasion by Turkey, which occupied the northern half of the island. Although a government has been established in "North Kibris," as it is called, it is wholly a creation of the Turkish government and no other country recognizes it as an independent state. As such, it is rather like Northern Ireland, the province of an across-the-channel state. As in Ireland, partition in Cyprus created one successor state, not two.

As a history of partition, this book is about the past. But because partition will almost certainly occur again—perhaps in Canada or Sri Lanka, Italy or Iraq, Israel or Burma—it is also a "history" of the future. My analysis of the past indicates that partition was less of a solution and more of a problem than diplomats, scholars, and politicians have been willing to recognize. If past experience were an accurate compass, one would expect future partitions to be as problematic as those in the past. But as a guide, the past is useful only up to a point, in part because the character of partition is changing.

For many years, partition is what powerful states did to weak ones. Today, one might say that partition is what weak states do to themselves. If the character of partition is changing—from something done by others to something done to oneself—then it may be difficult to predict the particular social outcomes of partition in the future. This point does not mean that past experience is useless but that future developments will not occur *only* as they have in the past.

This book represents a second intervention into the ongoing history of partition. I first became interested in partition in 1985 and completed *Warpaths: The Politics of Partition* in 1989. This history of great power partitions appeared just before another set of countries were divided by domestic forces in 1991–1992. These developments prompted me to take a second look at partition. This book recounts the analysis of partition from the first book and joins it with an examination of partitions in the 1990s and a discussion of movements that would partition other countries around the world. Because partition is an ongoing phenomenon and an enduring problem, I will likely return to it again in the future.

This book begins by examining the new interstate system that emerged during World War II. Chapter 1 explains why U.S. and Soviet leaders wanted to replace the old imperial system, how they used the idea of self-determination and the practice of decolonization to build a new system, and how problems associated with this enterprise led in some places to partition.

Chapters 2 and 3 look at British partition in Ireland, India, and Palestine, which divided former colonies along ethnic lines. Partition in these countries was a by-product of decolonization after World Wars I and II. Chapter 4 analyzes partitions in Korea, China, Vietnam, and Germany. In these countries, the United States and Soviet Union used partition to settle disputes related to the cold war and emerging spheres of influence.

Although the course of great power partition varied, it produced common problems in each of the divided states. Chapter 5 surveys the problems associated with massive cross-border migrations and the discriminatory policies adopted by divided states, policies that disenfranchised residual minority populations and compromised the meaning of citizenship. Chapter 6 reviews the ways that states contested the legitimacy of partition and attempted to abridge the sovereignty of their neighbors. These developments contributed to social conflict within and war between divided states. The eruption of civil and conventional wars, superpower intervention and nuclear threats, and the proliferation of nuclear weapons in divided states is examined in Chapter 7.

After this study of postwar, great-power partitions, we turn to more recent events. Chapter 8 examines the partitions of Pakistan and Cyprus, where regional powers played important roles. Chapter 9 looks at democratization and division in Yugoslavia, Ethiopia, the Soviet Union, and Czechoslovakia.

The last chapter faces the future of partition, not its past. It examines movements that would divide states to fulfill their demand for self-determination and looks at efforts that might solve or prevent problems related to partition.

NOTES

1. This quote is taken from Conor Cruise O'Brien in 1958, speaking as the ambassador of the Republic of Ireland to the United Nations during a UN debate about the future of Cyprus. Quoted in Stephen George Xydis, *Cyprus: Conflict and Conciliation, 1954–1958* (Columbus: Ohio State University Press, 1967), 405.

2. See, for example, my contribution to the literature on democratization: Robert K. Schaeffer, *Power to the People: Democratization Around the World* (Boulder, Colo.: Westview, 1997).

3. See Jane Jacobs, *The Question of Separatism: Quebec and the Struggle over Sovereignty* (New York: Random House, 1980).

O N E

A NEW WORLD ORDER

During World War II, American and Soviet leaders created a new world order. It was both a great success and a significant failure. As allies, the United States and Soviet Union successfully brought an end to centuries of colonialism. But as rivals, they started a decades-long cold war. While the new world order they created grew large and survived their mutual animosity, problems associated with decolonization and cold war led, in some countries, to partition.

The United States and Soviet Union became partners and rivals in 1941, after Axis powers launched surprise attacks on the two great republics. The German invasion in June and the Japanese assault in December joined the Soviet Union and United States as military allies. The expansion of war also persuaded President Franklin D. Roosevelt and Premier Joseph Stalin to prevent world war in the future. They could work together to wage and then prevent war because they agreed on the cause of war. Roosevelt and Stalin both believed that "colonialism" was to blame for World War II and for the Great Depression that preceded it.[1] Roosevelt thought that the competition for overseas colonies brought rival European and Asian empires into political conflict, while their exclusionary economic policies triggered economic turmoil. Because he held that colonialism was responsible for political and economic conflict, Roosevelt concluded that "the colonial system means war."[2]

Roosevelt was determined to see that colonialism would not survive war's end. "When we've won the war," he promised, "I will work with all my might and main to see to it that the United States is not wheedled into the position of accepting any plan that will further France's imperialistic ambitions, or that will aid and abet the British Empire in its imperial ambitions."[3] Stalin, who had long inveighed against imperialism, wholeheartedly concurred with Roosevelt.

Based on a shared opposition to imperialism, Roosevelt and Stalin agreed that the old colonial system should be dismantled and a new world order, based not on "empire" but on "republics" like themselves, should be established in its place. Their design for a new world order would be based on ideas and institutions derived from their predecessors: Woodrow Wilson and Vladimir Lenin.

The ideas used to develop a new world order after World War II were first advanced during World War I by Wilson and Lenin. They seem an unlikely pair. Wilson was a reformist Democrat and Lenin a revolutionary socialist. Wilson was applauded as a peacemaker for bringing the United States *into* war (he was awarded the Nobel Peace Prize in 1919), whereas Lenin was condemned as a spoiler for taking Russia *out* of war before its conclusion. But despite their many differences, both practiced what some historians have called a "New Diplomacy."[4] This diplomacy was based on an opposition to colonialism and "balance of power" politics, which in Wilson's view "had never produced anything but aggression, egotism and war."[5] And it was based on support for the idea of "self-determination."

Self-determination was a term first used by the socialist movement in the late nineteenth century. The Second International, meeting in London in 1896, declared, "[The International] stands for the full right of all nations to self-determination," which it rendered in German *Selbstbestimmungsrecht.*[6] But the word was popularized by Wilson, who argued that "all nations have a right to self-determination" and insisted that language upholding self-determination as a principle be inserted into the League of Nation's Covenant.[7] Lenin, meanwhile, argued that "the self-determination of nations means the separation of [national movements] from alien national bodies, and the formation of an independent national state."[8]

Wilson and Lenin believed that self-determination would permit oppressed peoples or "nations" to secede from colonial empires. Once they achieved their independence, Wilson and Lenin expected these nations to establish "republics" based on constitutional law and representative political institutions. These sovereign republics would then meet as equals with other independent states, establishing a new set of relations among states. As Wilson said, "The equality of nations upon which peace must be founded, if it is to last, must be an equality of rights."[9] A system of self-governing states, based on the principle of self-determination, would replace what Wilson called the "balance of power" politics practiced by colonial empires. In its place, he envisioned a new diplomacy based on "a league of power, a universal organized peace instead of organized rivalries."[10]

In this period, *self-determination* was synonymous with *decolonization*, the separation of colony from empire. Wilson did not believe that the right of self-determination should be extended to peoples within self-governing states. Indeed, a League of Nations commission concluded in 1921:

> To concede to minorities either of language or religion . . . the right of withdrawing from the community to which they belong . . . would be to destroy order and stability within states, to inaugurate anarchy in international life. It would be to uphold a theory incompatible with the very idea of the state as a territorial or political entity.[11]

Of course, when self-determination was established as an international principle after World War II, it was difficult to insist that it apply only to colonies and not also to nations within independent states. Robert Lansing, Wilson's secretary of state, warned that self-determination might be taken to mean the right to secede from sovereign states. In a confidential memo in 1918, Lansing argued that "the phrase [*self-determination*] is simply loaded with dynamite. It will raise hopes that can never be realized."[12]

Eventually, self-determination acquired this wider meaning, despite efforts to limit its application. Ironically, it would be used by groups in Soviet republics, who insisted on their right to secede as provided by the Soviet constitution. This right had been written into the constitution by early Bolsheviks, who argued that "the peoples of Russia" had a right to self-determination, "even to the point of separation and the formation of an independent state."[13] They never imagined that anyone would ever claim or exercise this right.

Although Wilson and Lenin agreed on the need for self-determination, they founded different organizations to promote decolonization. Wilson's League of Nations and Lenin's Communist International (Comintern), which were both founded in 1919, were designed to promote decolonization and establish a new world order based on sovereign states. Wilson, of course, hoped the League would promote reform, while Lenin expected the International to foment revolution. The League, which in 1934 had sixty members, met regularly in Geneva during the interwar period, though it collapsed in 1939 and was formally dissolved in 1946. The Comintern met regularly during the early 1920s, but after Lenin died in 1924, Stalin convened it infrequently.[14] He dissolved it, without consulting its members, in 1943, at President Roosevelt's request. Although both institutions survived the death of their founders, little came of either ef-

fort. Both succumbed because empires were still too strong, and the great republics and independence movements in the colonies too weak, to effect real
change. That would come only after World War II.

The League and Comintern failed for several reasons. First, European and
Asian empires resisted calls for self-determination in their colonies. One British minister insisted that "it may take generations or even *centuries* for the peoples in some parts of the colonies to achieve self-government [emphasis
added]."[15] At the 1918 Versailles Peace Conference, British and French leaders
were able to rebuff Wilson's call for widespread decolonization because they
had just won smashing electoral victories, while Wilson's position was undermined by disappointing elections in midterm congressional elections. Prime
Minister David Lloyd George of Britain and Premier Georges Clemenceau of
France were able not only to force Wilson to concede on the terms of the treaty
with Germany but also to enlarge their own empires with colonies and territories taken from German and Ottoman empires. As a result, the extent of the
world's territory under European colonial rule reached an all-time high.[16] Only
Ireland was allowed to depart from empire.

Second, the League and Comintern faltered because domestic politicians in
the great republics were not ready to support them. Wilson failed to secure
Senate approval for U.S. participation in the League. Then in 1920, Warren G.
Harding and isolationist Republicans swept into power, defeating James M.
Cox and his young running mate Franklin D. Roosevelt, who had supported
U.S. entry into the League. When Roosevelt later sought his party's presiden-
tial nomination in 1932, he repudiated his earlier support for the League to
secure William Randolph Hearst's newspaper endorsements. "The League,"
Roosevelt recanted, "was not in accord with fundamental American ideals."[17]
Isolationist domestic sentiment reduced U.S. demands for self-determination
to a whisper.

In the Soviet Union, Stalin, who bested Leon Trotsky in the battle for power
that followed Lenin's death, retreated from internationalism. The failure of
revolutions in Europe after World War I convinced Stalin that "there is no revolutionary movement in the West" and that the Comintern was useless as an
instrument of revolution.[18] For Stalin, the Comintern's only purpose would be
to defend the Soviet Union and its attempt to build socialism in one state. As
he subordinated the Comintern to the foreign policy needs of the Soviet state,
self-determination was no longer emphasized, in part because it encouraged
communist parties in other countries to imagine themselves as being indepen-

dent from the Soviet communist party, which Stalin would not allow.[19] As a result of Soviet isolationism, calls for self-determination were silenced.[20]

Still, the idea of self-determination gained widespread currency in the colonies. Before the war, movements had demanded only limited kinds of "home rule" or partial self-government. Before the war, for example, the Indian National Congress promised "unswerving loyalty to the British Crown."[21] But in the 1920s, encouraged by Wilson and Lenin's call for self-determination, Congress leaders demanded more, arguing that Britain should "Quit India" entirely.

The movements that emerged in the colonies to demand self-determination—or what they called *swaraj* in India, *doc lap* in Vietnam, and *sinparam* in Korea—found it difficult to make much headway.[22] British and French officials introduced reforms designed to placate and divide independence movements. Soviet leaders demanded that communist parties belonging to the Comintern mute their calls for revolution and adopt more modest goals.[23] Rivalry between movements—Indian National Congress versus Muslim League in India, and nationalists versus communists in China, Indonesia, Korea, and Vietnam—made it difficult to cooperate on joint strategies. The expansion of Japanese, Italian, and German empires in the 1930s and early 1940s compounded movement difficulties. Axis expansion subjected them to new masters, sometimes even to two sets of colonial overlords. In Vietnam, for example, the Viet Minh confronted not only Japanese occupying forces but also French colonial collaborators.

As a result of these developments, Wilson and Lenin's calls for self-determination and decolonization went unheeded during the interwar years. European and Asian empires turned a deaf ear to demands for change. The great republics became silent. And independence movements could not make themselves heard. This would eventually change during World War II, when demands for self-determination again found voice.

The latent anticolonialism of the great republics revived during World War II. U.S. and Soviet leaders renewed their predecessors' call for self-determination and promised to dismantle the colonial system. "The age of imperialism has ended," Undersecretary of State Sumner Wells declared in 1942.[24] They were determined to create a new world order or "interstate system" based on independent republics. "There are 1,100,000,000 brown people," Roosevelt observed. "In many Eastern countries, they are ruled by a handful of whites and they resent it. Our goal must be to help them achieve independence."[25]

To promote self-determination and construct a new set of relations among states, U.S. officials took several steps. They first decided that the United States should assume plenipotentiary or supersovereign powers to deal with wartime crisis. They then invited the other great powers—the Soviet Union, Great Britain, and sometimes Free France and Nationalist China—to participate in deliberations about the postwar world. At a series of summit meetings convened during the war—in Newfoundland, Cairo, Teheran, Yalta, and Potsdam—the executive committee of the "great powers" or, after 1944, the "superpowers" defined the principles and designed the institutions of the new interstate system.[26] They then invited other members of the "United Nations," which had signed Roosevelt's Atlantic Charter during the war, to ratify summit agreements at the United Nations' first general meeting in San Francisco in June 1945.[27] In their capacity as superpowers, the United States, Soviet Union, and Great Britain reserved for themselves important rights, such as permanent seats and veto power in the UN Security Council, that were not available to others.

Of course, it was an act of hubris to assert, as U.S. leaders did, that "in this global war there is literally no question, political or military, in which the United States is *not* interested" or to insist, as Stalin did, "that the large powers must dictate to the small."[28] But they did so in any event.

Having assumed constitutional powers, the United States and its superpower partners charged the United Nations with the responsibility for preventing a recurrence of war and Bretton Woods, which established the World Bank and International Monetary Fund (both were associated with the United Nations), with responsibility for preventing economic depression. Furthermore, the United States and Soviet Union insisted that members agree that participation in these institutions be "based on respect for the principle of equal rights and self-determination of peoples."[29] U.S. and Soviet leaders would then use decolonization, based on the principle of self-determination, as the way to dismantle the old colonial system and build a new republican one.

U.S. and Soviet leaders began by breaking up the empires of their wartime enemies. They not only liberated countries conquered *during* the war but deprived Axis power of lands they had acquired *before* the war. They detached Austria and Czechoslovakia from Germany; Tunisia, Libya, Somalia, Eritrea, and Ethiopia from Italy; and Taiwan, Manchuria, and Korea from Japan. At wartime summits, British and French leaders agreed to decolonize Axis empires, which they viewed as competitors. But they strenuously resisted calls for decolonizing their empires.[30] In one outburst at Yalta, Prime Minister Winston Churchill said he would never "consent to forty or fifty nations thrusting interfering fingers into the life's existence of the British empire," adding, "No one will induce me . . . to let any representatives of Great Britain to go to a conference where they will be placed in a dock and asked to justify our right to live in a world we have tried to save."[31] But this, of course, was exactly what U.S. and Soviet diplomats had in mind. After dispatching Axis empires, they soon turned their anticolonial guns on Allied empires.

At the United Nations, U.S. and Soviet diplomats authorized special commissions to investigate colonial conditions.[32] Colonial movements were encouraged to proffer petitions for independence to the General Assembly, which demanded that empires submit political information and fix time tables for eventual independence.[33]

When they had signed the UN Charter, the European colonial powers had agreed in Article 73 only to promise eventual "self-government," not "independence." But the anticolonial block in the United Nations soon revised the language and shifted the emphasis from "self-government" to "independence," a significant linguistic coup.[34] Churchill's fears were soon realized, as Britain and other colonial powers were placed "in a dock" by the United Nations and "asked to justify" continued colonial rule.

Naturally, the colonial powers objected to this treatment by their great republican allies. French leader Charles de Gaulle complained, "Roosevelt expected that the crowd of small nations would assault the position of the colonial power and assure the United States of an enormous political and economic clientele."[35] And Churchill complained that U.S. insistence on the extension of a permanent seat on the UN Security Council to China amounted to the creation of a "faggot vote" because he expected the Chinese republic to side with the United States "in an attempt to liquidate the British overseas empire."[36]

De Gaulle and Churchill correctly assessed the temper and direction of U.S. and Soviet policy, which was to dissolve empires and establish "a crowd" of independent republics as the constituent political units of the new interstate system. After the war, European empires could no longer avoid decolonization, they could only defer it.

Colonialism could not survive in the postwar environment for three reasons. First, the war had weakened and wrecked European colonial powers. Most of them had been crushed and occupied by German and Japanese forces during the war, a humiliation from which they never recovered. As de Gaulle observed, "In the Second World War, all the nations of Europe lost. Two were defeated."[37] Although Britain was not overrun in Europe, it capitulated to Japan in some southeast Asian colonies. And it, too, was crippled by war. As one member of parliament observed at war's end, "We are sitting here today as representatives of a victorious people, discussing the economic consequences of victory. [But] if a visitor were to come . . . from Mars, he might well be pardoned for thinking he was listening to the representatives of a vanquished people discussing the economic penalties of defeat."[38]

Military and economic weakness made the empires heavily dependent on U.S. aid for their survival. U.S. officials used their dependence on Lend-Lease aid, postwar loans, and Marshall Plan funds to wrest concessions from them. With each successive economic crisis, the colonial powers surrendered colonies and transferred their authority to the United States as payment for their debts.[39]

European colonies decolonized for a second reason: the United States and Soviet Union insisted on it. They pressed for decolonization *even after* cold war disputes divided the superpowers on other issues. Indeed, the great wave of decolonization (twenty-six countries in Africa and Asia gained their independence between 1956 and 1960) occurred during the height of the cold war.[40] The United States and Soviet Union never abandoned their mutual commitment to decolonization or quit the United Nations. Not only were they determined to end colonialism, but they possessed the means to destroy it. They were able to use their overwhelming economic and military powers to political advantage in the United Nations because they controlled its admission process. By limiting membership, more or less, to independent states, which allowed vast European empires only single votes, U.S. officials created a United Nations in which the United States and its republican allies outnumbered imperial states and their allies by a two-to-one margin.[41]

Of the fifty countries represented in San Francisco, thirty-three could be counted as republics, sixteen as governments representing European empires and colonies, and the rest as independent monarchies such as Luxembourg and Saudi Arabia. The domination of republican states, which provided the United States and Soviet Union with a working majority on issues related to decolonization, grew stronger over time as former colonies joined the United Nations. By 1960, UN membership had doubled, and the vast majority of new entrants were republics.[42] As the crowd of republics grew larger, their call for decolonization grew louder.

Finally, colonialism collapsed because independence movements had spread throughout the colonial world. Independence movements were first organized in the late nineteenth and early twentieth centuries. The Indian National Congress was founded in 1885, the Zionist movement in 1896, Ireland's

Sinn Fein in 1905, the Arab National Congress in 1913, a variety of Korean movements in 1919, the Chinese Communist Party in 1921, the Chinese Nationalist Party in 1922, and the Vietnamese Communist Party in 1925–1930.[43] After World War II, they were joined by movements across southeast Asia and Africa. Although the empires tried to deflect and divide these movements with partial and selective reforms, movements became more determined, some even making revolutions to secure their independence. The British governor-general's unilateral declaration of war against Germany on India's behalf, made without consulting Indian representatives, persuaded the Indian National Congress to launch a "noncooperation" campaign during World War II. The assassination of British minister of state Lord Moyne by Zionist irregulars in 1944 and the bombing of the King David Hotel in Jerusalem in 1946, the guerrilla uprising by the Viet Minh in Vietnam during World War II, and the Indonesian uprising in 1945 all demonstrated that independence movements could make serious trouble and impose significant costs on imperial governments.[44] As Muslim League leader Ali Jinnah said of "direct action" in India, "We have forged a pistol and are in a position to use it."[45] Although movements did not always fire their "pistols" in the postwar period, colonial authorities regarded independence movements everywhere as potentially armed and dangerous.

European empires often acted when violence became imminent, granting independence first to colonies where the threat or reality of violence was most acute: British Ireland after World War I, India in 1947, Burma and Ceylon in 1948, Palestine in 1948, Dutch Indonesia in 1949, and French Indochina in 1954. Independence for these colonies in turn contributed to pressure for independence elsewhere because leaders of postcolonial states in India, Vietnam, and Indonesia organized efforts to promote independence and, later, nonalignment.

The new republican interstate system that emerged after World War II differed in important respects from its imperial predecessor.[46] First, it dramatically increased the number of constituent states. From fifty in 1945, the number of member states doubled by 1960, tripled by 1990, and will nearly quadruple by the end of the century. Second, member states were much more homogeneous politically than their predecessors. Most regarded themselves as "republics."[47] Gone were states with diverse and complex sovereignties. Third, most states adopted "developmentalist" economic policies. Finally, this republican and developmentalist system discouraged the unilateral political and economic behavior that characterized the "balance of power" diplomacy and exclusionary economic behavior of the colonial system, promoting instead collective security and economic interdependence.

The construction of a new interstate system, which brought an end to colonialism, was a significant achievement. For U.S. and Soviet leaders, it realized long-held objectives. But problems associated with the decolonization process, with superpower relations, and with political structures in postcolonial states soon appeared. In some places, efforts to address these three problems led to partition.

Decolonization was a difficult, sometimes violent, and protracted process. European empires were reluctant to grant independence. Their evasions and delays frustrated popular aspirations in their colonies and persuaded some movements to force the issue. Violence, insurgency and military revolt in Algeria, Congo, Cyprus, Egypt, India, Indonesia, Kenya, Mozambique, Malaysia, Palestine, Rhodesia, and Vietnam preceded, accompanied, and followed decolonization. Although decolonization did not take "generations or even centuries" as some colonial authorities imagined, it still took decades, from 1945 to 1965. Even then, after most European empires had surrendered their colonies, holdouts such as Portugal remained. The dictatorship there clung to its African colonies until 1974, when guerrilla movements in Angola, Guinea-Bissau, and Mozambique and a revolt by leftist army officers in Portugal combined to overthrow the dictatorship, establish democracy in Portugal, and grant independence to the colonies.[48] Decolonization in Angola and Mozambique did not end matters but simply recast them. Struggles over political power in postcolonial states led to civil war, the creation of single-party regimes, and military intervention by foreign powers, which continued for another twenty years.[49]

In other postcolonial states, dictators and one-party regimes seized power, and successive revolts and coups became common. The dictators who took power then subverted the constitutional provisions and representative institutions bequeathed to them by independence movements and colonial powers. Although they continued to identify themselves as "republics," its meaning was corrupted. In some places, governments invaded and annexed neighboring territories and peoples not assigned to them by retiring colonial authorities or emerging superpowers. Indonesia invaded and annexed western New Guinea in 1962 and later invaded East Timor in 1975–1976. India forcibly incorporated princely states such as Hyderabad and Kashmir, which triggered war with Pakistan, and invaded Portuguese Goa, Daman, and Diu in 1961. Ethiopia incorporated Eritrea in 1962. The problems associated with protracted decolonization are too vast to examine in detail. But one problem deserves attention. In some places, particularly in British colonies where competing independence movements sought power on their terms, decolonization led to partition. This is what occurred in Ireland, India, and Palestine, the subject of the next chapter.

Wartime cooperation made it possible for the United States and Soviet Union to build a new interstate system. But superpower relations soon soured, leading to a second important problem: cold war.

Cooperation between Roosevelt and Stalin was based on a shared determination to end colonialism. It was also based on an agreement to divide the postwar world into U.S. and Soviet spheres of influence, though they sometimes denied that this was their intent. As Roosevelt told Churchill, "We must be careful to make it clear that we are not establishing any postwar spheres of influence."[50] And Churchill warned Stalin to describe "in diplomatic terms" a British-Soviet agreement on Balkan spheres. "[Do not] use the phrase 'dividing into spheres' because the Americans might be shocked."[51] Nonetheless, U.S. and Soviet leaders agreed to divide the world into spheres and recognize each other's authority in them because they wanted to preserve traditional diplomatic rights and consolidate hard-won military gains.

U.S. officials wanted to preserve rights given by the 1823 Monroe Doctrine, which had been designed to permit U.S. intervention in Latin America but prevent intervention in the region by European colonial powers, long a cornerstone of U.S. foreign policy. They worried that the U.S. Senate would not approve U.S. participation in the United Nations unless they could obtain recognition for the Monroe Doctrine, and they wanted to extend it to lands occupied by U.S. forces during the war.[52]

For his part, Stalin was willing to recognize U.S. Monroe Doctrine privileges in Latin America, Western Europe, and Japan, so long as Roosevelt reciprocated and recognized Soviet authority in Eastern Europe. "This war is not as in the past," Stalin argued. "Whoever occupies a territory also imposes on it his own social system," as far "as his army can reach."[53] By giving the United States a free hand in the administration of countries it had occupied during the war, Stalin was able to secure a free hand in Poland and much of Eastern Europe after the war. "Stalin shrewdly compared Soviet hegemony in Eastern Europe to Western dominance in Italy, France, Greece, and Japan," historian T. E. Vadney has argued. "Because Italy had surrendered first, in September 1943, the [U.S.] occupation and administration of the south provided the precedents for Stalin's position [on Poland and Eastern Europe] at Yalta."[54]

At wartime summits, the superpowers agreed to establish spheres of influence, and they placed this agreement *outside* UN consideration. At the UN's inaugural conference, Senator Arthur Vandenberg and Nelson Rockefeller, then a young assistant secretary of state, drafted articles recognizing the Monroe Doctrine and permitting the creation of political and military blocks outside UN authority. "We have preserved the Monroe Doctrine," Senator Vandenberg explained.[55] The adoption of Articles 51, 52, and 53 effectively recognized superpower spheres of influence and allowed the United States and Soviet Union to organize regional military, political, and economic alliances (such as the North Atlantic Treaty Organization and the Warsaw Pact) to maintain these spheres.

Roosevelt and Stalin agreed to divide the postwar world. But they did not carefully demarcate the boundaries of these spheres, deferring a final determination until war's end. By then, it was too late. U.S. and Soviet leaders soon began quarreling over the boundaries between emerging spheres, and they could not easily agree where boundaries fell. As Secretary of State John Foster Dulles explained, "There is a great attraction to this idea that we draw a line and say, 'If you cross this line, you get hit,' Well, we found that it was almost impossible to draw a line in terms of concrete, specific places and to say, 'this is it' and nothing else is it."[56] As each attempted to claim and expand their spheres and fix the boundaries between them, superpower relations deteriorated. Their disputes and disagreements over spheres of influence became known collectively as the "cold war."

The problems related to the cold war are many and complex. But the superpowers frequently adopted a common solution to some of their disputes. In some countries, partition would be a way for the superpowers to settle conflicts and fix boundaries along cold war frontiers in Germany, Korea, China, and Vietnam.

The division of the world into U.S. and Soviet spheres, and the partition of some countries along cold war frontiers, contributed to a third problem: dictatorship. Soon after World War II, the Soviets and then the Americans began installing one-party regimes or supporting military dictators in many of the new republics.[57] They did so because they believed that dictatorships could better secure borders against external, superpower threat, adopt domestic programs consistent with superpower policy, and suppress internal dissent. This last point was a major concern because people in many countries objected to having their foreign and domestic policy made by others. They were also determined to prevent countries from leaving their assigned superpower sphere.

Early on, some of the new republics objected to sphere of influence politics and exited superpower spheres. In 1948, Communist leader Josip Broz Tito

broke with Stalin and took Yugoslavia out of the Soviet sphere in Eastern Europe. After a coup overthrew the Egyptian monarchy in 1952, Gamal Abdel
Nasser took Egypt out of the U.S. sphere and into the Soviet sphere. And
Prime Minister Jawaharlal Nehru of India announced that "we will not attach
ourselves to any particular [superpower] group" and said he would stop "trying
to align ourselves with this great power or that and becoming its camp followers
in the hope that some crumbs might fall from their table."[58]

Tito, Nasser, and Nehru joined together and urged others to detach themselves from superpower spheres and adopt what they called "nonalignment."
Their call for nonaligned foreign policies at the 1955 Bandung Conference in
Indonesia, and at subsequent summits of "third world" countries, met with
some success.[59] Participation in non-aligned movement meetings grew from
twenty-nine countries in 1955 to forty-seven in 1964, fifty-three in 1970, and
eighty-five in 1976.[60]

Both superpowers objected to this development. In 1956, Secretary of State
Dulles denounced Indian "neutralism," as he called nonalignment, arguing
that it "pretends that a nation can best gain safety for itself by being indifferent
to the fate of others. This has become an obsolete conception and, except
under very exceptional circumstances, it is an immoral and short-sighted conception."[61]

The Soviets agreed with Dulles: "Neutralism, or the idea that these new
states could be a 'third force' between the two sides, was a rotten idea that only
served the interests of imperialism."[62]

The superpowers were determined to prevent countries from defecting
across cold war frontiers, which had been so difficult to demarcate. This fear
persuaded them to support dictators in decolonized and in divided states. In
the thirty years after World War II, the United States provided more than $70
billion in military aid to allied dictators; the Soviets furnished nearly $30 billion
to client regimes.[63]

Cold war dictatorships compromised the meaning of democracy in the new
republics. They commonly adopted language, education, and military policies
designed to create singular "national" identities. In multiethnic states, these
nation-building policies effectively discriminated against minority populations
and frequently roused them to fury. In Pakistan and Cyprus, ethnic groups that
were assaulted by dictatorships fought back, and their efforts led to partition
by regional powers: India and Turkey. Between 1974 and 1994, when the dictatorships that had been established during the early years of the cold war finally

fell, problems associated with democratization in Yugoslavia, Ethiopia, the Soviet Union, and Czechoslovakia would also lead to partition.

When European empires surrendered their colonies, they generally turned
over colonial lands and peoples to independence movements that took title to
unitary states. But in Ireland, India, and Palestine, British authorities did not
simple devolve power, they also divided it. Time and again the British advanced
partition as a way to solve problems associated with decolonization. For them,
the decision to split the colonies into two states was a way to settle differences
between competing independence movements, which demanded power on
their own terms. The next two chapters will examine why decolonization in
Ireland, India, and Palestine led to independence and to partition.

NOTES

1. Pollard argued that "the erection of closed economic blocs by fascist Germany in
Eastern Europe, Japan in the Far East, and Britain in the Commonwealth countries
had exacerbated economic rivalries and set the great powers on the road to war." Robert
A. Pollard, *Economic Security and the Origins of the Cold War, 1945–1950* (New York:
Columbia University Press, 1985), 8; Richard N. Gardner, *Sterling-Dollar Diplomacy
in Current Perspective: The Origins and the Prospects of Our International Economic
Order* (New York: Columbia University Press, 1980), 9.

2. William Roger Louis, *Imperialism at Bay: The United States and the Decolonization of the British Empire, 1941–45* (New York: Oxford University Press, 1978), 226.
On the eve of U.S. entry into war, Roosevelt told Prime Minister Winston Churchill, "I
can't believe that we can fight a war against fascist slavery and at the same time not
work to free people all over the world from a backward colonial policy." Louis, *Imperialism*, 212; Ruth B. Russell, *A History of the United Nations Charter: The Role of the
United States, 1940–45* (Washington, D.C.: The Brookings Institution, 1958), 14.

3. Louis, *Imperialism*, 28; John Foster Dulles and Gerald Ridinger, "The Anti-Colonial Policies of F.D.R.," *Political Science Quarterly* 70 (March 1955): 10.

4. Richard W. Van Alstyne, "Woodrow Wilson and the Idea of the Nation State,"
International Affairs 37, no. 3 (July 1961): 307. Van Alstyne argues:

It is a remarkable fact—one, I think, of tremendous historical significance—that
the concept of the "New Diplomacy" emerged simultaneously from Washington
and Petrograd. Although only dimly realized at that time, the U.S.A. and the
U.S.S.R. were already rivals in 1918. Wilson and Lenin are the prophets of the new
international order. Each in his own way, but in fulfilment of the peculiar mission

of his respective nations, struck a mortal blow at the classical system of nation States. Lenin conspired to extirpate the nation State and erect a wholly new type of society resting on the Communist revolution. Wilson was a Christian crusader, the author of a creed for a vague new international order wherein America would interpret the rules and the other nations merely signify their assent.

Van Alstyne, "Woodrow Wilson," 307. See also Geoffrey Barraclough, *An Introduction to Contemporary History* (New York: Penguin, 1967), 118–19; Rudolph Von Albertini, *Decolonization: The Administration and Future of the Colonies, 1919–1960* (Garden City, N.Y.: Doubleday, 1971), 8; Paul Kennedy, *The Rise and Fall of the Great Powers* (New York: Random House, 1987), 287; Gordon Levin, Jr., *Woodrow Wilson and World Politics* (New York: Oxford University Press, 1968), 1.

5. Jean-Baptiste Duroselle, *From Wilson to Roosevelt: Foreign Policy of the United States* (New York: Harper & Row, 1963), 75.

6. V. I. Lenin, *National Liberation, Socialism and Imperialism* (New York: International Publishers, 1968), 80; W. Ofautey-Kodjoe, *The Principle of Self-Determination in International Law* (New York: Nellen, 1977), 198–99.

7. David Cronon, *The Political Thought of Woodrow Wilson* (New York: Bobbs-Merrill, 1965), 455.

8. Lenin, *National Liberation*, 113, 47.

9. Alfred Cobban, *The Nation State and National Self-Determination* (New York: Crowell, 1970), 76.

10. Duroselle, *Wilson to Roosevelt*, 75.

11. J. N. Saxena, *Self-Determination: From Biafra to Bangladesh* (Delhi: University of Delhi Press, 1978), 10; Lee Burcheit, *Secession: The Legitimacy of Self-Determination* (New Haven: Yale University Press, 1978), 71–72.

12. Burcheit, *Secession*, 65–66.

13. Branko Lazitch and M. Drachkovitch, *Lenin and the Comintern* (Stanford: Hoover Institution Press, 1972), 369. The Soviet constitution provided in Article 17 that "the right to secede from the U.S.S.R. is reserved to every union republic." Burcheit, *Secession*, 100.

14. Lazitch and Drachkovitch, *Lenin and the Comintern*, 53.

15. Von Albertini, *Decolonization*, 85.

16. R. F. Holland, *European Decolonization, 1918–1981* (New York: St. Martin's, 1985), 1.

17. Robert Divine, *Roosevelt and World War II* (Baltimore, Md.: Johns Hopkins University Press, 1969), 54, 55.

18. Gunter Nollau, *International Communism and World Revolution* (New York: Praeger, 1961), 89. Isaac Deutscher, *Stalin* (New York: Oxford University Press, 1969), 392.

19. Nollau, *International Communism*, 78–79.

20. Fernando Claudin, *The Communist Movement: From Comintern to Cominform* (Harmondsworth, England: Penguin, 1975), 254.

21. B. N. Pandey, *The Breakup of British India* (New York: St. Martin's, 1969), 42, 114.

22. Jawaharlal Nehru, *Toward Freedom* (New York: John Day, 1942), 65. *Swaraj* means "self-government" as well as "freedom" or "independence." But because the British believed that India might be given self-government or "home rule" and still remain within the Commonwealth (not severing colonial ties completely), the Indian National Congress began using the phrase *purna swaraj*, or "complete independence," to distinguish its meaning from the British usage. Nehru, *Toward Freedom*, 388. Jean Lacouture, *Ho Chi Minh* (New York: Random House, 1968), 129. Lacouture says that "some translated '*Doc Lap*' as 'freedom,' others as 'independence'—Ho and his colleagues clearly favored the second interpretation." He adds: "Linguistically, they were certainly right. *Doc Lap* means 'to stand alone.'" Bruce Cumings, *The Origins of the Korean War* (Princeton, N.J.: Princeton University Press, 1981), 68. As the Korean writer Chong Kyong-mo explains, the word *sinparam*

> expresses the pathos, the inner joy, of a person moved to action not by coercion but by his own volition. *Param* is the sound of the wind; if a person is wafted along on this wind, songs burst from his lips and his legs dance with joy. A *sinparam* is a strange wind that billows in the hearts of people who have freed themselves from oppression, regained their freedom, and live in a society of mutual trust. This word, redolent with a shamanistic mystique, has a talisman-like appeal for Koreans.

23. During the 1920s, the Comintern advised communist parties in Asia to abandon revolution and work with the indigenous bourgeoisie on more modest reforms.

24. Russell, *A History of the United Nations Charter*, 83.

25. Peter W. Rodman, *More Precious Than Peace: The Cold War and the Struggle for the Third World* (New York: Scribner's, 1991), 42.

26. Russell, *A History of the United Nations Charter*, 103, 52–54, 165, 149; Peter J. Taylor, "Geopolitical World Orders," in *Political Geography of the Twentieth Century: A Global Analysis*, ed. Peter J. Taylor (New York: Wiley, 1993), 51.

27. Russell, *A History of the United Nations Charter*, 103, 52–54.

28. Diane S. Clemens, *Yalta* (London: Oxford University Press, 1970), p. 130; Russell, *A History of the United Nations Charter*, 478.

29. I. Brownlie, "An Essay in the History of the Principle of Self-Determination," in *Grotian Society Papers 1968*, ed. C. H. Alexandrowicz (The Hague: Nijhoff, 1970), 98; Bruce D. Marshall, *The French Colonial Myth* (New Haven, Conn.: Yale University Press, 1973), 182.

30. John Lewis Gaddis, *The Long Peace: Inquiries into the History of the Cold War* (New York: Oxford University Press, 1987), 84.

31. Louis, *Imperialism at Bay*, 458.

32. The term *decolonization* was first introduced by M. J. Bonn, a German economist who emigrated to Britain during the 1930s. See Von Albertini, *Decolonization*, 16–17.

33. Stanley Karnow, *Vietnam: A History* (New York: Viking, 1983), 137; Von Albertini, *Decolonization*, 24; Louis, *Imperialism at Bay*, 567; John Darwin, *Britain and Decolonisation: The Retreat from Empire in the Post-War World* (New York: St. Martin's, 1988), 43.

34. Von Albertini, *Decolonization*, 24.

35. Marshall, *French Colonial Myth*, 182.

36. Clemens, *Yalta*, 48.

37. Richard M. Nixon, *RN: The Memoirs of Richard Nixon* (New York: Warner, 1978), 461.

38. Malcolm Chalmers, *Paying for Defense* (London: Pluto, 1985), 37.

39. Darwin, *Britain and Decolonisation*, 223.

40. Darwin, *Britain and Decolonisation*, 167; Holland, *European Decolonization*, 281.

41. Russell, *A History of the United Nations Charter*, 1032.

42. Adam Robert and Benedict Kingsbury, "Introduction," in *United Nations, Divided World: The U.N.'s Roles in International Relations*, ed. Adam Robert and Benedict Kingsbury (Oxford: Clarendon, 1993), 6–7.

43. Lawrence McCaffrey, *The Irish Question, 1800–1922* (Lexington: University of Kentucky Press, 1968), 152.

44. John Gallagher discounted their role:

> Colonial resistance movements, a romantic term, are not going to help us through our problems. We need have no truck with the view that the downfall of this empire was brought about by colonial freedom fighters because, except in some Pickwickian sense, these processes involved next to no fighting . . [There were] no Dublin Post offices [in most colonial settings].

John Gallagher, *The Decline, Revival and Fall of the British Empire: The Ford Lectures and Other Essays* (Cambridge: Cambridge University Press, 1982), 73–74. But there *were* Dublin post offices or King David Hotels in some settings, and the absence of actual rebellion did not mean that the threat of violence did not loom large in the minds of colonial authorities.

45. H. V. Hodson, *The Great Divide* (Oxford: Oxford University Press, 1985), 166.

46. David Held, *Prospects for Democracy: North, South, East, West* (Stanford, Calif.: Stanford University Press, 1993), 29, 34.

47. There are, of course, different kinds of "republics." Socialist republics distinguish themselves by using adjectives such as "Democratic" or "People's" before "Republic" in their proper names; capitalist republics typically use the simple form, "Republic of . . . ," and Muslim states qualify "republic" with the adjective "Islamic."

48. See Robert K. Schaeffer, *Power to the People: Democratization Around the World* (Boulder, Colo.: Westview, 1997), chapter 4.

49. See Schaeffer, *Power to the People*, chapter 11.

50. Lloyd C. Gardner, *Architects of Illusion: Men and Ideas in American Foreign Policy, 1941–49* (Chicago: Quadrangle, 1970), 6; Gaddis Smith, *The Last Years of the Monroe Doctrine, 1945–1993* (New York: Hill & Wang, 1994), 130.

51. Walter LaFeber, *America, Russia and the Cold War, 1945–1984* (New York: Knopf, 1985), 13–14.

52. "The Monroe Doctrine is not now and never was an instrument of aggression; it is and always has been a cloak of protection," U.S. diplomats insisted. "The Doctrine is not a lance; it is a shield." Smith, *The Last Years of the Monroe Doctrine*, 34.

53. LaFeber, *America, Russia and the Cold War*, 13.

54. T. E. Vadney, *The World since 1945* (London: Penguin, 1992), 40.

55. Smith, *The Last Years of the Monroe Doctrine*, 54–5; LaFeber, *America, Russia and the Cold War*, 22.

56. Gaddis, *The Long Peace*, 103.

57. Schaeffer, *Power to the People*, 46–47.

58. Peter Willetts, *The Non-Aligned Movement: The Origins of a Third World Alliance* (London: Frances Pinter, 1978), 6.

59. The term third world was coined in 1952 by Alfred Sauvy, a French journalist, who used it to "describe countries that were not part of the industrial world or the Communist bloc." Barbard Crossette, "The 'Third World' Is Dead, But Spirits Linger," *New York Times*, November 13, 1994.

60. Willetts, *The Non-Aligned Movement*, 17, 15–16.

61. Rodman, *More Precious Than Peace*, 68; LaFeber, *America, Russia and the Cold War*, 171. Dulles conveniently ignored U.S. neutrality at the onset of two world wars and its 1955 decision to allow Austria to become an independent and *neutral* state. Audrey Kurth Cronin, *Great Power Politics and the Struggle Over Austria, 1945–1955* (Ithaca, N.Y.: Cornell University Press, 1986), 131, 165.

62. Gaddis, *The Long Peace*, 48–49.

63. Joel S. Migdal, *Strong Societies and Weak States: State-Society Relations and State Capabilities in the Third World* (Princeton, N.J.: Princeton University Press, 1988), 178. Another estimate of U.S. spending is $80.1 billion between 1950 and 1979. Vadney, *The World since 1945*, 98. Between 1973 and 1980, the Soviet Union also sold $59.6 billion in arms. Michael T. Klare, *American Arms Supermarket* (Austin: University of Texas Press, 1984), 9.

T W O

THE BRITISH BALANCING ACT

Even during the most robust phase of British colonialism, when the British Empire spanned the globe, the sun of its authority was already beginning to set over its nearest and oldest colony, Ireland. By the end of World War I, British rule in Ireland had been eclipsed: the partition of the island in 1920 reduced British rule to six northeast counties called Ulster.

A generation later, after World War II, British rule in India and Palestine would also be extinguished. And, as in Ireland, the devolution of British authority in these countries would result in partition.

In 1900, British officials would not have imagined that the devolution of British power was possible in its colonies. As Lord Salisbury said of the Irish, the inhabitants were no more capable of self-government than were African Hottentots.[1] Nor would they have believed that devolution, should it come, would result in the division of political power between two competing independence movements. But in Ireland, India, and Palestine, this is precisely what happened.

Although partition was not the inevitable consequence of devolution, it emerged time and again as the most practical solution British authorities could devise. When confronted with seemingly intractable "Troubles" in Ireland, British officials sought to find a solution that would secure devolution on terms favorable to themselves—what they called "dominion"—and minimize the risk of social conflict among the indigenous inhabitants. As it turned out, partition accomplished neither goal. British interests were irreparably damaged, partition altered the course of conflict but did not avert it, and the Troubles, be they in Ireland, India, or Palestine, continued.

British rule in Ireland, India, and Palestine was troubled by the rise of indig-

enous independence movements and by U.S. demands that Great Britain relinquish colonial authority in the name of self-determination. British officials
demonstrated some capacity to contain these internal and external political
forces by advancing various political reforms in Ireland before World War I
and in India and Palestine before World War II. But successive world wars
simultaneously strengthened the position of the independence movements and
the anticolonial states and weakened British authority in fundamental ways.
World War I forced the pace of devolution in Ireland and introduced the possibility of self-government in India and Palestine for the first time, with World
War II accelerating the progress of devolution there.

The awakening of anticolonial political forces and the rise of movements demanding independence made devolution an issue in colonial Ireland, India,
and Palestine. So long as these movements adhered to constitutional reforms
and subscribed to "dominion," the establishment of independent nation-states
was indefinitely postponed. But as elements within these movements grew
frustrated with the pace of reform and the structure of devolution, they began
to threaten violence.

    In Ireland, the slow but steady progress of an Irish Home Rule Bill frus-
trated both loyalist Protestants and independence-minded Catholics. First introduced in 1886, again in 1893, and for a third time in 1912, this modest bill
would have created an all-Irish parliament that could legislate on civil domestic
matters. Authority for trade, security, and foreign affairs would be retained by
the British parliament (in which the Irish would continue to have some modest
representation). The Protestant Irish minority objected to the bill because Irish
Catholics would command a majority in an all-Irish parliament. Without the
protection of their conservative allies in the British parliament, Irish Protestants feared that the Catholic majority would use this new forum to coerce
them. They wanted instead to keep Ireland within the British Union, where
they could ally with British conservatives to preserve their status in Ireland.
Their secessionism thus took a curious form: the Protestants threatened to secede from an all-Irish state so that they could maintain their "union" with the
colonial overlord, Great Britain. Irish Protestants and their conservative allies
had been able to defeat the Home Rule Bills of 1886 and 1893, but when it
became clear that some version of the 1912 bill would be approved by a Lib-
eral-dominated British parliament, Protestants began organizing an armed militia—the hundred thousand-member Ulster Volunteer Force—and threatened
to secede from a devolved Irish state, saying "Ulster will fight" rather than sub-

mit to Catholic Irish majority rule. Protestant leader Edward Carson even urged the formation of a provisional government. When, in March 1914, the British government took steps to protect its arsenals in Northern Ireland from possible assault and seizure by Protestant militias, British officers sympathetic to the Protestant cause announced that they would resign rather than suppress an incipient rebellion. The Curragh incident (named for the military base involved) and the threat of violence by the Ulster Volunteers tested British authority on the eve of world war and stimulated the Liberal government's search for a solution to the Irish problem.

The pace of reform, slowed by the alliance of Protestant unionists and British conservatives, and the character of reform, which would devolve to an Irish legislature only limited power over domestic affairs, frustrated independence-minded Catholics. And the growth of a stubborn, armed, Protestant movement opposed to Home Rule undermined the position of Catholic moderates (who would accept dominion Home Rule) and strengthened supporters of Irish independence. Irish republicans responded to the threat of Protestant violence by organizing an armed militia of their own—the Irish Volunteers—in the prewar years.[2] So long as British approval of an Irish Home Rule Bill appeared imminent, as it did from 1912 to 1914, Sinn Fein, the armed, independence-minded wing of the Irish independence movement, was held in check. Sinn Fein did not want to jeopardize chances for Home Rule, which was then supported by the moderate Catholic majority.

The outbreak of World War I in August 1914 shifted the ground under all the participants. The British government, which had labored to pass a Home Rule Bill in 1914, suspended it for the duration of the war. And the competing Irish movements moved to take advantage of the war, each in its own way. The Protestant minority rallied to the imperial war effort: The Ulster Volunteer Force transformed itself overnight from a group of rebellious secessionists to an embryonic national guard, which then marched off to be mauled in Flanders fields. The Catholic majority, having been denied Home Rule just when it finally appeared within their grasp, fulminated against imperialist war. The moderates became stubbornly uncooperative and demanded that the government commit itself to Home Rule as the price for their participation in the British war effort. The militants plotted revolution. The Easter Rebellion of 1916 announced the independence movement's willingness to use force to secure devolution, much as the Curragh incident had demonstrated the Protestant minority's determination to prevent it.

The suspension of the Home Rule Bill, the execution of the Easter Rebellion's leaders, and the attempt to extend conscription to a recalcitrant populace destroyed Catholic support for dominion and strengthened the republicans, who demanded unqualified independence. In the 1918 election, the moderate Irish Parliamentary Party won only six seats at Westminster. Sinn Fein won seventy-three.[3]

After the war, the Irish republicans withdrew from the British parliament, declared their independence on January 21, 1919, formed a legislature—the Dail—and began waging an irregular war to overthrow continued British rule in Ireland. British officials sent in the arms and enlisted Protestant irregulars— the Black and Tans and the Auxiliaries—to suppress the postwar rebellion.[4] By the fall of 1919, civil war had engulfed the island, continuing until 1920, when the British moved to devolve authority in most, though not all, of the country. Violence and the threat of violence by both loyalist and independence-minded Irish movements had tested British authority and patience. In the end, British officials were persuaded that Irish affairs were too troublesome to manage and that British colonial authority there would have to be surrendered.

Independence movements in India had supported the British war effort during World War I, and as a price for their participation, they extracted a promise that the British would work toward "the gradual development of self-governing institutions with a view to the progressive realization of responsible government in India as an integral part of the British Empire."[5] Postwar reforms, however, failed to advance self-government significantly in the subcontinent. So from 1920 to 1922, the Indian National Congress and the Muslim League, under Mahatma Gandhi's leadership, joined forces to mount a nonviolent protest campaign and to demand an end to British rule in India. Although the *satyagraha* or noncooperation campaign was predominantly peaceful, violence flared around its edges. Gandhi called off the campaign when it became clear that the independence movement could not control the spread of violence. But the point had been made: while the movement did not condone violence, the threat of popular riot and rebellion lay behind it.

British authorities were able to contain the independence movements during the interwar period. The India Act of 1935, like the Irish Home Rule Bill of 1912, was a moderate reform granting a measure of self-government to the independence movement at the local and provincial level. In the short run it assuaged Congress Party moderates who were swept into low-level government offices by huge electoral majorities. But it antagonized the Muslim League, which found itself unable to place its candidates in office, even in predominantly Moslem regions. Jinnah and League leaders began to worry that in any devolved state, the Moslem minority would be coerced by the Congress majority. Jinnah told the League conference in 1938 that the Congress would "bully you, tyrannize over you and intimidate you." A year later he said that the aim of the Congress was to get Moslems to "submit unconditionally to the Hindu raj. . . . The high command of the Congress is determined, absolutely determined, to crush all other communities and culture in this country and to establish [Hindu] raj."[6]

The outbreak of World War II altered the political landscape. The British viceroy declared war on India's behalf without consulting the independence movements. This unilateral declaration made a mockery of the 1935 reforms and effectively suspended any progress toward self-government as a British military government assumed control over the subcontinent. Frustrated by the abrogation of even modest reform and minimal participation in government, the Indian National Congress refused to support the war effort, withdrew from office, and launched a noncooperation campaign. Thousands of Congress Party members went to jail.[7] On July 6, 1942, the Congress, meeting in Bombay, passed a "Quit India" resolution demanding that the British withdraw from India. If the government refused, it would launch an active civil disobedience campaign. Hard-pressed British officials treated this demand as the nonviolent equivalent of the Easter Rebellion and the next day outlawed the Congress, arrested its leadership, and interned them for the duration of the war.[8]

The Muslim League, which had been hostile to British reform before the war, now saw a chance to make considerable gains by rallying to support the British war effort. The League rejected a Congress plea to join forces against the British and agreed instead to participate in the wartime government. The divergent attitudes of the two independence movements toward the war sharply divided the Congress and the League. While the Congress withdrew from participation in government and moved into nonviolent opposition, the League advanced its case for special political consideration in any future devolution of British power. At its 1940 conference in Lahore, the League resolved that

> no constitutional plan would be . . . acceptable unless it is designed on the following basic principle, viz: that geographical contiguous areas . . . in which Moslems are numerically in the majority . . . should be grouped to constitute 'independent states' in which the constituent units shall be autonomous and sovereign.[9]

This resolution constituted a demand for a separate Pakistan, an "Ulster" where the Moslem minority might find refuge from the Hindu majority. And in 1943, the League adopted the slogan that summarized its approach to devolution: "Divide and Quit."[10]

The League made considerable gains during the war. But these were threatened at war's end by British promises to move toward undivided devolution and by the Congress's return to public life. The League moved into the opposition after the war and raised the threat of violence as a way to secure devolution on favorable terms. On August 16, 1946, Jinnah announced that the League would move to "direct action" and would withdraw from government positions. "Never have we in the whole history of the League done anything except by constitutional methods and by constitutionalism," Jinnah said. "But now we are obliged and forced into this position. This day we bid goodbye to constitutional methods."[11]

According to a British participant in British-League negotiations prior to this announcement, Jinnah had said that "the British government and the Congress each held a pistol in its hand, the one of authority and arms, the other of mass struggle and non-cooperation. 'Today,' he declared, 'we have also forged a pistol and are in the position to use it.' "[12]

The League's threat immediately provoked widespread violence. In Calcutta alone, some twenty thousand people were killed or seriously injured in the days that followed.[13] The violence in Calcutta was the Muslim League's Curragh. It announced to British authorities and the Congress that Moslems would fight unless they could force devolution on favorable terms.

For its part, the Congress could not promise to restrain the riot and rebellion that pressed against its nonviolent front lines from behind.

The wartime and postwar strategies of the independence movements tested British authority in an effort to advance devolution. Unlike Ulster loyalists, however, wartime Muslim League loyalists would not settle for continued union with Britain. Like their counterparts in the Congress, they wanted independence—but on their own terms.

During World War I, Arab independence movements had assisted the British in their war against the Ottoman Empire, which ruled much of the Middle East. But these close wartime relations dissolved once the British and French claimed sizable mandates in what is now Lebanon, Syria, Jordan, and Israel and as the British permitted Jewish emigration into Palestine as a way to fulfill its promise (made in the second Balfour Declaration of 1917) to create a Jewish national home. After the war, Arab Palestinians rioted periodically—in 1920, 1921, and 1929—attacking British authorities and Jewish communities. With the creation of an Arab Independence Party in 1932, which helped organize widespread Christian and Moslem Arab opposition to continued British rule, sporadic rioting gave way to widespread rebellion in 1936. For three years, Arab Palestinians conducted an irregular war in an effort to force the British to devolve political power in Palestine to the Arab Palestinian majority, which would then move to block Zionist land purchases and curtail Jewish immigration.[14]

Although Zionist leaders pressed British authorities to permit Jewish immigration into Palestine, the movement did not directly challenge British rule during the interwar period. As a response to Arab Palestinian riots and revolt, though, they began to organize their own armed militias, of which the Haganah (Hebrew for "Defense") was the most prominent.[15]

British authorities responded to the 1936 Arab revolt by commissioning an investigation into its origins. The Peel Commission noted that "Arab nationalism is as intense a force as Jewish [nationalism]. The Arab leaders' demand for national self-government and the shutting down of the Jewish National Home has remained unchanged since 1920. . . . The gulf between the races is thus already wide and will continue to widen if the present Mandate is maintained."[16] The commission urged the partition of Palestine into separate Arab and Zionist states, with strategic and religious areas such as Jerusalem remaining under British rule.[17]

This proposal, like the Irish Home Rule Bill and the 1935 Indian reforms, frustrated the Arab Palestinian movement's hope for a unitary state and majority rule. And it disappointed militant Zionists who saw a two-state solution as a retreat from the Balfour Declaration. Continuing Arab Palestinian hostility— the Arab revolt resumed with renewed vigor after the report was issued—and Zionist criticism forced British authorities to commission another report. The 1939 White Paper on Palestine repealed the Peel Commission recommendations, ruled out partition, rejected the idea of an eventual Jewish state, and restricted Jewish immigration.

The outbreak of World War II did not immediately change the position of contending independence movements. The Arab Palestinian movement opposed participation in the British war effort (in contrast to their support for the British during World War I), and like the majority movements in Ireland and India, the Arab Palestinian movement pressed vigorously for devolution during the war. Some leaders even collaborated with the Axis. Most of the Zionist movement, however, rallied to support the British. Zionist leaders pressed for the creation of a Jewish division in the British army and many members of the Haganah joined the British armed forces.

By the end of the war, however, radical Zionist militias—the Stern Gang and Irgun (led by Avraham Stern and Menachem Begin, respectively)—began to use violence to force the British to devolve power to a Jewish state. The assassination in Cairo of British minister of state Lord Moyne in 1944 by Zionist irregulars marked the beginning of a campaign to oust the British by force. Although the British cabinet that year had again proposed the eventual partition of Palestine, the Moyne assassination put off any move to implement this policy.[18] After the war, Foreign Secretary Ernest Bevin announced that "Balfour is dead"—that Britain had retreated from its commitment to the creation of an independent Jewish state in Palestine.[19] The British retreat from the Balfour Declaration and the impact of the Holocaust destroyed the moderate Zionist position (much as Irish Catholic moderate position had been destroyed during World War I). Factions within the Zionist movement would move increasingly into armed confrontation with the British during the postwar years.

In Ireland, India, and Palestine, contending independence movements switched from cooperation to opposition, opposition that included the threat or use of force to achieve their ends. The effect of these oscillating threats was the appearance, to British authorities, of more or less continuous violence. Although the movements did not devise a common strategy—on the contrary, their tactics were based on opposition and opportunism—the effect was a sort of tag-team approach to devolution. First one movement opposed British rule by force, then took a cooperative breather while the other launched an attack.

Independence movement behavior, moreover, fell into another consistent pattern. During the world wars, majority movements—Catholic Irish republicans, the Indian National Congress, and Arab Palestinians—opposed the British war effort and used rebellion and noncooperation to test British authority. On the other hand, minority movements—Ulster Protestants, Indian Moslems, and Zionists in Palestine—rallied to support the British. The decision to oppose or support British authority during world war would have important consequences once the British moved to devolve power in these colonies. In addition, while independence movements within the empire pressed the British to relinquish power, the United States applied pressure from without. U.S. support for self-determination, as a means of encouraging colonial peoples to secede from the empire, remained consistent through two world wars. But it was during those wars, not the interwar period, that U.S. leaders actively demanded

British devolution. America-first isolationism in the 1920s and 1930s blunted U.S. enthusiasm for self-determination, and British officials were able to deflect half-hearted demands for devolution by the United States and the Soviet Union through their modest attempts to reform the empire. During the world wars, however, when U.S. leaders could demand a high price for their assistance, their demands for devolution sharpened, and British authorities found it more difficult to resist changing their colonial policies.

During World War I, U.S. interest in the devolution of British rule in Ireland was shaped by a large, vocal Irish immigrant constituency in the United States, which paid keen attention to developments in Ireland and persuaded U.S. political leaders to do the same. Balfour described this influential group as "coming from that part of Ireland which has never loved England."[20] The 1916 Easter Rebellion and the summary execution of its leaders angered Irish Americans and inflamed anti-British sentiment in the United States, which had not yet entered the war. Lloyd George, then minister of munitions, said that if Britain did not defend its response to the rebellion, "the Irish-American vote will go over to the German side, the Americans will break our blockade, and force an ignominious peace on us unless something is done even provisionally to satisfy America."[21] The British ambassador to the United States warned the cabinet that "the situation is much like that of a soda water bottle with the wires cut but the cork unexploded."[22] President Wilson, responding to congressional demands for Irish self-determination, had his ambassador tell Lloyd George that Britain's failure to advance Irish self-government prevented the United States from lending assistance to the British.[23] Balfour, visiting the United States, cabled the prime minister: "The Irish Question is apparently the only difficulty we have to face here, and its settlement would no doubt greatly facilitate the vigorous and lasting cooperation of the U.S. government in the war."[24]

The British responded to U.S. demands by reevaluating the suspension of the Irish Home Rule Bill and convening an Irish convention to negotiate a settlement that would secure Irish and American support for the faltering British war effort. As Lloyd George told Protestant leader Edward Carson in 1917, "We've got to settle the Irish Question now—in spite of you."[25] Negotiations failed to produce a satisfactory agreement, but U.S. leaders were assuaged by British assurances to devolve power after the war. The United States soon entered the war on Britain's side.

During World War II, the United States did not press Britain specifically to relinquish colonial power, but U.S. officials expressed concern about developments in India, where Indian National Congress obstructionism was seen as undermining Britain's ability to resist the Japanese advance through southeast Asia and Burma,[26] and in Palestine, where British restrictions on Jewish immigration were viewed as denying safe haven for Jews escaping the gathering holocaust in Europe. Like the anti-British Irish-American community during World War I, a vocal Jewish immigrant constituency in the United States was keenly interested in British colonial policy. British officials complained about the pressure exerted by this group during and after World War II in much the same terms that Balfour and Lloyd George complained about Irish Americans during World War I. In both instances, political constituencies in the United States stiffened presidential demands for the devolution of British colonial power.

The Indian independence movement did not possess an immigrant constituency in the United States, but they did not need one as much as the Zionist movement did. Indian movements' demands for devolution exerted considerable direct pressure on British authorities.

In an attempt to contain independence movements, British authorities themselves pressed for devolution. Prewar reforms—the Irish Home Rule Bill of 1912, the 1935 Government of India Act, and the 1937 Peel Commission report—demonstrated that the British were interested in some kind of devolution and were willing to take steps to implement it. But the pace of reform was extremely slow. The Irish Home Rule Bill was passed some twenty-eight years after it was first introduced. The 1935 Government of India Act and the Peel Commission proposals came two decades after the 1917 Balfour declarations promising some form of self-government in India and Palestine. At this leisurely pace, the managers of Britain's colonial empire would not have moved to devolve power fully until the 1960s.[27]

The world wars quickened the pace of devolution. To secure the assistance of independence movements in its colonies and of the United States during World War I, British authorities issued a series of declarations in 1917 promising to devolve significant power after the war. The nadir of the war for the British empire and its allies was 1917: revolution in Russia threatened to take that country out of the war and unleash German divisions from the eastern front against Britain and France. It is not surprising, then, that British officials moved to promise devolution as the price for political and military assistance. Ireland came first. On May 16, 1917, Lloyd George promised to reopen the question of devolution in Ireland.[28] This step was taken to rally support in Ireland so that the large British military forces stationed in Ireland in the aftermath of the Easter Rebellion could be reduced, so that Irish men could be recruited to fill European trenches, and so that the Irish Question would not obstruct U.S. intervention on the Allies' behalf. Then on August 20 and November 2 came the two Balfour Declarations, first in India and then in Palestine.

Taken together, these steps demonstrated British willingness to speed the devolution of power in its colonies, but after the war, British officials began to hedge these promises and burden them with qualifications and restrictions. Independence movements would later object to the British retreat from promises made under the duress of war, but Lloyd George, Balfour, and Churchill (then colonial secretary) had crafted their pledges and declarations in ambiguous terms so that they could later qualify them.[29] Still, the British could not entirely renege on wartime commitments. Although they managed to defer devolution in India and Palestine until after World War II, they could not do so in Ireland, where irregular war broke out in 1919. Churchill admitted that the war had changed almost everything in the modern world but that the deluge of war had not solved—or even altered—the Irish troubles: "As the deluge subsides and the waters fall short we see the dreary steeples of Fermanagh and Tyrone emerging once again. The integrity of their quarrel is one of the few institutions that has been unaltered in the cataclysm which has swept the world."[30] And so the war-weary British, in an attempt to rid themselves of continuing Irish troubles, agreed to devolve power in 1920.

World War II had much the same effect on the British. Then it was the Indian National Congress's turn to obstruct the war. To counter Congress opposition to the war, British viceroy Lord Linlithgow first promised the Muslim League in April 1940 that no postwar devolution plan would be made without the League's consent. Because the League had presented its demand for a separate Islamic state—Pakistan—to the viceroy just a few days before, Linlithgow's pledge marked a significant departure from the go-slow devolution policies of the interwar period.[31]

But as the war dragged on and the British experienced dramatic military reverses in southeast Asia, they sought to enlist the Congress's support for the war by offering devolution on more attractive terms. In 1942, Churchill commissioned a mission to India led by Sir Stafford Cripps, who proposed granting dominion status to India after the war.[32] Congress leaders, however, rejected the proposal because it deferred devolution until after the war and because it implied that the creation of a separate Moslem state might be possible. They then announced the beginning of a civil disobedience campaign. Nevertheless, Cripps's proposals more or less committed the British to some kind of devolution after the war.

Churchill was less eager to make wartime promises to independence movements in Palestine. After the Afrika Korps was defeated at El Alamein and the German threat to the Middle East receded in 1942, the British did not need to rally support in Palestine. Internal disturbances there posed less of a problem during most of the war than they did in India. Unlike Ireland and India, the British held Palestine under a League of Nations mandate, which meant that they had promised to relinquish power at some point. The problem for British officials in Palestine, therefore, was not *if* they would devolve power but *when* and *how* to do so.

Reform and war drove a wedge between independence movements in Ireland, India, and Palestine. As the devolution of British power approached, the conflict between competing independence movements sharpened. These movements began, in turn, violently and non-violently to press British authorities to devolve power. As these intramural conflicts sharpened, British officials began to look for ways to disengage quickly, and partition seemed the most expeditious option. In the postwar periods, then, the British would move simultaneously to devolve and divide power.

NOTES

1. Catherine B. Shannon, *Arthur J. Balfour and Ireland* (Washington, D.C.: Catholic University of America Press, 1988), 19. Salisbury was Arthur J. Balfour's uncle and mentor.

2. Shannon, *Balfour and Ireland*, 182.

3. Shannon, *Balfour and Ireland*, 243.

4. Shannon, *Balfour and Ireland*, 261.

5. Reginald Coupland, *The Indian Problem* (London: Oxford University Press, 1944), 52–53.

6. M. J. Akbar, *India: The Siege Within* (New York: Penguin, 1985), 27.

7. B. N. Pandey, *The Breakup of British India* (New York: St. Martin's, 1969), 160. As Gandhi said in 1940:

> The Congress claims for itself the right to protect civil liberty in this country, but must have the right to state freely what we feel about the war. . . . I claim the liberty of going through the streets of Bombay saying that I shall have nothing to

do with this war, because I do not believe in this war and in the fratricide that is going on in Europe.

Coupland, *Indian Problem*, 247.

8. Pandey, *Breakup of British India*, 166.

9. Coupland, *Indian Problem*, 206.

10. Pandey, *Breakup of British India*, 167.

11. Pandey, *Breakup of British India*, 183.

12. H. V. Hodson, *The Great Divide* (Oxford: Oxford University Press, 1985), 166.

13. Hodson, *The Great Divide*, 166. "If the Muslims gave the provocation and started the holocaust, they were certainly its worst victims, for they were a minority in the city . . . The police were inadequate and not wholly reliable." Hodson, *The Great Divide*, 166–67.

14. Michael J. Cohen, *The Origins and Evolution of the Arab-Zionist Conflict* (Berkeley: University of California Press, 1987), 90–93.

15. Amos Perlmutter, *Israel: The Partitioned State* (New York: Scribner's, 1985), 82–83.

16. Perlmutter, *Israel*, 55.

17. R. F. Holland, *European Decolonization, 1918–1981* (New York: St. Martin's, 1985), 114.

18. Michael J. Cohen, *Palestine and the Great Powers, 1945–48* (Princeton, N.J.: Princeton University Press, 1982), 9, 11.

19. William R. Louis, *The British Empire in the Middle East* (Oxford: Clarendon, 1984), 383.

20. Shannon, *Balfour and Ireland*, 215.

21. Shannon, *Balfour and Ireland*, 216.

22. Shannon, *Balfour and Ireland*, 226.

23. Shannon, *Balfour and Ireland*, 227.

24. Shannon, *Balfour and Ireland*, 232.

25. Shannon, *Balfour and Ireland*, 228.

26. Pandey, *Breakup of British India*, 161, 165.

27. Holland, *European Decolonization*, 281.

28. Shannon, *Balfour and Ireland*, 232.

29. As colonial secretary, Churchill played an important role in drafting these promises, and he wrote the official explanation of the second Balfour Declaration. Louis, *British Empire*, 385.

30. Tom Nairn, *The Breakup of Britain* (London: New Left Books, 1977), 223.

31. Pandey, *Breakup of British India*, 157–58.

32. Coupland, *Indian Problem*, 336–37.

THREE

"DIVIDE AND QUIT"

As the British devolved power in Ireland, India, and Palestine, they also divided it.

The British did not always do so. In Burma, Ceylon, and a host of other Asian and African colonies, they relinquished power to indigenous successors in unified states. But in Ireland, India, and Palestine, they divided power between competing independence movements and awarded them separate states. They did so for many of the same reasons: to protect minorities, reward wartime allies, avert civil war, and curry political support in Britain.

During debates over the course of devolution in Ireland, India, and Palestine, many British politicians expressed a determination to protect minority rights. When arguing against Irish Home Rule, Balfour invoked John Stuart Mill's warning against the "tyranny of the majority" to protest the imposition of Home Rule on the Protestant minority and said that "handing over Ulster to the tender mercies of the rest of Ireland is surely dishonorable as well as idiotic."[1] During his wartime mission to India in 1942, Stafford Cripps told Congress leaders that its suggestion that Congress form a national government in which its representatives would constitute a majority "would in fact constitute an absolute *dictatorship* of the majority [emphasis added]."[2] The 1937 Peel Commission in Palestine urged partition because each side feared the other would eventually become a tyrannical majority. Partition, the commissioners argued, would deliver Arabs "from the fear of being 'swamped' by the Jews and from the possibility of ultimate subjection to Jewish rule," and the Jews would be relieved "from the possibility of . . . being subjected in the future to Arab rule."[3] Minority movements echoed this sentiment. One Muslim League leader warned that "when sure of its power, [the Hindu majority] will, in the name of democracy and with the help of British bayonets, make use of it to coerce and crush us, its prey, into complete captivity."[4]

British concern for minorities grew out of a conservative political tradition, an identification with members of some minority groups in these countries, and a belief that majority and minority groups were irreconcilable. In reaction to the French and American Revolutions, conservative political theorists in nineteenth-century Britain lamented the development of mass-based democratic movements, which they regarded as incapable of responsible government. They argued that these new, majoritarian parties would be even more tyrannical than the despotic monarchs they had replaced and urged the preservation of rule by responsible minorities—men of education, property, and wealth. They consequently opposed the extension of the franchise to citizens who did not hold property or pay taxes, and they sought to prevent the diminution of the House of Lords' role in Parliament. It was only by having reduced the Lords' ability to veto legislation in 1911 that Asquith's Liberal government was able to advance Irish Home Rule legislation in 1912. In supporting the rights of some minorities, conservative British politicians also justified their own status as a well-to-do, educated elite.

Liberal British politicians, by contrast, tended to support the extension of the franchise at home and the devolution of what they called "responsible self-government" overseas. Winston Churchill, then a Liberal, lambasted Tory politicians whose defense of minority rights prevented any recognition of majority rule: "Coercion for four-fifths of Ireland is a healthful, exhilarating, salutary exercise but lay a finger upon the Tory fifth—sacrilege, tyranny, murder."[5]

British sympathy for minority groups had an ethnic dimension as well as a philosophical one. Many British authorities felt a kinship with certain minorities in Ireland, India, and Palestine that they did not feel toward majority groups. This kinship was based on a shared ethnic-religious identification. British officials tended to identify with Irish Protestants, many of whom had immigrated to Ireland from England, Scotland, and Wales. They felt less warmly toward Irish Catholics, whose confessional religion had been routed in England in the sixteenth and seventeenth centuries. In India, the British found that Islam, though distant from Protestant denominations, was at least monotheistic. Pantheistic Hindu religions stood at a greater distance from British faiths. And, as it happened, the British felt a stronger "racial" affinity with Moslems in India, descended from Aryan cultures to the north and west, than with non-Islamic Hindus. Yet while British officials might identify with Islamic Indians, they did not transfer this affinity to Moslem Arabs in Palestine. There they found a greater kinship with Jews—in part because there was a substantial Jewish population in Britain, in part because though Moslems stood closer to Protestant faiths than Hindus, Jews stood closer still.

British attitudes toward ethnicity and religion were thus based on a complex hierarchy, one much like the empire's Byzantine political structure. This hierarchy was based on relative, not absolute, characteristics, so support for Moslem Indians did not necessarily require support for Moslem Arabs. Insisting on systemwide consistency would have made it more difficult for the British to manage their heterogeneous empire by divide-and-rule tactics.

The British use of ethnic-religious characteristics to divide and rule imperial populations, moreover, tended to make these divisions *seem* permanent and irreconcilable. As Lloyd George said of Irish Protestants, they were "as alien in blood, in religious faith, in traditions, in outlook—as alien from the rest of Ireland in this respect as the inhabitants of [Scotland]."[6]

Although the two Indian movements had demonstrated a capacity to work together for independence, British reforms were designed to divide them, preventing the Muslim League and the Congress from acting in concert against British rule. In 1905, for example, the British Viceroy, Lord Curzon, divided Bengal into two provinces, one with a Moslem majority and the other with a Hindu majority.[7] The division of Bengal effectively split the Muslim League from the Congress: the League saw partition as a chance to gain power in the Islamic province, whereas the Congress viewed it as an attempt to weaken its power, prompting it to demand independence for the first time and organize its first boycott of British goods.[8] (King George V reunited Bengal in 1911, which of course antagonized the Muslim League and exacerbated its differences with the Congress.) One year later, Curzon established separate electorates for Moslems and Hindus throughout the subcontinent, which had the same polarizing effect as the partition of Bengal. The British would retain this practice until the reforms of 1935 eliminated separate electorates and created provincial governments to which the Congress could elect majorities, thus antagonizing the Muslim League. Linlithgow's unilateral decision to go to war in 1939 hammered home the wedge between the two independence movements and divided them further.

By the 1940s, the British authorities had come to view the two movements as permanently antagonistic. After having engineered the partition of India in 1947, Lord Mountbatten wrote, "The responsibility for this mad decision [must lie] squarely on Indian shoulders in the eyes of the world, for one day they will bitterly regret the decision they are about to make."[9] In the end, then,

Mountbatten blamed partition on Indian divisiveness, which, he failed to note, had largely been a British creation.[10]

British pragmatism also contributed to division as devolution approached. Because devolution occurred after the conclusion of world wars, the British gave some weight in devolution deliberations to the wartime roles of independence movements. They were inclined to view the claims of cooperative independence movements more favorably than those of obstructionist, uncooperative, or rebellious movements. As discussed in chapter 2, minority independence movements—Irish Protestants, Muslim League Indians, and Zionists—had rallied to the British side during World Wars I and II, while the majority independence movements—Irish Catholics, Congress Party Indians, and Arab Palestinians—had obstructed the imperial war effort. Minority movements, moreover, supported partition; majority movements opposed it. And as devolution approached, partition was a convenient way for British officials to reward their wartime allies and punish wartime foes.

British officials also hoped that by granting independence and awarding state power to each movement, partition would avert civil war, which threatened from both sides. Minority movements successfully exploited British fears of civil war in the postwar years, demonstrating (particularly in Ireland and Palestine) that they were willing to wage irregular war to achieve devolution on favorable terms. British authorities took the threat of civil war particularly seriously in Ireland because many British officials had actively encouraged it. Before World War I, British Conservatives announced their support for Ulster unionist intransigence. Conservative Party leader Andrew Bonar Law, who would become prime minister in 1922, declared in 1912 that "there are things stronger than parliamentary majorities" and that "I can imagine no lengths of resistance to which Ulster can go in which I am not prepared to support them."[11] This kind of incendiary talk prompted Winston Churchill to remark that advocating civil war was a strange way of preventing it.[12]

Domestic political considerations played an important role in British officials' decision to divide Ireland, India, and Palestine. Conservative politicians sided with Ulster unionists against Home Rule as a means to attack the Liberals, who had won smashing electoral victories in 1906 and 1910. For Conservatives, the Irish Question could be used to undermine the Liberals' ability to maintain power. As U.S. ambassador Walter Hines Page explained:

> The Conservatives have used Ulster and its army as a club to drive the Liberals out of power; and they have gone to the very brink of civil war. They don't really

care about Ulster. I doubt whether they care very much about Home Rule. They'd slip Ireland out to sea without much worry—except their own financial loss. It's the Lloyd George programme that infuriates them, and Ulster and anti-Home Rule are all mere weapons to stop the general Liberal Revolution.[13]

After the war, however, the Conservatives conceded that Home Rule was necessary, the Liberals agreed that some separate provision for Ulster was necessary, and together they agreed to devolve power so that Britain could retain some measure of power—dominion—in Ireland. Lloyd George and the Liberals were willing to concede a separate Ulster because the continuation of war in Ireland undermined the war-weary public's support for the Liberal government.

Domestic considerations also persuaded British officials to move toward devolution and division in India and Palestine. The Labour government, which had replaced Churchill's wartime coalition government in 1945, wanted to devolve power quickly in India and Palestine so that it could pursue its domestic social agenda, which was hampered by continued administrative and military expenditures in the two colonies. Division promised a way to devolve power more rapidly in India because it eliminated the necessity for negotiating and drafting an intricate, power-sharing constitution or for providing British guarantees during a potentially difficult transition period. In Palestine, the haste with which the British abandoned their mandate to the United Nations meant that they did not even have time to divide the country before leaving. They left that task to the United Nations.

In their desire to protect minorities, reward allies, prevent war, and maintain domestic support, British officials increased the weight of minority claims. Ulster unionists could claim to represent only one-fifth of the Irish, the Muslim League only one-quarter of the Indians; Zionists, one-third to two-fifths of the inhabitants in Palestine. Yet British authorities treated them as having an *equal* claim on power. Without weighing their own concerns and issues in the balance, British authorities would not have extended to these minorities the kind of consideration that they refused to extend to other minorities—Catholic unionists in Ireland, Sikhs and princes in India, Christian Arabs in Palestine. Devolution tended to polarize and restrict political definitions. Groups that did not fit into the two great camps, which were increasingly seen as the only legitimate contenders for power, were ignored and their claims shunted aside.

Before World War I, a substantial segment of moderate Catholic Irish opinion favored Dominion Home Rule. But they were squeezed out of the picture by the suspension of Home Rule at the beginning of the war, by the Easter Rebellion and British repression during the war, and by the irregular war after it. Partition, no matter how carefully drawn, would not give representation to all. Ulster unionists, for example, wanted nine northeastern counties included in a secessionist state. Three of these counties, however, had substantial but minority, Protestant populations. The dilemma was this: if they were excluded, substantial Protestant populations would be subjected to rule by Catholic majorities, precisely what partition was supposed to prevent; but if they were included, Catholic majorities in these counties would be subject to rule by the statewide Protestant majority, and their inclusion would narrow the numerical majority that Protestants enjoyed. (A six-county state would give the Protestants a substantial majority; a nine-county state would give them a much narrower majority.)

Even pro-Ulster Balfour admitted, "If you have a Hibernia Irredenta within the province of Ulster, you will greatly add to the difficulties of the Ulster parliament; you will reproduce on a small scale all of the trouble which we had at Westminster during the [last] forty years."[14]

But a Catholic minority would be subject to Protestant rule whether the British created a six- or a nine-county Ulster. De Valera argued that it was impossible to create an Ulster that did not include in it substantial Catholic minorities, who deserved the same protection that the British wanted to extend to the Protestants:

> [Lloyd George] can't take six counties, no, nor four. Why he can't even take Antrim, because it hasn't a complete Ulster representation. He can't take Belfast, because in Belfast there are more nationalists than in the City of Cork. Therefore, Lloyd George can't himself find the boundary of his Ulster. His homogeneous Ulster does not exist.[15]

The same was true in India. Various large, minority populations were excluded from a two-part devolution. The Sikhs in the Punjab argued that if Moslems could use religion as the basis for their claim to a separate state, they could too. So did the Pathans on the northwest frontier, Nagas on the Assam-Burma border, the Adibasi of Bihar and Orissa, inhabitants of Darjeeling, and Dravidians in the south.[16] But the British excluded Sikhs from any meaningful role in devolution negotiations, as they did the princes who ruled some 565 states with varying degrees of autonomy and the untouchables.[17] These groups did not have the social-political weight, the mass-based political parties, to participate as *equals* in the devolution process.

As in Ireland, where supporters of Ulster wrestled with the six- versus nine-county question, the Muslim League struggled to define a large "homogeneous" Pakistan and prevent the creation of what Jinnah called "a moth-eaten Pakistan."[18] But India's problem mirrored Ireland's. If regions with large minority populations were included, Pakistan, like Ulster, would grow in size, but at the same time reducing the power of the newly created majority. This would become a particularly difficult problem in the Kashmir, which had a Moslem majority but a Hindu ruling prince; the struggle for control of the province would eventually lead to war between the two new countries after devolution and partition.

In Palestine, the British made some attempt to include Christians in their calculations—recommending at various times the neutralization of Jerusalem so that it could be accessible to all faiths—but the interests of Christians and other non-Islamic Arabs and non-Zionist Jewish groups were swept aside by the two main antagonists.

As a result of this British policy to treat the two big contending movements as equals and to drop smaller movements out of the equation altogether, and as a result of their own separate strategies, the independence movements split apart. As devolution approached, minority and majority movements were persuaded, even coerced, to accept partition as a condition of independence.

In Ireland, the decision to accept partition as the price of independence tore Sinn Fein apart. Following World War I, Sinn Fein had conducted an irregular guerrilla war to force the British to relinquish control of the island. British authorities recruited Ulster unionists to suppress the uprising, and after two years of fighting, the British passed legislation providing for the partition of Ireland and for continued British control over trade and defense. However, the 1920 Government of Ireland Bill failed to end the war. In late 1921, the British agreed to direct negotiations with Sinn Fein to end the war and devolve British power.

In the negotiations, the bipartisan British team (which consisted of Lloyd George, Balfour, and Churchill) offered dominion status to Sinn Fein representatives (led by De Valera and Michael Collins) if they would also accept partition and the creation of a separate Ulster. When Sinn Fein representatives refused, the British offered a carrot and brandished a stick. To make partition palatable, the British promised to hold a reunification referendum in the North and South that would determine whether the separate states would be reunited, two years after partition went into effect. But they also said that if Sinn

Fein did not immediately accept this offer, the British would abrogate the cease-fire, send new troops to Ireland, and crush the rebellion by force.[19]

At this critical juncture, De Valera was absent from the negotiations. Collins, believing that partition would be temporary and that renewed British intervention could be deterred, agreed to accept British terms. He did not, or could not, consult with De Valera. The decision to accept partition split Sinn Fein. A narrow majority of the Dail—sixty-four to fifty-seven—supported partition and dominion, whereas a large minority, led by De Valera, violently opposed the Anglo-Irish Treaty and took up arms to prevent its implementation.[20] After two more years of irregular internecine war, during which Collins was killed, the majority suppressed minority resistance and De Valera surrendered. The British, meanwhile, reneged on their promise of reunification elections, and the countrywide referendum was never held.

At the British-sponsored 1930 Roundtable Conference in India, Muslim League leader Dr. Shafa'a Ahmad Khan said, "We have never tried to create an Ulster in India; that has never been our wish."[21] But ten years later, at the League conference in Lahore, Jinnah demanded that such a separate state be provided for Moslems, saying, "It is a dream that Hindus and Moslems can ever evolve a common identity."[22] The 1935 reforms, which increased the political power of the Congress and diminished that of the League, persuaded Jinnah that the League could not compete with the Congress in a single state. During the war, however, the Congress rejected the demand for creation of Pakistan. As Maulana Abul Kalam Azad, a Moslem leader of the Congress, said of Jinnah's decision to push for a separate state, "Whether we like it or not, we have now become an Indian nation, united and indivisible. No fantasy or artificial scheming to separate and divide can break this unity."[23]

Other Congress leaders viewed partition with ambivalence. Gandhi rejected the two-nations theory advanced by the League, saying, "Hindus and Muslims of India are not two nations. Those whom God has made one, man will never be able to divide."[24] Yet he also borrowed Lenin's argument that self-determination was like the right to divorce: "The Muslims must have the same right of self-determination that the rest of India has. We are at present a joint family. Any member may claim a division."[25] Indeed, he told the 1942 Cripps Mission that

> if the vast majority of Muslims regard themselves as a separate nation . . . no power on earth can compel them to think otherwise. And if they want to partition India on that basis, they must have that partition, unless Hindus want to fight

against such a division. So far as I can see, such a preparation is silently going on on behalf of both parties. That way lies suicide.[26]

Other Congress leaders refused to consider partition at this date (as late as 1946 they refused to negotiate with the League on anything less than a unified government based on majority rule[27]), but they accepted partition as a temporary expedient in 1947. In April 1947, Nehru said that "the Muslim League can have Pakistan if they want to but on the condition that they do not take away other parts of India which do not wish to join Pakistan."[28] The Congress working committee formally accepted partition in principle on May 1, 1947, less than four months before the British relinquished power.[29]

The Congress was persuaded to accept partition in much the same way that Sinn Fein negotiators were. When Mountbatten arrived in India in February 1947, he announced that the British would withdraw in June 1948. But he soon decided to move up the departure date to August 15, 1947, in the hope that this shortened deadline would force the Congress and the League to agree on devolution more quickly. In negotiations with the Irish, the British had imposed a deadline and then threatened to *intervene* if a satisfactory agreement was not reached. In India, they imposed a deadline (of several months rather than days) and threatened to *leave* if negotiations were not concluded. The effect was the same: the Congress was forced to put partition on the bargaining table. To make it easier for the Congress to negotiate on these terms, Mountbatten, like his predecessors, promised to arrange for reunification elections after partition was completed. And like Michael Collins, Nehru decided that "perhaps the best way [to reunify the country] is to go through some kind of partition now."[30]

The rapid devolution of British power, together with the promise of reunification elections down the road, made partition easier for the Congress to accept. As Azad said of partition on June 16, 1947, "The division [of India] is only on the map of the country and not in the hearts of the people, and I am sure it is going to be a short-lived partition."[31]

In Palestine, by contrast, the Zionists moved toward partition as the British retreated from it. When the Peel Commission first advanced partition in 1937, the twentieth Zionist Congress commended the report but refrained from endorsing partition in principle.[32] The various political factions within the Zionist movement were sharply divided about the British proposal, but after the British retreated from partition in the 1939 white paper, important segments of the movement began to regard partition as the pragmatic alternative to minority status in a unitary Palestine.

David Ben-Gurion pushed for partition early on. He welcomed the Peel Commission report because it was "the first document since the Mandate which strengthens our moral and political status . . . it gives us control over the coast of Palestine; large immigration; a Jewish army, systematic colonization under state control."[33] A pragmatist, Ben-Gurion believed (like Jinnah) that by obtaining even a small, "moth-eaten" Palestine, the Zionists could control the means—immigration, colonization, and an army—necessary to build up that state.[34]

Some Zionists, like Ze'ev Jabotinsky, opposed this strategy and rejected partition because they wanted to establish a Jewish state over all of mandated Palestine. Others, like Shlomo Kaplansky, opposed it because they believed that a binational settlement with Arab Palestinians was necessary. And some, like Dr. Judah Magnes, opposed it because they viewed partition as a way to advance unfairly the Jewish minority at the expense of the Arab majority.[35]

Ben-Gurion began to press for partition during the war. At the 1942 American Zionist Conference held at the Biltmore Hotel in New York City, Ben-Gurion joined forces with Rabbi Hillel Silver and passed, over Chaim Weizmann's objections, a proposal demanding "that the gates of Palestine be opened [to Jewish immigration]; that the Jewish Agency be vested with the necessary authority for upbuilding the country . . . ; and that Palestine be established as a Jewish commonwealth integrated in the structure of the new democratic world."[36] The Biltmore program viewed devolution as a process resulting in the creation of a Jewish nation state that would be a member of the emerging interstate system—the "new democratic world"—then being created by the superpowers and their allies. Although it did not explicitly advance partition (as the 1940 Lahore meeting of the Muslim League did), the Biltmore program was consistent with it, and it was promoted by Ben-Gurion, who favored partition. After the war, on August 5, 1946, Ben-Gurion convinced the Jewish Agency to officially adopt partition as the official policy of the Zionist movement.[37]

While the Zionist movement adopted the pro-partition strategy of minority movements in Ireland and India, British authorities, uncharacteristically, moved away from it, though they never abandoned it. Devolution in Palestine took a somewhat different course, for a time, than it did in Ireland and India, because the British devolved power not to indigenous successors but to an intermediary—the United Nations. The United Nations then simultaneously devolved power and advanced partition. Although the devolution process was different in some respects, its result—partition—would be the same. But British authorities could disassociate themselves from the outcome in Palestine in a way that was impossible in Ireland and India.

Although British authorities were sensitive to foreign demands for devolution in Ireland and India and were particularly alert to American views on Ireland during World War I, they did not invite or permit the United States or any international organization to participate in the devolution of its nearest and dearest colonies. They took a different view of Palestine, inviting participation in the devolution process in part because the territory was a League of Nations mandate (and therefore gave it a different international standing than Ireland or India) and in part because it was a costly property—not the kind of colony from which Britain could reap the kind of financial rewards that it had long extracted from Ireland and India.

The British first explored the possibility of U.S. participation after World War II; a joint Anglo-American Committee of Inquiry was sent to Palestine in the spring of 1946. In April this committee (the Morrison-Grady Commission) issued its report, which stated:

> In order to dispose, once and for all, of the *exclusive* claims of Jews and Arabs to Palestine, we regard it as essential that a clear statement of the following principles be made: 1. That Jew shall not dominate Arab and Arab shall not dominate Jew in Palestine. 2. That Palestine shall be neither a Jewish state nor an Arab state. 3. That the form of government ultimately to be established, shall, under international guarantees, fully protect and preserve the interests in the Holy Land of Christendom and of the Moslem and Jewish faiths. Thus Palestine must ultimately become a state which guards the rights of Moslems, Jews and Christians alike; and accords to the inhabitants, as a *whole*, the fullest measure of self-government, consistent with the principles set forth above [emphasis added].[38]

The report also recommended that the British mandate given by the now-defunct League of Nations be converted into a trusteeship of the newly formed United Nations.[39]

The Anglo-American report reiterated the British position expressed in the 1939 White Paper, which had rejected the 1937 Peel Commission's recommendation that Palestine be partitioned. But the recommendations made by the joint committee were rejected by President Truman on October 4, 1946. Zionists persuaded Truman that partition would be preferable to a unitary state in which Jews would be a minority.[40]

After the British attempt to enlist U.S. support for its devolution policy in Palestine failed, the Attlee government decided to force the pace of devolution and adopted Winston Churchill's suggestion (of August 1, 1946) that the "one rightful, reasonable, simple and compulsive lever which we held was and is a sincere readiness to lay our mandate at the feet of the United Nations Organization and thereafter evacuate the country."[41] So on February 18, 1947, the British announced that it would delegate its authority in Palestine to the United Nations.[42]

The timing of the British announcement is significant. On February 18, the Attlee government announced the end of British rule in Palestine. Two days later, on February 20, Lord Mountbatten announced the departure of Britain from India. Like the two Balfour Declarations of 1917 and the reforms of the mid-1930s, the February 1947 announcements synchronized British movements in India and Palestine. Devolution in both countries proceeded according to the same clock.

When he first announced the British decision to depart from India, Mountbatten gave a June 1948 devolution date. He subsequently sped up the process and devolved power on August 15, 1947. While Attlee did not at first set a date for British withdrawal from Palestine—he announced the actual date of withdrawal on September 26, 1947, after the UN Commission on Palestine recommended partition—the British actually withdrew on May 15, 1948, thereby keeping to Mountbatten's original schedule for devolution in India.[43] The synchronicity of developments in India and Palestine undoubtedly contributed to their singular outcome.

Britain's under-the-gun approach to the devolution process in Palestine quickened developments there, as it had in India. The United Nations assembled a multilateral committee in May 1947 to investigate the issues in Palestine. The committee then traveled to Palestine and returned with its recommendations on August 31. The majority recommended the partition of Palestine into a Jewish and an Arab state, with Jerusalem assigned to an international trusteeship. The minority report proposed the creation of a single, federal Palestinian government, which would consist of two states (states in the American sense of the term, as in North and South Carolina), one Jewish and one Arab.[44] The majority report essentially dusted off the 1937 Peel Commission report, adopted its tripartite partition, modified its boundaries slightly, and passed along the updated version to the United Nations for ratification.[45]

The UN committee also recommended that the British stay on to supervise partition. The British demurred from this onerous task. According to the minutes of a September 20 cabinet meeting:

The Prime Minister [Attlee] said that in his view there was a close parallel between the position in Palestine and the recent situation in India. He did not think it reasonable to ask the British administration in Palestine to continue in present conditions, and he hoped that salutary results would be produced by a clear announcement that His Majesty's Government intended to relinquish the Mandate and, failing a peaceful settlement, to withdraw the British administration and British forces [emphasis added].[46]

On September 26, the British announced that they were going to terminate unilaterally their mandate in Palestine and withdraw on May 15, 1948.[47]

President Truman endorsed the UN recommendation for partition in October. On November 29, the United Nations, with U.S. and Soviet support, adopted the commission's recommendation and endorsed the partition of Palestine.[48] The Soviets, Lenin's heirs, supported partition because they viewed it as a way to end British colonialism and to promote self-determination. Andrei Gromyko, the Soviet delegate to the United Nations, said:

We cannot agree with the assertion which implies that the decision on the Partition of Palestine is aimed against Arabs and Arab countries. It is our deep conviction that this decision corresponds to the fundamental interests of both Arabs and Jews. . . . The Soviet Union supports . . . the aspirations of any state and any people, no matter how small its weight in international affairs, in the struggle against foreign dependence and remnants of colonial oppression.[49]

The day before the British withdrew, Ben-Gurion read a declaration of independence and announced the formation of a Jewish state: Israel. War broke out the following day and continued until a truce was established in the spring of 1949. Separate armistices were signed between February and July.[50]

Unlike majority movements or factions of majority movements in Ireland and India, Arab Palestinians and their allies in neighboring states never viewed partition as an acceptable by-product of devolution. Had the British not delegated authority for devolution to the United Nations and its U.S.-Soviet architects, Arab Palestinians might have been able to forestall partition. But having failed to create a unified, mass-based political party (such as Sinn Fein or the Indian National Congress), they relied heavily on neighboring states and the Arab League to act on their behalf; this approach was not effective.[51] As the venue changed from unilateral British decision making, where the Arabs had some influence, to multilateral U.N. decision making, where they could exert less pressure and the American-based Zionists could exert more, partition was impossible to deter.

British authorities moved toward devolution and partition in Ireland, India, and Palestine at two speeds. For years, they had adopted a slow, plodding, deliberate pace: they formed commissions of inquiry and enacted modest reforms that inched movements in its colonies toward self-government. But after World War I in Ireland and World War II in India and Palestine, the British discarded reform, set deadlines, and raced toward devolution at breakneck speed. When they abandoned deliberate managerialism and adopted under-the-gun devolution, partition became a more attractive solution to the problems confronting British authorities, primarily because it could be implemented in a hurry. It did not require a continuing British presence, which would be necessary if a more complex, long-term constitutional solution were adopted. Partition also seemed advantageous because it was the only solution to which most or all parties could agree. It offered something for everyone, at least in the short run. It promised to retain certain privileges—dominion—for British authorities in Ireland and India; it promised to break up the colonial empire and advance the creation of independent nation-states for the anticolonial superpowers, and it awarded a measure of state power to the competing independence movements. Politically, partition was the lowest common denominator.

In their rush to partition, the British attempted to defer some important issues. They attempted to put aside the decision as to whether partition would be a temporary or permanent by-product of devolution. British officials told majority parties that partition would be temporary and provided for reunification elections in Ireland and India. But these provisions were not carefully written and did not provide any authority to administer them. It was left to now-independent states to determine whether they wanted to hold elections that might abolish themselves. But few states wither away of their own accord. Not surprisingly, neither Northern Ireland nor Pakistan wanted to exercise this provision of the devolution agreement, and neither Ireland nor India could compel them to do so.

The British also deferred the issue of boundaries. In Ireland and India, British officials set up boundary commissions, staffed with political cartographers, to adjucate disputed territorial claims. But theirs proved an impossible task. The lines they drew satisfied no one. No matter how carefully they might be drawn, boundaries between divided states left too many people on the wrong side. The same ethnic population would be part of a majority or a minority depending on where the line was drawn. The result was the creation of a territorial basis for irredentist claims.

In Ireland, the British gave Northern Ireland six counties, not the nine counties claimed by Protestants. And when the Hindu maharaja of Kashmir, a predominantly Moslem state lying between India and West Pakistan, joined India, military forces from both countries fought for control of the state. After inconclusive fighting, they divided it between them, a subdivision that neither regarded as permanent.[52]

In Palestine, no boundary commission was established. It was left to Zionist and Arab military forces to draw the lines. When the first Arab-Israeli War ended in 1949, Israel was 21 percent larger than the territory assigned to it by the United Nations' partition plan and possessed 80 percent of the area assigned to Palestine under the League of Nations' mandate.[53]

NOTES

1. Catherine B. Shannon, *Arthur J. Balfour and Ireland* (Washington, D.C.: Catholic University of America Press, 1988), 65, 178.

2. Nicholas Mansergh, *The Irish Question, 1840–1921* (London: George Allen and Unwin, 1975), 299.

3. Michael J. Cohen, *The Origins and Evolution of the Arab-Zionist Conflict* (Berkeley: University of California Press, 1987), 154.

4. Reginald Coupland, *The Indian Problem* (London: Oxford University Press, 1944), 201. And Jinnah said that democracy based on majority rule could not work in India. Coupland, *Indian Problem*, 310.

5. Mary C. Bromage, *Churchill and Ireland* (Notre Dame, Ind.: University of Notre Dame Press, 1964), 42.

6. Mansergh, *Irish Question*, 229.

7. M. J. Akbar, *India: The Siege Within* (New York: Penguin, 1985), 25.

8. William J. Barnds, *India, Pakistan and the Great Powers* (New York: Praeger, 1972), 16; B. N. Pandey, *The Breakup of British India* (New York: St. Martin's, 1969), 47.

9. Akbar, *India*, 35.

10. As the historian B. N. Pandey notes, "The British Raj was not the originator of communalism. But it did nourish Muslim separatism as a useful ally against Congress nationalism. . . . British policy made Pakistan feasible and Congress, by lacking a definite policy towards the League, made it attainable." Pandey, *Breakup of British India*, 215–16.

11. Shannon, *Balfour and Ireland*, 176.

12. Shannon, *Balfour and Ireland*, 286.

13. Shannon, *Balfour and Ireland*, 206.

14. Shannon, *Balfour and Ireland*, 254.

15. John Bowman, *De Valera and the Ulster Question* (Oxford: Clarendon, 1982), 40.

16. Pandey, *Breakup of British India*, 198.

17. H. V. Hodson, *The Great Divide* (Oxford: Oxford University Press, 1985), 367–68.

18. Pandey, *Breakup of British India*, 177.

19. At a cabinet meeting in which British officials discussed what the imposition of full-scale martial law would mean, General MacCready said that one hundred rebels would be shot the first week. Shannon, *Balfour and Ireland*, 274.

20. Michael Farrell, *Northern Ireland: The Orange State* (London: Pluto, 1980), 47.

21. Coupland, *Indian Problem*, 121.

22. Akbar, *India*, 20.

23. C. H. Philips and M. D. Wainwright, *The Partition of India* (Cambridge, Mass.: MIT Press, 1970), 209.

24. Philips and Wainwright, *Partition of India*, 209.

25. Philips and Wainwright, *Partition of India*, 210.

26. Coupland, *Indian Problem*, vol. II, 298.

27. R. F. Holland, *European Decolonization, 1918–1981* (New York: St. Martin's, 1985), 75.

28. Philips and Wainwright, *Partition of India*, 219. Nehru indicated, however, that he had reached this conclusion earlier, in 1944.

29. Philips and Wainwright, *Partition of India*, 20.

30. A. Jeyartnam Wilson and D. Dalton, *The States of South Asia* (Honolulu: University of Hawaii Press, 1982), 51. Other leaders agreed. "V. P. Menon urged [Nehru] to accept quick partition in order to avert the further spread of communal bitterness and to prepare for later reunification." Wilson and Dalton, *States of South Asia*, 51.

31. Philips and Wainwright, *Partition of India*, 220.

32. Amos Perlmutter, *Israel: The Partitioned State* (New York: Scribner's, 1985), 56.

33. Perlmutter, *Israel*, 70.

34. Perlmutter, *Israel*, 70.

35. Perlmutter, *Israel*, 58–73. The day after the United Nations approved partition in Palestine, Magnes predicted, "It looks like trouble." Walter Laqueur, *A History of Zionism* (New York: Schocken, 1976), 582.

36. Laqueur, *History of Zionism*, 546.

37. Perlmutter, *Israel*, 111.

38. Cohen, *Arab-Zionist Conflict*, 160.

39. J. C. Hurewitz, *The Struggle for Palestine* (New York: Schocken, 1976), 245.

40. Richie Ovendale, *The Origins of the Arab-Israeli Wars* (London: Longman, 1984), 97; Laqueur, *History of Zionism*, 573.

41. Laqueur, *History of Zionism*, 577–78.

42. Laqueur, *History of Zionism*, 577. The British government did not recommend to the United Nations either the conclusions of the Peel Commission or the white paper of the Anglo-American Commission because it was of two minds about partition.

43. Holland, *European Decolonization*, 120.

44. Hurewitz, *Struggle for Palestine*, 296.

45. Compare the 1937 Peel partition plan (Cohen, *Arab-Zionist Conflict*, 94) with the UN plan (Hurewitz, *Struggle for Palestine*, 297).

46. William R. Louis, *The British Empire in the Middle East* (Oxford: Clarendon, 1984), 475. On August 9, 1947, *The Economist* had suggested, "in any situation of complete deadlock, the only hope is to introduce a completely new factor—a catalyst—such as was found in India [and for that matter Ireland] when the Government announced a date for the transfer of power. If the policy of catalyst worked there, could it not work in Palestine?" Louis, *British Empire*, 476.

47. Holland, *European Decolonization*, 118.

48. Cohen, *Arab-Zionist Conflict*, 126–27. See also Louis, *British Empire*, 387.

49. Gromyko said this on April 18, 1948, after the UN vote but before partition went into affect. Hashim S. H. Behbahani, *The Soviet Union and Arab Nationalism, 1917–1966* (London: KPI, 1986), 58–59.

50. Laqueur, *History of Zionism*, 586; Avi Shlaim, *Collusion across the Jordan* (New York: Columbia University Press, 1988), 386.

51. Holland, *European Decolonization*, 113.

52. Barnds, *Great Powers*, 38–43.

53. Ovendale, *Arab-Israeli Wars*, 123.

F O U R

COLD WAR PARTITION

After World War II, the devolution of military power in Germany, Korea, China, and Vietnam also resulted in partition. Partition in these countries has to be understood in the context of two developments: the creation of a new interstate system and the division of that system into "spheres of influence."

The new interstate system created by U.S. and Soviet leaders during and just after the war was based on independent nation-states. It was intended to replace the old system based on colonial empires and heterogeneous states. Although U.S. and Soviet officials disagreed about many things in the postwar period (as they did about the devolution of power in European and Asian countries), both superpowers nonetheless remained committed to the breakup of colonial empires and to the consolidation of the new interstate system. The United States and the Soviet Union thus supported the devolution of British power in Palestine and India, as well as devolution throughout Asia and the Middle East. They also remained committed to the United Nations as the institutional expression of the new system.

Even at the nadir of U.S.–Soviet relations in the late 1940s and early 1950s, neither country abandoned the joint effort to create this new interstate system or attempted to construct an alternative to it. The United States did not abandon the task or retreat to "America-first" isolationism as it had after World War I because the new system afforded it considerable economic, political, and military advantages. And the Soviet Union, which might have been expected to retreat to Soviet-first isolationism in response to U.S.-sponsored policy defeats in the United Nations, did not do so. The Soviets' UN Security Council veto helped them to retain their influence in the United Nations even though they were regularly outvoted by substantial majorities.

Both countries remained committed to the fundamental features of the system they created as wartime allies throughout the postwar period. Indeed, U.S. officials worried that the Soviet Union might permanently withdraw from the United Nations during the Korean War and start a rival organization, and they were relieved when the Soviets did not.

Despite sharp disagreements and dramatic fluctuations in bilateral relations, the continued participation of both superpowers in the interstate system is *the* central fact of the postwar period. Despite disagreements over the course of devolution in Europe, Asia, and the Middle East, they generally agreed to disagree and frequently found that partition was a practical way to do so. Through partition, they managed to contain their disagreements and avoid a third world war.

The superpowers could agree to disagree because they had provided for a division of the world into spheres of influence when they constructed the new interstate system at Yalta and Potsdam, as well as under the U.S.-sponsored amendments to the UN Charter. At the end of the war, these spheres were regional and limited in scope. Neither superpower claimed or recognized spheres of influence extending around the globe.

Although the superpowers recognized each other's right to claim a sphere, these claims were not carefully defined at the wartime summits, a consequence of the fluid character of world war. The superpowers sketched the outline of some spheres and divided between them the responsibility for occupying certain countries—Germany, Austria, Korea, China, and Vietnam—but these partitions were intended to be temporary, to be sorted out after the war was concluded.

The allocation of spheres of influence and the division of particular states was not inconsistent with the creation of a new interstate system. Although nominally egalitarian, the United States and the Soviet Union intended to fashion a system in which they could wield their newfound power. Spheres of influence permitted each to exercise its hegemony over some, though not all, states in the system. And because superpower partition would in each case result in the creation of two more or less independent nation-states, the devolution of power in Germany, Korea, China, and Vietnam would not impede the development of the new system. In fact, the creation of multiple states conformed to the principle of self-determination and augmented the weight of nation-states, as opposed to colonial empires, in the interstate system as a whole.

Although U.S. and Soviet officials agreed in general terms to allocate some spheres and divide some countries, they disagreed as to the particulars of devolution and division. As tensions rose during the course of the cold war, U.S. and Soviet spheres of influence widened, and the division of particular countries deepened. The modest spheres originally claimed by the superpowers expanded dramatically during the decade after World War II, and the temporary division of Germany, Korea, China, and Vietnam was made permanent. (The partition of Austria was undone in 1955. Austria became a neutral, unified state that was placed outside superpower blocs[1]).

The globalization of superpower spheres and the hardening of wartime partitions began and ended in Germany. The attempt to define U.S. and Soviet spheres in the heart of Europe led to sharp disagreement, and during the period from 1945 to 1962, Germany was twice divided. In 1948–1949 the country was partitioned along lines defined by wartime occupation zones. Then, in 1961–1962, Berlin was subdivided, and the partition of Germany was set in concrete.

In the interim, the superpowers also participated in the division of Korea, China, and Vietnam on a permanent basis, leading to the expansion of their respective spheres of influence. By the end of this period, the superpowers defined their spheres on a global basis.

In 1944, Stalin told Milovan Djilas, a Yugoslavian communist leader, "This war is not as in the past. Whoever occupies a territory also imposes on it his own social system" as far "as his army can reach."[2] This did not happen right away. It took time to devolve power in these territories to regimes resembling the superpower occupiers. But in the decade after the war, both the United States and Soviet Union established states and social systems in their own image in Germany, Korea, China, and Vietnam.

The shifting focus of U.S.–Soviet relations, which moved geographically around the world, expanded their leaders' definition of spheres of influence and deepened their interest in the division of these countries as a way to defend these spheres.

To understand the simultaneous expansion of U.S. and Soviet spheres and the division of countries within their spheres, it is necessary to examine the course of devolution and partition in these four countries. Events in Germany contributed to developments in Asia, which in turn contributed to developments in Germany. For the most part, these developments were sequential. They began in Germany, moved to Korea and then China, and returned to Germany by way of Vietnam.

The superpowers agreed to divide Germany, Korea, and Vietnam during the war. Although they gave considerable attention to Germany at wartime summit conferences, they devoted only passing attention to the disposition of Korea and Vietnam. After the war they retreated from their collective decision to divide these countries; within a few years, however, they returned to their initial plans.

During the war, all of the Allied leaders proposed that Germany be dismembered, though they each had somewhat different ideas about how this might best be accomplished.

Roosevelt argued that "the war-breeding gangs of militarists must be rooted out of Germany if we are to have any real assurance of future peace."[3] To do this he first suggested that latent separatist tendencies be encouraged so that Germans could divide themselves and return to the disassembled condition of German states that had existed prior to 1871. But if that did not occur, he said, "Germany must be divided into several states."[4] Dismemberment, he told British foreign secretary Anthony Eden, was the "only wholly satisfactory solution" to the German problem.[5] Roosevelt first suggested Germany be divided into three states, and later five.[6] His successor, Harry Truman, initially agreed with Roosevelt and told Admiral Leahy prior to the Potsdam summit that "the separation of Germany into separate sovereign states would be advantageous to future peace and security."[7] Churchill was of like mind, proposing in 1943 that the southern German states be detached and united with Austria and Hungary in a "Danubian Confederacy."[8]

Stalin, moreover, told Churchill and Roosevelt in November 1943 that they all "preferred" partition and that he endorsed a threefold partition, which would include a North and East German state, a Rhineland-Ruhr state, and a "Catholic Republic" in Bavaria and Württemburg.[9] De Gaulle also indicated his preference for "another Peace of Westphalia, which had once set the seal on the division of Germany into petty principalities and vassal states."[10]

After agreeing to partition at the Teheran summit in late November 1943, the superpower leaders deferred the question of how German division and devolution would actually occur. In the meantime, a working group called the European Advisory Commission was formed to allocate responsibilities for the occupation of Germany pending its ultimate disposition. In January 1944, the British proposed a three-part division of occupation zones, under which the Soviets would occupy an eastern zone, the British a northwestern zone, and the Americans a central western and southern zone.[11] After some discussion about the boundaries of each zone, the U.S. and Soviet governments accepted the British proposal in June 1944. (These boundaries were subsequently adjusted to create a French zone in the southwest.) This occupation-zone division of Germany during the war would become the basis for partition after it.

Although the superpowers did not agree to the particulars of partition during the war, U.S. officials prepared plans detailing the division and devolution of power in Germany. Two competing proposals emerged. The first, called the "Program to Prevent Germany from Starting World War Three," was drafted by Treasury Secretary Henry Morgenthau and his assistant Harry White. It provided for the annexation of parts of Germany to neighboring Denmark, Poland, and France and for the creation of two independent states, one in the south and west and one in the north and east.[12] Partition would be accompanied by deindustrialization—the closing of all mines and dismantling of "all industrial plants and equipment not destroyed by military action"—which would transform the two Germanies into countries that would be "primarily agricultural and pastoral in character."[13]

Roosevelt initially endorsed the plan and told Morgenthau in August 1944, "We have got to be tough with Germany and I mean the German people not just the Nazis, we either have to castrate the German people or you have got to treat them in such a manner so they can't just go on reproducing people who want to continue the way they have in the past."[14] But he later backed away from extreme deindustrialization, saying, "No one wants to make Germany a wholly agricultural nation again."[15]

The State Department had rather different plans. It opposed partition and urged that Germany be retained as an economic unit. State Department planners also opposed the deindustrialization scheme because they believed it would make it difficult for the Germans to make reparations payments to the Soviets, reparations that U.S. officials had agreed in principle to deliver. They feared that the Morgenthau plan would repeat the errors of the Versailles settlement, under which the United States had subsidized the Germans so that they could make reparation payments to the Allies. Under the Treasury proposal, the State Department argued, the United States would have to do the same in order for the Germans to meet post–World War II reparation obligations, for only a reconstructed Germany could make reparations.[16] As Secretary of State Henry Stimson told Truman, Morganthau's punitive partition plan would be a "grave mistake":

> Punish her war criminals in full measure. Deprive her permanently of her weapons, her General Staff and perhaps her entire army. Guard her governmental action until the Nazi educated generation has passed from the stage—admittedly a

long job. But do not deprive her of a means of building up ultimately a contented Germany interested in following non-militaristic methods of civilization. . . . It is to the interests of the whole world that [the Germans] should not be driven by stress of hardship into a non-democratic and perhaps predatory habit of life.[17]

The Treasury–State Department debate over the future of Germany indicates that U.S. planners were of two minds. During the war they favored Morgenthau's punitive plan. After the war, however, they retreated from it and endorsed the State Department's approach to devolution in Germany, which advocated its reconstruction. Then, during 1947–1948, they adopted parts of each. U.S. officials simultaneously advanced partition, which the Treasury Department had urged, and German reconstruction, which the State Department advocated. The result would be the reconstruction of a separate West German state.

The future of Korea was not high on the superpower's agenda during the war, though it did come up at superpower summits. At the Cairo summit, the Pacific war allies—Roosevelt, Churchill, and Chiang Kai-shek (Stalin was not present because the Soviet Union was not then at war with Japan)—issued a declaration that stated, "The aforesaid three powers, mindful of the enslavement of the people of Korea [by Japan], are determined that in due course Korea shall become free and independent."[18]

Before power could be devolved to a "free and independent" Korea, however, Roosevelt thought it should pass through a period of four-power superpower trusteeship (under the United States, China, Great Britain, and the Soviet Union), which would last some thirty or forty years. Roosevelt raised the issue of Korea with Stalin at the Teheran and Yalta conferences, even though the Soviet Union had not yet declared war on Japan, and Stalin endorsed the idea with one qualification: "The shorter the period [of trusteeship] the better."[19]

After the Soviet Union declared war against Japan in the summer of 1945, two junior U.S. military officers were assigned the task of fixing U.S. and Soviet occupation zones in Korea. On the night of August 10–11, Col. C. H. Bonesteel III and Col. Dean Rusk (who would later be secretary of state under Presidents Kennedy and Johnson) were given thirty minutes to complete the task.[20] They hastily took out a map and drew a line across Korea at the 38th parallel, choosing this latitude because it roughly divided the country in half and placed the Korean capitol of Seoul in the U.S. zone.[21] Although Rusk and other U.S. officials worried that the Soviets would not accept this arbitrary division because Soviet troops could have occupied the whole peninsula before U.S. forces could land, Stalin did halt the Soviet advance at the 38th parallel. Truman later recalled that "the 38th parallel . . . was not debated over nor bargained for by either side."[22]

During this process, Roosevelt's idea of a four-power trusteeship was shunted aside. Unlike Germany, where Great Britain and France were given occupation zones, the other two Asian powers—Great Britain and China— were not allocated zones in Korea. But as in Germany, the occupation-zone partition of Korea was supposed to be temporary. After Japan surrendered, the superpowers would devolve power to a unified country. But within a few years of the war's end, they would divide the country, along wartime lines, on a permanent basis.

While the United States and Soviet Union shunted aside their European and Asian allies in Korea, they found a role for them in the postwar occupation of Vietnam.

In 1943, Roosevelt suggested that Vietnam, like Korea and Germany, be made a four-power trusteeship, again under the United States, Soviet Union, Great Britain, and China, and that power devolve to an indigenous government after twenty or thirty years.[23] At one point he even offered to give a major role to China. He reportedly asked Chiang Kai-shek, "Do you want Indo-China?" Chiang replied, "It's no help to us. We don't want it. They are not Chinese. They would not assimilate into the Chinese people."[24]

Although Roosevelt was opposed to continued French colonialism in Indochina, he suggested after the Yalta summit that the French be permitted to reassume their authority in the area provided they promise to devolve power to indigenous groups in a short time.[25] Roosevelt took this step because the other allies were either unwilling or unable to assume such responsibility. After Truman took office, U.S. officials in May 1945 recognized French claims in Indochina.[26] But because the French were then incapable of immediately acting on such claims, the superpowers meeting at Potsdam assigned responsibility to the Chinese and the British for accepting the anticipated Japanese surrender and for occupying Vietnam. British troops were assigned an occupation zone south of the 16th parallel and Nationalist Chinese forces, the zone north of that line.[27] Both countries assumed that their occupation responsibilities would be brief and that they would devolve their authority to the French.

In August 1945, however, the superpower disposition of Vietnam was interrupted by Ho Chi Minh, who announced the creation of an independent Vietnamese republic. But despite Ho's pleas, the Soviet Union, which had endorsed the Potsdam plan for Vietnam, refused to recognize the new regime.[28] The British and Chinese proceeded to occupy their respective zones. Without superpower recognition, Vietnamese independence was stillborn. In March 1946, the British and Chinese began to withdraw their forces in favor of the French.

The superpowers would return to the devolution of French rule in Indochina in 1954, when they would again agree to divide the country, this time at the 17th parallel.

The superpowers took a somewhat different view of China during the war. Unlike Korea and Vietnam, China had not been overrun by the Japanese, though Japanese forces controlled much of the country. For the superpowers, the problem was how to devolve power in Japanese-occupied China, not in China as a whole. No formal assignment of Allied occupation zones was made, as in Germany, Korea, and Vietnam. A sort of free-for-all ensued as the United States and the Soviet Union—and Nationalist and Communist Chinese forces—rushed to occupy territories held by the Japanese. The Soviets occupied much of Manchuria and North China, where the Chinese Communists were strong, and the United States sent the Marines into central and western China to secure these areas for the Nationalists. The superpowers might have agreed to create occupation zones and partition China into north and south, but they did not do so.[29]

The U.S. officials persuaded the Soviets to recognize the Nationalist Chinese government and devolve power in the occupied areas to them in return for Chinese territorial concessions to the Soviet Union: leases on some Chinese ports, railway concessions, and the creation of an independent Outer Mongolia.[30] The Soviets then permitted Nationalist troops to enter much of their occupied territories ahead of the Communists. The Soviets and the Nationalists even signed a Treaty of Friendship.[31] As Soviet foreign minister Vyacheslav Molotov told U.S. officials at the end of 1945, "It was without question that we all agreed to support Chiang Kai-Shek and that the Soviet Union has embodied this in writing [at Potsdam]."[32]

During and immediately after the war, then, the superpowers opposed the partition of China. It would only be in 1950, as a result of developments elsewhere—in Germany and Korea—that they would change their minds.

Wartime agreements may have provided for the de facto division of Germany, Korea, and Vietnam, but partition did not become de jure until 1948 in Germany and Korea and 1954 in Vietnam. It was not immediately apparent that these countries would be divided. After the war, in fact, U.S. and Soviet officials retreated from partition and promoted unification, albeit on their own terms. But after a few years, conflicting political and economic needs persuaded both superpowers to advance partition. In Germany and Korea, partition moved forward at the same pace, almost in lockstep.

In Germany, the American and Soviet leadership were of the same mind. Each wanted a unified German economy and a polity that would serve its own interests. The problem was that they had separate interests. The United States wanted to create a German economy that would assist the reconstruction of Western Europe. As policy planner George Kennan said, "To talk about the recovery of Europe and to oppose the recovery of Germany is nonsense. People can have both or they can have neither."[33] Germany would assist European recovery not by paying its reparations in cash or in kind (sending industrial equipment in lieu of cash) but by providing the goods—coal, industrial products—then in short supply throughout Europe, in exchange for foodstuffs, which were scarce in Germany.

The United States also wanted a German government that would resist both a resurgence of indigenous militarism and the importation of communism. A neutral or rather neutralizing government would fit U.S. specifications. But the strongest political party in a united Germany would probably have been the Social Democrats, who were seen by the United States as antifascist but not sufficiently anticommunist, which meant they could not keep a united Germany neutral.[34]

The Soviets wanted the postwar German economy to assist the recovery of the Soviet Union and then that of Eastern Europe. But because they had suffered devastating wartime economic losses, they wanted Germany to make direct contributions to the Soviet Union with very little in exchange. The Soviets first wanted to receive some $10 billion in reparations, which would be paid for by the Germans in industrial equipment or raw materials, followed by the creation of a German economy that could participate in a wider European recovery.[35]

Like the United States, the Soviets also wanted a neutralizing government, one that could resist resurgent militarism. But they believed that a communist government, or one friendly to the Soviet Union, could best ensure this. They distrusted the Social Democrats as insufficiently antifascist because they had been unable to prevent the rise of Nazi power in the interwar period.

U.S. officials opposed using the German economy to aid Soviet economic recovery, because they believed such a policy would forestall the recovery of the other war-battered European economies. Unless other European economies recovered quickly, communist political movements would grow and the United States could find itself subsidizing Germany and Europe—with much of the aid going to the Soviet Union—without laying the basis for long-term recovery. U.S. officials thus began taking unilateral steps to prevent the Soviet Union from extracting reparations from Germany. A U.S. directive in 1947 stated that "an orderly, prosperous Europe requires the economic contribution of a stable and productive Germany" and that reparations "should not permanently limit Germany's industrial capacity."[36] U.S. officials subsequently refused to fulfill superpower reparations agreements. In the fall of 1946, the United States moved to unify the three western occupation zones in Germany into a single economic unit, which excluded the Soviets, and on June 20, 1948, introduced currency reform in the western zones.[37] The German economy was then integrated into the Western European economy,[38] which received generous Marshall Plan assistance.

By issuing a new currency, U.S. officials hoped to eliminate inflation and the black market. At the time, the preferred unit of exchange in the western zones was Lucky Strike cigarettes (one carton equaled 23,000 reichmarks or $2,300 U.S.). This system encouraged the hoarding of food and consumer goods. According to one U.S. official, the currency reform "transformed the German scene from one day to the next. On June 21, goods reappeared in the stores, money resumed its normal function, and the black and grey markets reverted to a minor role."[39] The Soviets responded to these measures by introducing their own currency two days later and by blockading Allied access to Berlin. Throughout the process that followed, the Soviets matched U.S. moves with nearly identical policies of their own.

The growing division of economic life was followed by the increased separation of political life. After the currency reform, U.S. officials instructed the minister-presidents of eleven West German states to convene a constituent assembly and draw up a "Basic Law" that would guide the development of political institutions and the devolution of Allied occupation authority to an indigenous German government.[40] Administrators of the western zones agreed to allow Germans "those governmental responsibilities which are compatible with the minimum requirements of occupation and control and which ultimately enable them to assume full governmental responsibility."[41] According to the U.S. State Department, this meant reconstituting western Germany "as a political entity capable of participating in and contributing to the reconstruction of Europe."[42]

However, the creation of a full-fledged, all-German constitution, which would establish a wholly sovereign state independent of U.S. and Soviet authority, was deferred. The Basic Law was approved by the constituent assembly in May 1949 and soon ratified by the individual German states and the occupation authorities. Representatives were subsequently elected to the newly created parliament, the Bundestag.[43] During the same period, the Soviets moved to establish a People's Congress in East Germany, which ratified a constitution in March 1949 and established a government in the eastern zone on October 7.[44]

Both the United States and the Soviet Union wanted German reunification on their own terms, which were defined by separate economic needs. Failing that, they decided to pursue their separate economic agendas—reconstruction and integration in the West, reparation and integration in the East—in their separate occupation zones. The economic and the political partition of Germany was initiated by a series of unilateral U.S. actions, to which the Soviets responded in kind. Because the United States could not accomplish its economic objectives in the whole of Germany, officials such as George Kennan recommended early on (in March 1946) that the United States and its allies "carry to its own logical conclusion the process of *partition* . . . and to endeavor to rescue [the] western zones of Germany by *walling them off* against eastern penetration and integrating them into [the economic and political] pattern of Western Europe [emphasis added]."[45] Kennan later said, "I hope we won't shrink from carrying out that partition rather than giving the Russians the chance to dominate the whole country."[46]

U.S. officials heeded Kennan's prophetic advice. American actions led to partition, though curiously it was the Soviets, not the Americans, who actually built walls. Responding to U.S. initiatives in Germany, the Soviets first blockaded Allied access to Berlin and closed the inter-German border in 1948–1949. They finally sealed off West Berlin with concrete barriers in 1961. But it was the Western Allies that had initially called for these walls. As British foreign minister Ernest Bevin said in January 1948, the United States and its allies needed "to reinforce the physical barriers which guard our Western civilization."[47]

Partition in Germany led to the expansion of U.S. and then Soviet spheres of influence in Europe. As a result of developments in Europe, and particularly in Germany, the United States gradually increased its political, economic, and military commitments to Europe after the war, most notably in 1947, through the Truman Doctrine and the Marshall Plan. Although the United States had increased its political and economic commitments, it was not prepared in 1947 to make a permanent military commitment. But events in early 1948—the Communist-led coup in Czechoslovakia and, more important, the partition of Germany and the subsequent Soviet blockade of Berlin—changed all that. The British asked the United States to consider forming a military alliance to "protect" Western Europe from communist intervention and "permit" U.S. intervention on Western Europe's behalf, in much the same way that the Monroe Doctrine enabled the United States to "protect" Latin America from interference by colonial European powers and to "permit" U.S. intervention in the region. That summer, as the United States began its airlift of supplies to West Berlin, U.S. officials began exploratory talks with the Western European states on the creation of a military security organization. By April 1949, U.S. and European diplomats agreed to establish a U.S.-dominated, collective security institution in Europe: the North Atlantic Treaty Organization (NATO).[48]

To secure Senate approval of the NATO Treaty, Secretary of State Dean Acheson insisted that the United States would not rearm Germany. "We are very clear," he told senators, "that the disarmament and demilitarization of Germany must be complete and absolute."[49] He said that NATO would not be used to prevent internal subversion in Western European states, that U.S. participation in NATO did not imply its acceptance of European colonialism, and that NATO would not be a permanent alliance (the treaty was to remain in effect for only twenty years). When asked whether substantial numbers of U.S. troops would have to be sent to Europe to fulfill its commitment to the new alliance, Acheson replied, "The answer . . . is a clear and absolute 'no.' "[50]

As it turned out, Acheson would be wrong on every count. Germany would be rearmed by the United States and its allies in 1955, an act that prompted the formation of the Warsaw Pact by the Soviet Union. The United States used NATO and various covert means to prevent anti-NATO political parties from coming to power in allied countries (Article 4 of the treaty permitted use of troops from member states to suppress uprisings within member states).[51] The United States would support French colonialism in Vietnam as a means of securing French participation in NATO. NATO would become a permanent alliance, and the United States would assign a "substantial" number of troops—some 345,000 in 1988—to NATO in Europe.

Together with the Truman Doctrine and the Marshall Plan, NATO increased U.S. commitments to Europe. These commitments "protected" Western Europe from interference by the Soviet Union while simultaneously "permitting" American political, economic, and military intervention in the region. These developments effectively extended the U.S. sphere of influence to include all of Western Europe. As Senator Tom Connally, chairman of the Foreign Relations Committee, said of the NATO Treaty during the Senate debate, "The Atlantic Pact [NATO Treaty] is but the logical extension of the principle of the Monroe Doctrine."[52]

But when the treaty was ratified by the Senate on July 21, 1949, NATO was not yet the military alliance it would become. It was, in Bevin's words, "a sort of spiritual alliance of the West."[53] It would take developments elsewhere—in Korea, China, and Vietnam—to activate the new Monroe Doctrine in Europe and give substance to the West's spiritual federation.

The Soviet Union, meanwhile, strengthened political and economic ties within its sphere of influence in Eastern Europe and extended its own version of the Monroe Doctrine there. The Soviets agreed to permit the creation of collective security regimes in the UN Charter, which allowed the United States to retain Monroe Doctrine foreign policy in the Americas, because it wanted to establish its own sphere of influence in Eastern Europe after the war, a sphere recognized by Roosevelt and Truman at the wartime and postwar summits.

At the end of World War II, Soviet troops occupied much of Eastern Europe, but they did not immediately devolve power to friendly, indigenous communist parties. As the United States was constructing its European sphere of influence under the Truman Doctrine, the Marshall Plan, and the partition of Germany, however, the Soviets organized the Communist Information Bureau (Cominform) in 1947 as its own version of the Truman Doctrine, and in 1949 they organized the Council of Mutual Economic Assistance (Comecon) to develop economic and trade relations as its own version of the Marshall Plan.[54]

Moreover, between 1946 and 1949, as the partition of Germany proceeded, the Soviets consolidated their sphere of influence in Eastern Europe, establishing friendly communist regimes in Bulgaria, Poland, Romania, Czechoslovakia, and Hungary. In 1947, the Soviets also concluded a treaty with Finland that effectively neutralized that nation. Only Yugoslavia successfully resisted incorporation into the Soviet sphere. Marshal Tito broke from the Soviet Union and participation in the Cominform in 1948 and pursued a nonaligned, though socialist, foreign and domestic policy.

The superpower march toward partition in Korea moved in step with developments in Germany, though it did so for different reasons. Whereas economic considerations forced the pace of partition in Germany, political considerations set the tempo in Korea. Whereas partition in Germany led both superpowers to dig in their heels—keeping their occupation armies in place on a permanent basis—they took to their heels in Korea: after separate states were created, both superpowers began withdrawing occupation forces from the peninsula. Although partition in Germany stimulated the expansion of U.S. and Soviet spheres of influence and their respective "Monroe Doctrines" in Europe, partition in Asia did not. The deployment of military forces in Korea strained U.S. and Soviet military capacity. Whereas Germany and Japan could sustain the presence of occupying armies—with some difficulty—a poor country such as Korea could not. U.S. and Soviet forces in Korea were wholly dependent on long, external supply lines. Additionally, in Korea, unlike Germany, indigenous movements of the right and left were quite vigorous and equally determined to get rid of superpower occupation.[55]

Neither the United States nor the Soviet Union intended to stay in Korea. They both wanted to devolve power to indigenous successors. The problem was how to manage this devolution so that friendly political parties would play a prominent role in the devolved state. At the end of 1945, the United States and the Soviet Union agreed that the devolution of political power would best be managed by a four-power commission—consisting of the United States, the Soviet Union, Nationalist China, and Great Britain—which would act as a trustee for five years. The joint commission would set up a provisional government and assist "the political, economic and social progress of the Korean people, and the development of national independence of Korea."[56]

This plan initially aroused the opposition of all the political parties in the South, though it came to be supported by the leftist parties after a time. When the joint commission met for the first time in early 1946, discussions stalled because neither the United States nor the Soviet Union was prepared to create a unified economy or polity that would put its indigenous allies at a disadvantage.[57] U.S. occupation officials began promoting rightist parties, particularly the party led by Syngman Rhee, and suppressing leftist parties that had led strikes or protests in the South. The Soviets, meanwhile, suppressed noncommunist parties in the North.[58]

The joint commission met again in May 1947 in an attempt to establish political ground rules for the creation of a provisional government composed of parties from the North and South. But the superpowers differed as to which parties would be recognized as legitimate participants in the political process. The Soviet delegation argued that rightist parties, which had opposed the trusteeship plan, should not be allowed to participate; U.S. representatives argued that leftist parties were over-represented.[59]

When the second commission meeting failed to produce a satisfactory plan for devolution, U.S. officials asked the United Nations in September 1947 to establish a commission on Korea that would oversee the election of a national assembly, which would then establish a unified government.[60] (Curiously, U.S. officials seem to have borrowed the strategy adopted by the British in Palestine in the same year, though no conclusive evidence suggests that U.S. officials consciously imitated the British move.) The UN General Assembly adopted the U.S. proposal over Soviet objections (the Soviet bloc abstained), established a UN Temporary Commission on Korea, and began preparing for "the observance of elections in all Korea, and if that is impossible, *in as much of Korea as is accessible to it* [emphasis added]."[61]

Commission members themselves disagreed sharply over whether they should participate in a partial election that would result in a permanent division of the country, a fear borne out after the Soviets and their allies in the North refused to participate in the U.S.–UN–sponsored election, which was held on May 10, 1948. (This was four days before the UN-sponsored partition of Palestine took place.) This election resulted in an overwhelming majority—190 of 198 seats—for Syngman Rhee's and Kim Song-su's rightist parties. A constituent assembly convened on May 31, adopted a constitution on July 12 (which claimed to represent all of Korea), elected Rhee as its first president on July 20, and inaugurated the Republic of Korea—and the end of U.S. military rule—on August 15.[62] The Soviets thereupon convened a North Korean assembly that ratified its own constitution on September 3 and elected Kim Il Sung as the premier of the Democratic People's Republic of Korea, which was officially established on September 10 and quickly recognized by the Soviet Union.[63]

Although U.S. and Soviet officials could not agree on how devolution in Korea should be managed—and partition was the solution that provided some satisfaction to each—they agreed that political power should be devolved and superpower occupation forces withdrawn. Viewing the U.S.–Soviet impasse, American occupation commander Lt. Gen. John Hodge said, "Under present condition with no corrective action forthcoming, I would go so far as to recommend we give serious consideration to an agreement with Russia that both the United States and Russia withdraw forces from Korea simultaneously and leave Korea to its own devices and an *inevitable internal upheaval for its self-purification* [emphasis added]."[64] And this is what was eventually done.

The Soviets announced the withdrawal of their troops from the North by

December 31, 1948, and President Truman announced that "every effort should be made to create conditions for the withdrawal of occupation forces by 31 December 1948," though the withdrawal of U.S. forces was not completed until March 1949.[65] The U.S. decision to withdraw reflected Pentagon and State Department opinion

> that Korea is of little strategic value to the United States and that any commitment to United States' use of military force in Korea would be ill-advised and impracticable in view of the overall world situation and of our heavy international obligations as compared to our current military strength.[66]

One general, when asked by Congress whether there was any strategic disadvantage in not having a toehold like South Korea in Asia, replied, "It would be a very, very minor disadvantage."[67]

Even as the United States and Soviet Union moved toward partition in Germany and Korea in the years between 1945 and 1948, they abandoned their attempt to shape the political future of China and Vietnam. By 1945, in fact, the superpowers had withdrawn their troops and were prepared to abandon both countries to contesting political-military forces: Communists and Nationalists in China, Communists and French colonialists in Vietnam.

For all intents and purposes, China and Vietnam (as well as Korea) lay *outside* the spheres of influence claimed by the United States and the Soviet Union. This would change with the outbreak of the Korean War in 1950. But for a brief period, developments in China and Vietnam would be shaped primarily by local forces.

At the end of World War II in China, the Soviet Union and the United States both recognized the Nationalist government as the legitimate successor to receding Japanese colonialism and agreed that Japanese-held Taiwan (a colony since 1895) would be returned to Chinese authority. Both sought to prevent the Chinese Communists from challenging Nationalist rule. The United States supported Chiang Kai-shek, and, curiously, so did the Soviets. As Mao later said of the Soviets, "They [would] not allow China to make revolution. This was in 1945 when Stalin tried to prevent the Chinese revolution by saying there should not be any civil war and that we must collaborate with Chiang Kai-shek."[68]

The Chinese Communists did not heed this advice and a mammoth civil war broke out. Nationalist forces, which were strong in South China, moved to occupy northern China, the Communist stronghold. But Nationalist forces over-extended themselves and were cut off and destroyed by Communist troops, which began to advance to the south, routing huge Nationalist armies. In 1948 and 1949, Chaing Kai-shek and his Kuomintang forces fled the mainland to Taiwan, where they dug in for a last stand. Some four hundred thousand Nationalist forces and many more civilians, some two million in all, swamped the island and imposed military rule on the indigenous inhabitants.[69] One U.S. State Department official said the new rulers displayed a "genius for mismanagement" in Taiwan. Independence movements in Taiwan resisted the reimposition of mainland rule and in February and March 1947 demonstrated against the new government and demanded reform. The Kuomintang governor massacred ten thousand to twenty thousand Taiwanese demonstrators to crush the incipient revolt.[70]

Chinese Communist defiance and Chinese Nationalist negligence alienated their respective superpower allies. The Soviet Union maintained diplomatic recognition of the Nationalists until the very end and was the only foreign power to move its embassy from Nanking to Canton with the retreating Kuomintang.[71] And U.S. officials toyed with the idea of supporting the Taiwanese independence movement's claims for autonomy from both Communist *and* Nationalist rule.[72]

The Soviets finally recognized the Chinese Communist government in October 1949, but relations were cool and negotiations to establish political and economic relations were difficult and protracted.[73] Because the Chinese had made their revolution on their own initiative and with little Soviet assistance, the Soviets feared that China would follow an independent course, perhaps like Tito in Yugoslavia, and would not be easily included in the Soviet "sphere" in the same way that East Germany was then being incorporated. Communist governments in East Germany and China were both established in October 1949, but the Soviet Union was far more cordial to the former than the latter.[74]

As the Nationalist government collapsed on the mainland and retreated to Taiwan, the United States prepared to abandon the Nationalists. In 1947, U.S. officials ranked China thirteenth on a list of countries considered vital to U.S. security and a year later it dropped to seventeenth.[75] On January 5, 1950, just three months after the Communists established a government in Peking, President Truman announced that the United States would no longer interfere in China and that it would not defend Nationalist government claims to Taiwan, placing Taiwan outside the U.S. sphere of influence:

> The United States has no predatory design on Formosa or any other Chinese territory. . . . Nor does it have any intention of utilizing its armed forces to inter-

fere in the present situation. The U.S. government will not pursue a course which will lead to involvement in the civil conflict in China.[76]

By 1950, then, the United States and the Soviet Union had both retreated from China and abandoned their attempt to establish compliant client regimes there. China had been split apart, but it was not yet formally divided.

Much as the United States and the Soviet Union detested French colonialism, particularly in Indochina, they nonetheless retreated from their halfhearted attempt during the war to displace the French and establish a trusteeship in the region that would lead eventually to indigenous rule. At Potsdam, the superpowers assigned British troops responsibility for occupying the southern half of Vietnam and Nationalist Chinese troops the northern half. After the Japanese surrender in August, British and Kuomintang forces occupied the country. At the same time, Viet Minh insurgents moved into the cities and announced the formation of a Vietnamese republic. However, neither the United States nor the Soviet Union recognized Ho Chi Minh's government, despite Ho's pleas. He told an Office of Strategic Services officer in the summer of 1945:

> I have a government that is organized and ready to go. Your statesmen make eloquent speeches about helping those with self-determination. We are self-determined. Why not help us? Am I any different from Nehru, Quezon—even your George Washington? I too want to set my people free.[77]

In December 1945, Ho confessed that Vietnamese independence was still-born:

> Though five months have passed since we declared independence, no foreign countries have recognized us. Though our soldiers have fought gloriously, we are still far from victory . . . [W]e could ascribe these setbacks to the fact that our regime is young, or make other excuses. But no. Our successes are due to the efforts of our citizens, and our shortcomings are our own fault.[78]

When Chinese forces decided in February 1946 to turn over North Vietnam to the French, the Viet Minh were forced to negotiate. In March they agreed to let French colonial troops return to the North in return for French recognition of the Vietnam Republic as a "free state having its own government, parliament, army and finances, *and* forming part of the Indochinese federation and the French Union [emphasis added]."[79]

Although this decision might seem a step toward independence, it was really a retreat from it. French officials' conception of "Union"—their version of imperial reform—effectively subordinated peripheral peoples to metropolitan

French control. Once its military forces were built up by the end of 1946, the French launched assaults on the Viet Minh throughout the country. They began their counterattack by bombarding the port city of Haiphong, killing some six thousand people in November 1946.[80] The Viet Minh retreated from the cities to the countryside, and the war for independence began. It would not end until 1954.

After a few years, French authorities set about to create an indigenous Vietnamese government led by Bao Dai, the Vietnamese emperor who had abdicated in 1945 when Ho Chi Minh founded the Vietnam Republic, and integrated this government into the French Union as its representative in Vietnam.[81] In the agreement establishing the Republic of Vietnam on March 8, 1949, France retained control of Vietnam's foreign policy, finance, and national defense.

U.S. officials, however, were not eager to endorse the reimposition of French colonialism or the creation of a puppet regime. After the Bao Dai government was created, a State Department report recommended neither "full support . . . of French imperialism" nor "unlimited support of militant nationalism" and urged that the United States "should attempt to have the French transfer sovereignty in Indochina to a noncommunist indigenous regime."[82] But by the end of 1949, as the partitions of Germany and Korea hardened and Communists came to power in China, the United States moved toward recognizing the Bao Dai regime. Dean Rusk, the former colonel who had drawn occupation zones in Korea and now a State Department official, said on October 26, "We must support against aggressive pressure from the outside even states which we regard unfavorably. We must preserve them merely as states. . . . Our first concern is not with the *internal* structure of states but with their safety from aggression."[83]

While U.S. officials began to lean toward supporting the French in Vietnam, Soviet authorities offered encouragement to the Viet Minh. As in China, the Soviets withheld wholehearted support for indigenous communist movements they did not control. They refused to recognize either Chinese or Vietnamese Communist parties as legitimate governments throughout the late 1940s, and the civil wars for independence in China and Vietnam proceeded at the initiative of indigenous movements, not at the behest of the Soviets. The Soviets finally recognized the Chinese Communist government in October 1949 (just as Rusk was moving the U.S. toward recognition of Bao Dai), and the day after the French government ratified its pact with Bao Dai in January 1950, the Soviets recognized the Viet Minh. The British and U.S. governments then quickly decided to recognize Bao Dai and similar French puppet governments in Laos and Cambodia.[84]

The extension of U.S. and Soviet diplomatic recognition to contending Vietnamese parties did not immediately widen their spheres of influence. Rather, it left the resolution of conflict in Vietnam to indigenous forces that neither superpower controlled. It would not be until after the Korean War that the superpowers would begin to claim spheres of influence in the region and not until after the collapse of French colonialism in 1954 that they would intervene directly and attempt to devolve French colonial power to indigenous successors as they had in Germany and Korea.

Whereas in Germany partition stimulated the expansion of U.S. and Soviet spheres of influence and the extension of their respective "Monroe Doctrines," in Asia the partition of 1945 enabled the United States and Soviet Union to withdraw and limit their involvement—for a time. U.S. Secretary of State Dean Acheson described the U.S. withdrawal to the National Press Club on January 12, 1950. He placed Korea, Taiwan, and Indochina outside the "defensive perimeter" of the United States:

> So far as the military security of other areas of the Pacific is concerned, it must be clear that no person can guarantee these areas against military attack. . . . Should such an attack occur . . . the initial reliance must be on the people attacked to resist it and then upon the commitments of the entire civilized world under the Charter of the United Nations.[85]

Although Soviet officials did not make a corresponding announcement, subsequent events would demonstrate that they, too, placed Asia outside their defensive perimeter and let their nominal allies fend for themselves. They would not introduce Soviet troops into any of the Asian conflicts that emerged after 1950.

It was in this context that indigenous movements began to assert their independence. In Korea (and also in China and Vietnam), indigenous movements sought to undo de facto partition, unify their countries, and conclude conflicts that had been waged since the end of World War II. The attempt to undo superpower partition and reunify a country by force led to the outbreak of war in Korea in June 1950. The Korean War then precipitated a series of sweeping geopolitical developments in Asia and Europe between 1950 and 1955, triggering superpower intervention, solidifying partition, expanding U.S. and Soviet spheres of influence in Asia, and deepening the division of Europe into U.S. and Soviet blocs.

The Korean War was the product of an ongoing conflict between indigenous forces, a conflict that predated the cold war and the devolution of U.S. and Soviet authority in their respective occupation zones. It thus cannot be said to be a product of the cold war or an expression of superpower conflict in the peninsula. Rather, having agreed to divide Korea and withdraw, the superpowers left indigenous forces on their own to conclude this contest for power.

The North Koreans started the war by sending troops south across the 38th parallel on June 25, 1950. U.S. officials believed that Stalin directed the North Korean attack. In their view, the Korean War was an expression of the cold war and the North Koreans merely Soviet surrogates. But according to Nikita Khrushchev, it was North Korean leader Kim Il Sung who proposed the attack; Stalin and Mao Tse-tung merely agreed.[86] After it began, the Soviets did not participate in the war. Indeed, Andrei Gromyko told the Truman administration that the conflict was "a civil war among Koreans" and the Soviet Union would not intervene in it.[87] When the U.S.-led United Nations army swept into North Korea, the Soviets did not mass troops on the Soviet-Korean border or intervene in the conflict. The Chinese, however, did. According to Huang Hua, a member of the Chinese leadership, Stalin initially opposed Chinese intervention because "[Chinese] action would anger the United States, thus triggering World War III."[88] The Soviets did not at first even provide the Chinese with military supplies.

The superpowers may have approved or welcomed Korean attempts to unify the country on their own, but they did not initiate these efforts or themselves start the war. The Koreans had every reason to act on their own. Since 1946, they had been involved in a violent contest for power that had preceded the superpower partition of their country.

Between 1946 and 1950, civil and irregular war within and between the North and South claimed one hundred thousand lives.[89] Urban riots and strikes in 1946, large-scale insurrection on Cheju island in 1948–1949, border clashes at the 38th parallel, and irregular warfare by indigenous southern guerrillas and infiltrators from the North rocked the southern half of Korea throughout this period. To resolve this ongoing conflict, both Syngman Rhee and Kim Il Sung had vowed to reunify the country by force *before* full-scale conventional war broke out in 1950. As early as 1946, Syngman Rhee said, "On my returning to Korea I advocated unification . . . so that we could drive the Russians from North Korea. . . . As soon as the time comes, I will instruct you. Then you should be prepared to shed blood."[90] And on December 30, 1949, he reiterated his determination to reunify the country despite superpower partition: "In the coming year, we shall unanimously strive to regain lost territory . . . through our own efforts."[91] During this period, Kim Il Sung expressed a similar desire to use North Korea "as a democratic base for Korean unification."[92] The withdrawal of superpower occupation forces merely cleared the way for the two Korean governments to pursue reunification on their own. As it happened, the North Koreans struck first.

Although indigenous in origin, the Korean War quickly widened. And the war in Korea triggered U.S. intervention, not only in that country but also in China and Vietnam.

With the Soviets absent from the UN Security Council, the United Nations passed a U.S.-sponsored resolution on June 27 providing for UN participation, and assigned command of U.S. and UN forces to Gen. Douglas MacArthur. When he arrived in Korea to assume command, MacArthur announced that the 38th parallel was a "barrier [that] must and will be torn down. Nothing shall prevent the ultimate unity of your people."[93]

Although sixteen countries contributed soldiers and equipment to the UN forces in Korea, the United States directed the campaigns, made the decision to cross the 38th parallel and occupy the North as a prelude to reunification, contemplated the use of nuclear weapons during the course of the conflict, and conducted negotiations that would conclude the war. As MacArthur said of the U.S. role, "The entire control of my command and everything I did came from our own [U.S.] Chiefs of Staff. Even reports which were normally made by me to the United Nations were subject to censorship by our State and Defense Departments."[94]

On the day the United States obtained UN participation in the Korean War, President Truman ordered the Seventh Fleet into the Taiwan Strait

> to prevent any attack on Formosa [by Communist China]. As a corollary of this action, I am calling on the Chinese Government on Formosa to cease all air and sea operations against the mainland. . . . The determination of the future status of Formosa must await the restoration of security in the Pacific, a peace settlement with Japan, or consideration by the United Nations.[95]

Truman took this action to prevent the invasion of Taiwan by mainland forces, which were then preparing for a seaborne assault to unify the country under Communist rule. Truman's action would have important consequences for the conduct of war in Korea.[96]

On June 28, Truman ordered that U.S. aid to the French in Vietnam be accelerated; he even began sending military assistance before legislation providing that aid could be drafted and approved by Congress.[97] The administration announced in July that "the United States does not intend to permit further extension of Communist domination on the Continent of Asia or in the Southeast Asia area."[98]

U.S. actions in Korea, China, and Vietnam began to define and extend the U.S. sphere of influence in Asia, a process that by 1954 would result in the solidification of partition in these three countries. In concrete terms, military intervention in Korea and China, multilateral recognition of the Nationalist government in Taiwan, the creation of new security organizations—ANZUS in 1951 and SEATO in 1954—and the intervention in Vietnam on behalf of the French and, later, its South Vietnamese successor defined and extended the U.S. sphere.

Until 1950, the United States argued that Taiwan was part of China and that its reincorporation was a foregone conclusion. This attitude changed with the onset of the Korean War and the imposition of U.S. naval forces between the island and mainland. But unless the United States could persuade other countries to recognize the Kuomintang government as legitimate, U.S. officials could not permanently prevent the forcible reunification of China. Many countries, including Great Britain, had broken ties with the Nationalists and recognized the Communist government in Peking, and others threatened to do the same. Early in 1950, the United States blocked the Soviet attempt to unseat the Kuomintang delegation to the United Nations. But this was a temporary action. Events in Korea, however, enabled the United States to defend the Kuomintang in the United Nations, which deepened the partition of China.

At the beginning of the war, North Korean troops drove south and forced U.S.–UN and South Korean forces to retreat to a small enclave near the southern port city of Pusan. In September, MacArthur launched a successful amphibious invasion at Inchon, near the South Korean capital of Seoul (midway up the western side of the peninsula), and North Korean troops withdrew from the southern half of the peninsula and retreated behind the 38th parallel. In late September, UN forces headed north across the 38th parallel to destroy the North Korean army and fulfill MacArthur's promise to reunify the country. North Korean forces were driven back to enclaves along the Sino-Korean border, and on November 24, MacArthur launched an "end-the-war offensive" to eliminate North Korean resistance up to the Yalu River, the border with China. Two days later, the Chinese intervened in the war and counterattacked, driving UN forces out of North Korea and, by January 1951, back across the 38th parallel. During 1951, the opposing armies checked each other and the war stalemated. Peace negotiations began in the summer of 1951 but dragged on for two more years until July 27, 1953, when the country was again divided at the 38th parallel. Korea was three times divided at the 38th parallel: in 1945, 1948, and 1953.

It is important to note that by blocking the incipient Communist Chinese invasion of Taiwan, the United States made it possible for the Chinese to invade Korea as MacArthur's armies approached the Yalu. Chinese intervention in Korea was only possible if the Chinese transferred their army preparing to invade Taiwan to the north. By all accounts, this was a difficult decision, because the Communist leadership was more eager to unify China than unify Korea.[99] It is perhaps ironic that U.S. action at the outset of the Korean War *prevented* the Chinese invasion of Taiwan but *permitted* its invasion of Korea. However, the result in both Korea and Taiwan was the same: U.S. action and Communist China's response led to the deepening of partition not only in Korea but also in China.

With the outbreak of the Korean War and the imposition of the U.S. Seventh Fleet in the straits in the summer of 1950, the breech between China and Taiwan widened. Toward the end of that war, in 1953, President Eisenhower quietly removed the fleet,[100] but one year later, in the fall of 1954, mainland forces began shelling the islands of Quemoy and Matsu, which were held by the Kuomintang, perhaps in preparation for a renewed attempt to invade Taiwan. In January 1955, the U.S. Congress gave Eisenhower authority to take steps to defend Taiwan, and he sent the navy once more into the Taiwan Strait, where it would stay until 1969.[101] During a second Quemoy-Matsu crisis in 1958, when Communist shelling intensified and troops moved into coastal areas near the offshore islands, Eisenhower dispatched an armada—130 warships, including seven of the thirteen U.S. aircraft carriers[102]—into the strait. This naval screen effectively detached Taiwan from China and reconfirmed the division of China into separate states.

The division of China was effected primarily at U.S. initiative; the Soviet Union played only a minor role. During the first Quemoy-Matsu crisis in 1954, the U.S. ambassador to Moscow reported that the Soviet Union was probably not prepared "to run [a] serious risk of involvement in [a] major war over Chinese claims to Formosa."[103] Eisenhower told his press secretary in 1955, "I have a feeling that the Chinese Communists are acting on their own on this, and that is considerably disturbing to the Russians."[104]

The Soviets did little to support Chinese attempts to reclaim Taiwan or to stop the U.S.-initiated division of China. As the Soviets and Chinese began to differ on a host of other issues and the split between them widened in the late

1950s and early 1960s, the Soviets adopted their own quiet "two Chinas" policy. In the mid-1960s they even referred to Taiwan as a separate "state" or "country."[105] Nor did the Soviets actively challenge the Taiwanese delegation's claim to represent China in the United Nations or link the recognition of China to other issues at various superpower summits with the United States.

The outbreak of the Korean War also led to an intensification of the conflict in Vietnam. The French used the Korean War, and the accompanying extension of the U.S. sphere of influence in Asia, to press for increased U.S. support. The French successfully persuaded U.S. officials to discard long-standing reservations about French colonialism and the Bao Dai regime and to increase financial and military aid. By 1954, the United States was paying about one-third of the annual cost of the French war effort.[106] With U.S. political support and financial assistance, the French embarked on a major military campaign to defeat the Viet Minh insurgents before the United States changed its mind. Premier Georges Bidault of France feared that U.S. support might evaporate "if peace were reestablished in Korea while the war continued in Indochina."[107]

After the Korean armistice was signed in the summer of 1953, General Navarre, the French military commander in Vietnam, drew up a plan for a decisive military campaign. In November, he parachuted troops into a remote valley in northeastern Vietnam, there to build a fortress that would invite Viet Minh attack. Confident that superior French fire power and coordinated air strikes would decimate Viet Minh attackers and inflict a decisive defeat on his guerrilla opponents, General Henri Navarre said of the long-running war, "Now we can see it clearly—like light at the end of a tunnel."[108] But it would not be the French who found light in a place called Dien Bien Phu. It would be their Viet Minh opponents. There, on May 7, 1954, French colonialism was extinguished. Some fifty thousand Viet Minh troops overwhelmed the French garrison of thirteen thousand on the very day that Vietnamese peace talks opened in Geneva.[109]

Despite the Viet Minh's victory at Dien Bien Phu, the representatives of indigenous Vietnamese, Laotian, and Cambodian movements were shunted aside at the peace conference and were pressured to agree to decisions made by the great powers Great Britain, France, the United States, the Soviet Union, and China. Great Britain had helped to organize the peace conference, and Prime Minister Churchill urged "some form of partition" as a solution.[110] Likewise, French premier Pierre Mendes-France, who had just won election on the promise to withdraw French troops from Indochina, persuaded Chinese premier and foreign minister Chou En-lai to agree to partition, as least on a temporary basis, until reunification elections could be held. The French wanted to divide the country at the 18th parallel: this would give them a majority of the country's land and population even though the Viet Minh controlled three-quarters of the country, including large areas in the South. The French wanted to put off elections until an electoral majority could be built in the South.

The Viet Minh, persuaded that some form of partition was the only settlement the superpowers would accept, proposed partition at the 13th parallel. They also advocated early elections, within six months of a cease-fire, which they were confident they could win.[111] As Eisenhower later remarked, "I have never talked or corresponded with a person knowledgeable in Indochinese affairs who did not agree that had elections been held at the time of the fighting, possibly 80 percent of the population would have voted for the Communist Ho Chi Minh as their leader rather than Chief of State Bao Dai."[112]

Chou En-lai and Soviet foreign minister Molotov then mediated the difference, proposing *unequal* concessions by the French and the Viet Minh. As Chou En-lai told Mendes-France, "The two parties should take a few steps toward each other—which doesn't mean that each has to take the same number of steps," adding, "We are here to reestablish peace, not to back the Viet Minh."[113] When French and Viet Minh negotiators deadlocked, Molotov simply told the participants, "Let's agree on the 17th [parallel]."[114] The French thus had to take only one step to reach agreement with Molotov; the Viet Minh took four. And on elections—Mendes-France wanted an open timetable, whereas Viet Minh representative Pham Van Dong had revised his initial request for elections from within six months to a year or more—Molotov firmly suggested, "Shall we say two years?"[115]

And so it was done. The agreement reached on July 20, 1954, provided for the separation of three states—Vietnam, Laos, and Cambodia—from French Indochina and the partition of one: Vietnam. Vietnam would be divided at the 17th parallel pending reunification elections in the North and South in two years.[116] The agreement also prohibited the North Vietnamese from joining a military alliance or establishing foreign military bases on their soil. But it left the door open for South Vietnam to join a military alliance—it would join SEATO later that year—and the development of a massive U.S. military presence.[117]

The representatives of indigenous movements in Vietnam, however, were frustrated by the course of negotiations at the Geneva conference and by the fact that partition was drawn by non-Vietnamese hands. South Vietnamese representative Tran Van Do said:

> We fought desperately against partition. . . . [But it was] absolutely impossible to surmount the hostility of our enemies and the perfidy of false friends. Unusual procedures paralyzed the action of our delegation. All arrangements were signed in privacy. We express deepest sorrow in this total failure of our mission.[118]

The Viet Minh delegation also expressed frustration at having been denied at the conference table what had been won on the battlefield and having been pressured by its allies to accept an agreement that would forestall the unification of the country.[119] As Ho Chi Minh asked rhetorically, "Suppose we Vietnamese . . . proposed ourselves for a peacekeeping role in Europe. What would you Europeans think?"[120]

U.S. delegates to the conference took a low profile. Secretary of State John Foster Dulles had initially objected to a conference that included a Chinese Communist delegation and had been unenthusiastic about the British proposal to divide the country, but he agreed to back partition as a way to make the best of a bad situation. He was completely opposed to reunification elections, however, fearing that such a plebiscite would undermine U.S. efforts to replace French colonialism with U.S. assistance and establish a strong anticommunist regime in the South. As Dulles told reporters, "At the present time in a country which is politically immature, which has been the scene of civil war and disruption, we would doubt whether the immediate conditions would be conducive to a result which would really reflect the will of the people."[121]

The United States then moved quickly to establish a viable southern regime, persuading Bao Dai to appoint Ngo Dinh Diem as prime minister and then retire to Paris, organizing SEATO to provide collective security for South Vietnam, and supplying military-political advisers and financial assistance to the new government. Between 1955 and 1960, the United States provided nearly $15 billion to the regime in Saigon.[122] In addition, as in South Korea, Diem (with U.S. support) preempted countrywide reunification elections by holding a South-only referendum at the end of 1955, which elected Diem as president of the new "Government of Vietnam."[123]

U.S. officials had been willing to assist the French and assume greater responsibility in Vietnam because they wanted to increase French participation in NATO and defend partition in Germany. The war in Vietnam prevented the French from returning seasoned troops to Europe, and the cost of the war slowed French postwar economic recovery, considered essential to general European economic development.[124] A U.S. intelligence report in 1952 said that the "financial and manpower drain" of the war in Vietnam "seriously reduce[d] France's ability to meet its NATO obligations and maintain the power position on the continent which is necessary to balance a rearmed Germany."[125]

Moreover, with the outbreak of the Korean War and the commitment of U.S. troops to Asia, the Truman administration realized that it would need military assistance from other European countries to shore up its NATO defenses. With one-half of the French army tied down in Vietnam[126] and the British tied down all over the world, U.S. officials wanted West Germany to provide much needed, skilled military manpower to NATO. As one U.S. analyst observed, "the outbreak of the Korean War . . . brought the German rearmament issue to the forefront of alliance politics."[127] In September 1950, Secretary of State Acheson proposed the creation of a ten-division West German army.[128] German chancellor Konrad Adenauer welcomed this development because he worried that "Stalin was planning the same procedure for Western Germany as had been used in Korea."[129]

The French, like the Soviets and most other Europeans, opposed West German rearmament. The French had agreed to join NATO only on the condition that West Germany be excluded.[130] Therefore, in the early 1950s, U.S. officials hoped that if the French could conclude the war in Vietnam on favorable terms and return their troops to Europe, where they could shore up NATO, West German rearmament could be forestalled. The United States assisted the French with this in mind.

But developments in Asia prevented U.S. hopes from being realized. The French were defeated at Dien Bein Phu, and, after the 1954 Geneva peace conference divided the country at the 17th parallel, they withdrew. The United States then moved in to assist the new South Vietnamese government in France's absence. Because the United States had to expand its military and financial commitments in Vietnam as a result of the French defeat, it was still eager to lessen is responsibilities in Europe, despite the return of French troops to Europe. To do this it sought to increase both French and West German military participation in NATO. Thus, although French troops were returned to Europe, they were no longer sufficient, under the new conditions, to eliminate the need for West German rearmament. Moreover, because the United States had taken over for the French in Vietnam, the French could not easily refuse U.S. requests to rearm West Germany, and in December 1954, Mendes-France persuaded the French assembly to permit West German participation in NATO. The Federal Republic of Germany joined NATO the following May.[131]

The expansion of the U.S. sphere of influence in Europe and Asia was matched, to some extent, by a corresponding extension of a Soviet sphere. Although the Soviets did not respond to the creation of NATO in 1949 by creating their own regional security regime, the subsequent U.S. insistence on West German rearmament and participation in NATO did provoke this response. On May 14, 1955, just nine days after West Germany joined NATO, the Soviets organized the Eastern European states under its control into the Warsaw Pact. Like NATO, the Warsaw Pact was a common security organization formed outside the United Nations that would be used to deny Western intervention in Eastern Europe and, at the same time, permit Soviet intervention there. The pact, in short, was a Soviet version of the Monroe Doctrine and deepened its sphere of influence in Europe.

The mutual division of Europe into spheres, first begun at wartime summits, was recognized as a legitimate undertaking by both superpowers. When the Soviet Union exercised its Monroe Doctrine prerogatives—sometimes called the Khrushchev Doctrine or the Brezhnev Doctrine—in East Germany in 1953, Hungary in 1956, and Czechoslovakia in 1968, the United States and its Western European allies did nothing. NATO intervention in the Soviet sphere would have undermined the prohibition against Soviet intervention in the U.S. sphere.

But the symmetry between U.S. and Soviet Monroe Doctrines does not mean they were equal. The Soviets exercised their "rights" and intervened in a dramatic fashion in Eastern Europe. The United States, by contrast, did not have to send its tanks into Paris, London, or Rome. The Soviets intervened, and the United States did not, because the regimes established by the Soviets in Eastern Europe were weaker—had less indigenous popular support—than those in Western Europe after World War II.

In Asia, the Soviet sphere of influence expanded as a result of developments in Korea, China, and Vietnam, but it was not as well defined or developed as the corresponding U.S. sphere in Asia. Soviet influence in North Korea, mainland China, and North Vietnam increased during the wars in Korea and Vietnam as various *individual* military treaties, providing financial and military assistance, were negotiated by these regimes and the Soviet Union. But the Soviets did not organize a regional, Asian counterpart to ANZUS and SEATO, nor did their treaties have Monroe Doctrine features: they did not declare Asian communist states as within their sphere, which would prevent U.S. intervention and permit Soviet intervention there.

The Soviets did not intervene in the Korean War, even though two of its allies were embroiled in the war and even though the conflict bordered on the Soviet Union. Nor did the Soviets intervene in Vietnam. The Soviet "sphere" in Asia was less developed and more dependent on informal relations than on formal political, economic, or military institutions. They were less developed because indigenous movements were more developed.

By and large, regimes in North Korea, China, and North Vietnam were far stronger, with far greater indigenous popular support, than those in Eastern Europe or, for that matter, than their southern and island counterparts. They had won widespread popular support during their long anticolonial wars, they had considerable experience at force of arms, and they were determined to secure their independence from colonial empires and superpower states. North Korean, mainland Chinese, and North Vietnamese regimes repeatedly displayed a capacity for independent initiative: the North Koreans initiated a conventional war with neighboring South Korea; the Chinese launched a civil war in 1946 despite Soviet objections, planned to invade Taiwan on their own initiative, and intervened in the Korean conflict on their own; and the North Vietnamese waged an insurrectionary war against French colonialism for four years before the Soviet Union recognized them as a legitimate political entity. Although these Asian movements were influenced by and to some extent dependent on the Soviet Union, they resisted the extension of a Soviet "sphere" in Asia.

The United States, on the other hand, extended its sphere in Asia because the indigenous movements and regimes that it supported were weak. In contrast to Europe, where U.S.-supported governments were strong and Soviet-supported regimes were weak, U.S.-supported regimes in South Korea, Taiwan, and South Vietnam were weak and their communist rivals strong. The weakness of regimes in South Korea and Taiwan was made evident by the Korean War, just as the war in Vietnam demonstrated the frailty of Bao Dai's regime. Without U.S. assistance, all three would have been overwhelmed. So while the Soviet Union intervened in Eastern Europe (but not Asia) to shore up allied regimes, the United States did likewise in Asia (but not Western Europe).

It is a mistake to attribute all these developments to superpower competition. Many of these conflicts had indigenous origins and predate the outbreak of U.S.–Soviet hostilities in 1946–1947, while several others were between superpowers and indigenous movements: between the Soviet Union and indigenous movements in East Germany, Hungary, Yugoslavia, and Czechoslovakia; between the United States and indigenous movements in Korea, China, and

Vietnam. The superpowers regularly described their opponents as agents of the other superpower, justifying their interventions by claiming such actions prevented the other superpower from encroaching on their legitimate sphere of influence, but both really intervened to protect weak indigenous allies from strong indigenous opponents. They just did so in different corners of the world: the Soviet Union in Eastern Europe; the United States in East Asia.

The history of devolution and partition differs from one country to the next. But two distinct patterns can be identified: those of British colonies—Ireland, India, and Palestine—and those subject to great or superpower military occupation at the end of World War II—Germany, Korea, China, and Vietnam.

Partition in the British colonies was a unilateral affair. Although indigenous movements played a part, it was a British decision to divide Ireland and India and devolve power to two, separate indigenous movements. Other powerful states did not participate in any meaningful way, though they did pressure the British to get rid of their colonies. Even in Palestine, where a great many states participated in partition, they were merely implementing a solution first advanced by the British. Ireland, India, and Palestine were divided along "ethnic" lines, and power devolved to movements representing Catholics and Protestants, Hindus and Moslems, Arabs and Jews. These identities, however, were recent social constructions and were defined and developed during the protracted process of devolution in each setting. In this process, the British used the record of indigenous movements in world wars to weigh their claims to power in the devolving states. Partition in the British colonies, furthermore, coincided with the contraction of the British sphere of influence around the world. In Ireland, British authority retreated to an enclave in the northeast. And in India and Palestine, devolution and partition resulted in the complete withdrawal of British influence, bag and baggage.

By contrast, partition in Germany, Korea, China, and Vietnam—states subjected to military occupation after World War II—was a multilateral process. The United States and the Soviet Union were the principal actors, but they did not act alone. Great Britain and France participated in the division of Germany and Vietnam, and China played a role in the later stages of partition in Korea and Vietnam. And the United Nations, representing a host of countries, took part in the partitions of Korea. Only in China did the United States exercise nearly unilateral initiative. In other countries, the United States practiced what one diplomat described as "unilateral concerted action,"[132] taking unilateral initiatives that would be supported by an increasingly dense network of allies around the world. The Soviet Union also practiced this kind of diplomacy, though with less success.

Unlike Britain, the United States and the Soviet Union did not attempt to use religious or ethnic characteristics to determine their choice of successors in devolving states. They divided states along ideological lines, not ethnic ones, and devolved power in separate states to indigenous movements that could be characterized as "capitalist" or "communist." In Germany, the superpowers enlisted movements that closely resembled themselves, but they met with less success in Asia, where indigenous capitalist and communist movements did not always imitate superpower ideology or practice. Movements in Asia were quite capable of taking their own initiative and departing from superpower expectations.

Moreover, while devolution and partition in the British colonies helped to contract the British sphere of influence in the world, partition in Europe and Asia contributed to the expansion of U.S. and Soviet spheres. As partition in Germany, Korea, China, and Vietnam deepened, the United States and the Soviet Union expanded their spheres and applied their respective "Monroe Doctrines" to places that lay beyond the perimeters of their power at the end of World War II.

But regardless of whether devolution was a unilateral or multilateral affair, whether it preceded along ethnic or secular lines, or whether it resulted in the contraction or expansion of spheres of influence, the result was the same: permanent partition.

The lines dividing states at the 38th and 17th parallels, in Kashmir or the Negev, were not drawn by indigenous movements but by superpower hands. Partition was supposed to be temporary—the dividers of states typically provided for reunification elections once tempers had cooled. But reunification elections were never held. Partition solidified.

Partition was supposed to permit self-determination, protect residual minorities and superpower interests, and prevent war. But for indigenous movements that had set independence, *swaraj*, *sinparam*, or *doc lap* as their goal, partition would compromise the meaning of self-determination in important ways. Frustration with the limits placed on their independence prompted indigenous movements to reclaim their legacy by force. Ideological movements, no less than ethnic ones, would fight tenaciously for the kind of independence that partition had denied them.

NOTES

1. See Audrey Kurth Cronin, *Great Power Politics and the Struggle over Austria, 1945–1955* (Ithaca, N.Y.: Cornell University Press, 1986).

2. Walter Lafeber, *America, Russia and the Cold War, 1945–85* (New York: Knopf, 1985), 13.

3. John L. Gaddis, *The United States and the Origins of the Cold War* (New York: Columbia University Press, 1972), 100.

4. Gabriel Kolko, *The Politics of War* (New York: Vintage, 1968), 316.

5. Bruce Kuklick, *American Policy and the Division of Germany* (Ithaca, N.Y.: Cornell University Press, 1972), 25.

6. Kolko, *Politics of War*, 316; Kuklick, *Division of Germany*, 25.

7. Truman would later claim that he always wanted "a unified Germany with a centralized government in Berlin." John L. Snell, *Dilemma over Germany* (New Orleans, La.: Phauser, 1959), 200.

8. Snell, *Dilemma over Germany*, 49.

9. Kuklick, *Division of Germany*, 30; Snell, *Dilemma over Germany*, 125, 142.

10. Snell, *Dilemma over Germany*, 109.

11. Snell, *Dilemma over Germany*, 55.

12. Snell, *Dilemma over Germany*, 75–76.

13. Snell, *Dilemma over Germany*, 79. Morgenthau told White during their deliberation, "I don't care what happens to the population. . . . I would take every mine, every mill and factory and wreck it . . . Steel, coal, everything. Just close it down." Gaddis, *Origins of the Cold War*, 120.

14. Gaddis, *Origins of the Cold War*, 119.

15. Gaddis, *Origins of the Cold War*, 120.

16. Kuklick, *Division of Germany*, 22–23, 69.

17. Gaddis, *Origins of the Cold War*, 236.

18. Bong-youn Choy, *A History of the Korean Reunification Movement* (Peoria, Ill.: Institute of International Studies, Bradley University, 1984), 10.

19. Choy, *Korean Reunification Movement*, 10; see also Joyce and Gabriel Kolko, *The Limits of Power* (New York: Harper & Row, 1972), 278.

20. Peter Lowe, *The Origins of the Korean War* (London: Longman, 1986), 14; James I. Matray, "Captive of the Cold War: Decision to Divide Korea at the 38th Parallel," *Pacific Historical Review* 5, no. 2 (May 1981): 164; John Sullivan, *Two Koreas— One Future?* (Lanham, Md.: University Press of America, 1987), 7; Choy, *Korean Reunification Movement*, 12.

21. Coincidentally, Russia and Japan had twice discussed dividing Korea at the 38th Parallel, first in 1896 and again in 1903. Choy, *Korean Reunification Movement*, 13.

22. Matray, "Captive of the Cold War," 166.

23. Lowe, *Origins of the Korean War*, 90–91; LaFeber, *Cold War*, 107.

24. John T. McAlister, *Vietnam* (New York: Knopf, 1970), 275.

25. LaFeber, *Cold War*, 107; Andrew J. Rotter, *The Path to Vietnam* (Ithaca, N.Y.: Cornell University Press, 1987), 93.

26. Stanley Karnow, *Vietnam: A History* (New York: Viking, 1983), 137.

27. Karnow, *Vietnam*, 147.

28. Karnow, *Vietnam*, 152.

29. John King Fairbank, *The United States and China* (Cambridge, Mass.: Harvard University Press, 1983), 341–42.

30. LaFeber, *Cold War*, 30–31.

31. Kolko, *Limits of Power*, 255; Lowe, *Origins of the Korean War*, 99–100.

32. Kolko, *Limits of Power*, 255.

33. Frank Ninkovich, *Germany and the United States* (Boston: Twayne, 1988), 58.

34. Snell, *Dilemma over Germany*, 227.

35. LaFeber, *Cold War*, 75.

36. Ninkovich, *Germany and the United States*, 60.

37. Snell, *Dilemma over Germany*, 224.

38. Ninkovich, *Germany and the United States*, 60.

39. Ninkovich, *Germany and the United States*, 43, 62.

40. Ninkovich, *Germany and the United States*, 69.

41. John L. Gaddis, *The Long Peace* (New York: Oxford University Press, 1987), 64.

42. Gaddis, *Long Peace*, 64.

43. Ninkovich, *Germany and the United States*, 71.

44. Ninkovich, *Germany and the United States*, 72; Henry Ashby Turner, Jr., *The Two Germanies since 1945* (New Haven, Conn.: Yale University Press, 1987), 50.

45. Gaddis, *Long Peace*, 54.

46. Gaddis, *Long Peace*, 55.

47. Gaddis, *Long Peace*, 62.

48. Lawrence S. Kaplan, *NATO and the United States* (Boston: Twayne, 1988), 17–30, 33.

49. LaFeber, *Cold War*, 83.

50. LaFeber, *Cold War*, 83.

51. Rotter, *Path to Vietnam*, 99.

52. LaFeber, *Cold War*, 84.

53. Rotter, *Path to Vietnam*, 14–15; see also Kaplan, *NATO*, 33.

54. LeFeber, *Cold War*, 69, 70.

55. See Kolko, *Limits of Power*, 33, 56; Ralph B. Clough, *Embattled Korea* (Boulder, Colo.: Westview, 1987), 20; Turner, *Two Germanies*, 36.

56. Choy, *Korean Reunification Movement*, 41–42.

57. Choy, *Korean Reunification Movement*, 45.

58. Choy, *Korean Reunification Movement*, 46–48.

59. Choy, *Korean Reunification Movement*, 49.

60. Choy, *Korean Reunification Movement*, 50–51.

61. Choy, *Korean Reunification Movement*, 52.

62. Choy, *Korean Reunification Movement*, 52, 54.

63. Choy, *Korean Reunification Movement*, 55.

64. Bruce Cumings, *The Origins of the Korean War* (Princeton, N.J.: Princeton University Press, 1981), 211; Lowe, *Origins of the Korean War*, 35.

65. Lowe, *Origins of the Korean War*, 48, 49; Bruce Cumings, *Child of Conflict: The Korean-American Relationship* (Seattle: University of Washington Press, 1983), 189. The initial decision to withdraw was made in the fall of 1947, when the United States asked the UN to supervise the devolution process. Gaddis, *Long Peace*, 94.

66. Clough, *Embattled Korea*, 20; Gaddis, *Long Peace*, 94.

67. Robert Blum, *Drawing the Line* (New York: Norton, 1982), 71.

68. Seymour Topping, *Journey Between Two Chinas* (New York: Harper Colophon, 1972), 54; Roy Medvedev, *China and the Superpowers* (London: Blackwell, 1986), 90.

69. Lowe, *Origins of the Korean War*, 114.

70. Topping, *Journey between Two Chinas*, 53.

71. Lowe, *Origins of the Korean War*, 108.

72. Gaddis, *Long Peace*, 81. George Kennan, for instance, argued that "Formosan separatism is the only concept which has sufficient grassroots appeal to resist communism." Gaddis, *Long Peace*, 81. And Secretary of State Dean Acheson hoped to satisfy "the legitimate demands of indigenous Formosans for self-determination either under a U.N. trusteeship or through independence." Cumings, *Child of Conflict*, 47. But these schemes foundered because the Kuomintang was strong, Taiwanese independence movements weak, and the United States had already agreed to return Taiwan to China. A State Department memo warned that an attempt to detach the island "would outrage *all* Chinese elements and as a resort to naked expediency would destroy our standing with the smaller countries of the world." Gaddis, *Long Peace*, 83.

73. Medvedev, *China and the Superpowers*, 21.

74. The Soviet historian Roy Medvedev observes:
No personal letter to Mao Zedong . . . came from Stalin . . . whose silence was all the more unusual in that only 10 days later, on the occasion of the proclamation of the German Democratic Republic, he would send a long personal letter to the first President of the GDR, Wilhelm Pieck, and to the Prime Minister, Otto Grotewohl."
Medvedev, *China and the Superpowers*, 21.

75. Gaddis, *Long Peace*, 78.

76. June M. Grasso, *Truman's Two-China Policy* (Armonk, N.Y.: M. E. Sharpe, 1987), 113.

77. Lloyd C. Gardner, *Approaching Vietnam* (New York: W. W. Norton, 1988), 62.

78. Karnow, *Vietnam*, 152.

79. Blum, *Drawing the Line*, 106.

80. Gardner, *Approaching Vietnam*, 75.

81. Blum, *Drawing the Line*, 107. Bao Dai was a notorious playboy. Following his return to Vietnam, the emperor took up with a blonde who was supposedly part of a documentary film crew. When officials told him they doubted she could use a camera and was merely masquerading as part of the crew, Bao Dai replied, "Yes, I know. But really that girl is quite extraordinary in bed." Then he added, "She is only plying her trade. Of the two I am the real whore." Rotter, *Vietnam*, 95.

82. Rotter, *Path to Vietnam*, 96.

83. Rotter, *Path to Vietnam*, 113.

84. Rotter, *Path to Vietnam*, 169–70.

85. Lowe, *Origins of the Korean War*, 119; Grasso, *Truman's Two-China Policy*, 127.

86. Lowe, *Origins of the Korean War*, 156; Ralph B. Levering, *The Cold War 1945–87* (Arlington Heights, Ill.: Harlan Davidson, 1988), 44.

87. LaFeber, *Cold War*, 103.

88. Melvin Gurtov and Byong-Moo Huang, *China under Threat* (Baltimore, Md.: Johns Hopkins University Press, 1980), 54.

89. LaFeber, *Cold War*, 99.

90. Choy, *Korean Reunification Movement*, 61.

91. Choy, *Korean Reunification Movement*, 61; Kolko, *Limits of Power*, 568.

92. Choy, *Korean Reunification Movement*, 61.

93. Cumings, *Child of Conflict*, 187.

94. LaFeber, *Cold War*, 105.

95. Grasso, *Truman's Two-China Policy*, 128, 141.

96. U.S. conservatives, who opposed the Truman administration's policy of placing Korea and Taiwan outside the U.S. defensive perimeter in Asia, welcomed this policy change. Senator H. Alexander Smith said of Truman's action, "It was all very wonderful and an answer to prayer. The saving of Formosa was clearly God guided." Gaddis, *Long Peace*, 87.

97. Karnow, *Vietnam*, 177.

98. Rotter, *Path to Vietnam*, 104.

99. More than fifty thousand Chinese troops assigned to the invasion-of-Taiwan army were moved north to the Korean frontier. Gurtov and Huang, *China under Threat*, 49.

100. Eisenhower said that the "Seventh Fleet [should] no longer be employed to shield Communist China." Gardner, *Approaching Vietnam*, 129. This move was a neat reverse. When Truman first sent the fleet into the Strait, he did so to protect Taiwan from mainland attack and also to halt Kuomintang raids on the mainland, which had caused considerable damage. So to assuage congressional critics of the move, Eisenhower claimed he was removing the fleet so that it would no longer protect the mainland from nationalist attack. But this was a thin charade.

101. Medvedev, *China and the Superpowers*, 85; Ilpyong Kim, *The Strategic Alliance* (New York: Paragon House, 1987), 185.

102. Medvedev, *China and the Superpowers*, 87.

103. Gaddis, *Long Peace*, 185.

104. Gaddis, *Long Peace*, 185.

105. Kim, *Strategic Alliance*, 196.

106. Gardner, *Approaching Vietnam*, 116.

107. Karnow, *Vietnam*, 191.

108. Gardner, *Approaching Vietnam*, 153.

109. R. F. Holland, *European Decolonization, 1918–1981* (New York: St. Martin's, 1985), 100; Gardner, *Approaching Vietnam*, 179.

110. Rotter, *Path to Vietnam*, 215.

111. Karnow, *Vietnam*, 202.

112. Gardner, *Approaching Vietnam*, 316.

113. Karnow, *Vietnam*, 202, 201.

114. Karnow, *Vietnam*, 202–04.

115. Karnow, *Vietnam*, 204.

116. Gardner, *Approaching Vietnam*, 284.

117. Gardner, *Approaching Vietnam*, 313.

118. Gardner, *Approaching Vietnam*, 281.

119. Topping, *Journey between Two Chinas*, 151; Gardner, *Approaching Vietnam*, 298.

120. Malcolm Chalmers, *Paying for Defense* (London: Pluto, 1985), 83.

121. Gardner, *Approaching Vietnam*, 298.

122. Gardner, *Approaching Vietnam*, 340.

123. Gabriel Kolko, *The Roots of American Foreign Policy* (Boston: Beacon, 1969), 111; Topping, *Journey between Two Chinas*, 151.

124. Rotter, *Path to Vietnam*, 180. As the historian Andrew Rotter notes, "A strong France [was] a prerequisite to an integrated Europe that included West Germany. The Americans pursued [this objective] . . . with increasing vigor in the spring of 1950, but it quickly became clear to them that this goal was incompatible with the continuation of the French military effort in Indochina." Rotter, *Path to Vietnam*, 166.

125. Rotter, *Path to Vietnam*, 217.

126. Rotter, *Path to Vietnam*, 184.

127. Rotter, *Path to Vietnam*, 211.

128. LaFeber, *Cold War*, 109.

129. Kaplan, *NATO*, 44.

130. Ninkovich, *Germany and the United States*, 84–85.

131. Rotter, *Path to Vietnam*, 218–19.

132. Gardner, *Approaching Vietnam*, 189.

F I V E

CITIZENSHIP DIMINISHED

Partition transformed the social landscape in unexpected ways. In its aftermath, millions fled their homes, families were divided, and refugees poured across newly created borders. Almost overnight, members of majority populations became minorities. Minorities became majorities.

Once they assumed power, independence movements sought to strengthen their political position and guarantee the rule of the empowered "majority." This effort typically restricted, qualified, or abrogated the meaning of "citizenship" for minority populations, who found they could not participate as full-fledged members of the polity in divided states Mahatma Gandhi once said, "One can judge a nation by the way it treats its minorities."[1] By this measure, partition has not fared well.

At the same time, the officials governing devolved states sought to exercise their newfound independence. But sibling states and superpowers, as well as other members of the interstate system, challenged their right to rule and restricted their sovereignty in important ways. International recognition often proved difficult to secure and maintain. Officials in divided states found they could not participate as equal members in the interstate system. Partition thus proved a bitter disappointment for movements that had championed democracy and independence. In the years following partition, citizenship would be compromised, sovereignty abridged, and democracy impoverished.

As the meaning of citizenship eroded, minority social movements emerged to reclaim lost rights. When constitutional and legal redress was blocked, they frequently threatened violence, much as their predecessors had, to achieve self-determination. Where sovereignty was abridged, state officials sought to reassert their independence—and when diplomacy failed to establish an unchallenged claim, they frequently turned to war to recover their state's lost sovereignty. The result in many divided states was that democracy remained unrealized.

The abrogation of citizenship and sovereignty would lead to social conflict and war within and between divided states. Partition was supposed to deflect incipient social conflict and deter war. But it did neither. In the decades that followed partition, such conflict instead became obdurate and irremediable.

The import and export of huge populations during partition dramatically altered the social landscape, catching state officials unprepared and creating problems that would be felt for generations. In the partitioned states, the scale of migration ranged from modest to massive. By comparison with the other divided states (and by comparison with mass emigration of the nineteenth century), Ireland's partition-induced migration was relatively small-scale. Some twenty-five thousand Catholics fled Northern Ireland between 1922 and 1924, and in roughly the same period, 1920–1926, twelve thousand Protestants left southern Ireland.[2] The larger Catholic migration was due to anti-Catholic violence in the North, while there was little comparable violence directed at southern Protestants after the Anglo-Irish Treaty was concluded.

Migration on a more considerable scale took place in the ideologically divided states—Korea, China, Vietnam, and Germany. In the years preceding the outbreak of the Korean War, 1.8 million people left the North (and parts of northeastern China) for the South, and another 1.2 million moved South during the course of the war.[3] Although estimates vary, it is generally recognized that between 25 and 30 percent of North Korea's population had migrated south by 1953.[4] Likewise, during the last stages of the civil war between Chinese Communists and Nationalists, about 1.5 million Nationalist troops and refugees from the mainland fled to Taiwan, which at the time had some eight million indigenous inhabitants.[5] The heavily armed refugees from the mainland solidified Kuomintang control of the island, and in November 1949, Chiang Kai-shek established Taipei as the seat of the Nationalist government. In Vietnam, as in Korea, nine hundred thousand people, mostly Catholic, left the North for the South.[6] The execution of many landlords and French collaborators undoubtedly encouraged many to flee.

Although the sibling states in Korea, China, and Vietnam sealed their borders and stopped the flow of migrants soon after partition, migration in Germany continued after partition in 1949, until Berlin was subdivided and the border sealed in 1961. In that period, between two and three million people, roughly one-sixth of East Germany's population, left for the West.[7] There was also considerable migration of ethnic Germans from other Eastern European countries into West Germany.[8] The exodus from East to West, primarily through Berlin, increased in 1953 as a result of the uprising in the East, then remained fairly steady until 1960–1961, when it jumped dramatically. In the first eight months of 1961, 155,000 residents of East Germany fled to the West.[9] This outflow prompted East German and Soviet officials to build the Berlin Wall, which greatly slowed East German emigration (at least until the recent exodus in 1989).

But it was the partition in India that led to what may have been the largest, swiftest population transfer in history. In the months that followed the August 1947 partition, 17.2 million people crossed the new borders; Moslems and Hindus were uprooted in roughly equal numbers.[10] People fled singly and in huge human caravans that stretched for miles. Lord Mountbatten observed that one refugee column in the Punjab was "drawn up in good marching order along some 50 miles of road."[11]

This massive exodus was stimulated by widespread violence throughout the subcontinent. Nearly one million people were killed in the three-month carnage that followed partition.[12] In many places, whole villages were massacred. Refugee columns often passed down the same road, traveling in opposite directions. Such columns met, fought, and killed on the highways in Kashmir, Bengal, and the Punjab.

Neither the departing British administrators nor the newly installed Indian and Pakistani officials were prepared to cope with the flood of refugees or the scale of the violence. Pendrel Moon, a government minister in Bahawalpur, Pakistan, said:

> I foresaw, of course, a terrific upheaval . . . but I quite failed to grasp the speed with which disturbances and displacements of population . . . would resolve themselves into a vast movement of mass migration. . . . Punjabis in general were strangely unprepared for what was coming.[13]

The result was chaos. A large-scale war was waged by armies of civilians, many of them neighbors. One noncommissioned officer in Bengal wrote:

> This country has become a battlefield since the 16th August. One village attacks another village and one community another community. Nobody could sleep for a week. Villages are being destroyed and thousands are being killed or wounded. Smoke-fires are seen everywhere all around my village.[14]

The size and murderousness of the Indo-Pakistani migration was without precedent. In relative terms, however, partition-related migration in Palestine involved fewer people but a much larger percentage of the population, and the violence practiced there was smaller only on a numerical scale.

As a result of partition in Palestine, a vast population swap took place. The bulk of the Arab Palestinian population was removed and replaced by a Jewish Israeli population, turning the prepartition Arab majority into a minority. Before partition in 1948, Jews had been a minority in Palestine. Slow, uneven immigration increased the percentage of Jews from about 11 percent of the population prior to World War I to about 22 percent in 1948.[15] On the eve of partition, Moslem Arab Palestinians made up more than 68 percent of the population and owned 90 percent of the land, and Christian Arab Palestinians about 9 percent of the population.[16]

During the war that accompanied partition, between December 1947 and July 1949, most of the Moslem and Christian Arab Palestinian population fled Israeli-held territory. (During the course of the war, the Israelis occupied and claimed territories not awarded to them by the United Nations partition plan. The size of Israel after the 1949 cease-fire was 27 percent larger than the territory allotted it by the United Nations.) Estimates on the number of Arab refugees vary, from 520,000 according to Israeli sources to 900,000 according to Arab sources. UN observers said the real figure was somewhere in between, about 726,000.[17] As a result of partition-induced migration, the Arab population inside Israel dropped to 11 percent. Most fled to Arab-held lands on the West Bank, which was subsequently annexed by Jordan, and to the Gaza Strip, which was under Egyptian control.[18]

In Palestine, as in most of the other divided states, violence and coercion encouraged people to flee. An Israeli Defense Force study of Arab migration between January 1947 and June 1948 found that most Arabs left their homes as a result of (in order of importance) "1) Direct, hostile Jewish operations against Arab settlements; 2) The effect of our hostile operations on nearby settlements . . . especially the fall of large neighboring cities; and 3) Operations of the [Israeli] dissidents [such as the Irgun and Stern Gang]."[19] Arabs did not leave because they were encouraged to do so by Arab state radio broadcasts. Indeed, according to Israeli historian Benny Morris, "The Arab Higher Committee decided to impose restrictions and issued threats, punishments and propaganda in the radio and press to *curb* [Arab] emigration [emphasis added]."[20] The Arabs left because, like most persons in a war zone, they sought to avoid attack.

The Israelis and Arabs, like the Indians and Pakistanis, were surprised by the size of the Arab exodus from the war zone. Arab leaders thought that it was a temporary problem and that the refugee columns would return home after the shooting stopped. Israeli officials, after seeing large Arab cities such as Jaffa empty during the fighting, decided to encourage Arabs to leave during the war and then moved to block their return. Military assaults on Arab villages, orders to evacuate towns, and psychological campaigns aimed at obtaining an Arab evacuation all stimulated Arab flight. About 350 Arab towns and villages were depopulated during the war, and Israeli demolition teams razed many of them. The majority of these sites were either completely or partly in ruins or uninhabitable. Demolition was so pervasive that Israeli dynamite supplies ran short. This widespread practice was slowed when officials decided that evacuated villages should be kept intact to provide housing for the expected influx of Jewish immigrants.[21]

The Israeli army then blocked the return of Arab Palestinian refugees. On June 16, 1948, the Israeli cabinet ratified this policy. Ben-Gurion argued, "I believe we should prevent their return. . . . [W]e must prevent their return at all costs."[22] Later that month, the government issued emergency regulations that provided for the seizure of any Arab land or property in an "abandoned area" and transferred the land directly to Jewish settlers or to private Jewish agencies that leased Arab properties to Jews.[23] In November, while the war was still in progress, the government conducted a census. Any Arab not registered was regarded as an "absentee," which meant they could not claim their "abandoned" property or obtain Israeli citizenship. Refugees who returned to their homes were regarded as "illegal immigrants" and were deported to neighboring states.[24] At war's end, Foreign Ministry Director General Walter Eytan wrote:

> The war that was fought in Palestine was bitter and destructive, and it would be doing the refugees a disservice to let them persist in the belief that if they returned, they would find their homes or shops or fields intact. In certain cases, it would be difficult for them even to identify the sites upon which their villages once stood. . . . Generally, it can be said that any Arab house that survived the impact of the war . . . now shelters a Jewish family.[25]

After Arab Palestinians were exported from Israel, Jews were imported. During the decade that followed partition, nearly one million Jews from around the world—half of them from the Middle East and Africa and half from Europe—immigrated to Israel.[26]

The Arab Palestinian population remained a small minority in Israel until 1967. Then, during the Six-Day War, Israeli forces occupied the Gaza Strip and the West Bank, bringing 1.4 million Arab inhabitants under its jurisdiction.[27] Israel annexed East Jerusalem immediately and a portion of the Golan Heights in 1981, but it did not formally annex the West Bank or Gaza. By 1984, Arab Palestinians made up 42.5 percent of the total population of Israel and occupied Palestine.[28] Of the two million Arab-Palestinians there, about one-quarter are considered "citizens" of Israel, though they do not have the same legal standing as Jewish citizens, one-half of the total were treated (until recently) as Jordanian nationals with the status of enemy aliens; and one-quarter were viewed as stateless enemy aliens in Gaza.[29]

In most of the divided states, violence or the threat of violence played a major role in the migrations that accompanied partition. Only Germany was spared the kind of civil and conventional war that punctuated partition in the other divided states. But in its place was the threat of superpower conflict and nuclear annihilation.

Although in many instances refugees left their homes voluntarily, hoping to improve their lot in a state where they could participate as full-fledged citizens, many were also gripped by fear. Fear provided the push, hope the pull. Whether they felt push or pull more strongly, whether their fears and hopes were real or imagined, the experience of partition-related migration was wrenching for millions of people. Moreover, most of the population transfers were sudden, occurring immediately prior to or following partition. Migration across the inter-German border was more protracted than most, but there, as in most divided states, the common border was eventually sealed and the flow of migration staunched for twenty-eight years. The inter-Irish and Indo-Pakistani borders, though, have remained relatively porous. Migration across them continues to this day. But these remain exceptions to the rule; the borders of other divided states present much more formidable barriers, and movement across them is full of risk.

After the great migrations waned and the flood of refugees receded, the social landscape of the divided states emerged transformed. The most important and obvious transformation was that minorities had become majorities and vice versa. Protestants in Ireland, Jews in Palestine, and Moslems in India, minorities all, found themselves rulers of states in which they now commanded a majority. Conversely, Catholics in Northern Ireland, Arab Palestinians in Israel, and Hindus in Pakistan—all members of majority populations in undivided states—discovered that they had each become a minority in their homeland.

In the other divided states, people who had previously expected to rule as a majority over a unified territory found that they could not. Moreover, minority political parties found themselves in control of truncated states. In Korea, China, and Vietnam, communist parties fully expected to assume state power over a unified country. Without the intervention of the superpowers, they probably would have done so. They could claim, with some justification, to represent the majority of the inhabitants, though the identification of a majority based on political ideologies (as opposed to religious belief, ethnic identity, and linguistic practice) is fairly transient, particularly during war. Communists in East Germany could not lay claim to represent a majority of the population, though in the fractured political context of postwar Germany, no single party could make that claim. In any case, communists and their sympathizers in South Korea, South Vietnam, and West Germany found that they had become unwelcome political minorities. By the same token, noncommunists in North Korea, North Vietnam, and East Germany found themselves excluded from participation in government or public life.

If partition was supposed to create states where homogeneous ethnic and secular political groups could exercise self-determination without interference, it was a singular failure. Despite huge population transfers, partition did not result in the creation of homogeneous polities as significant minority populations remained behind. Thus, despite the transfer of seventeen million people across the Indo-Pakistani border, as many Moslems remained in India as lived in East and West Pakistan. Despite violence and coercion, many Catholics remained in Northern Ireland, and some Protestants remained in the South. Between 1950 and 1967, Arab Palestinians made up 11 percent of the population in Israel, a proportion that increased to more than 40 percent (of Israeli-held territory) after 1967. In Korea, China, Vietnam, and Germany, residual minority populations living on the "wrong" side of the border contested majority rule.

Majority rule in the divided states was further complicated by the fact that minority populations retained their links to families, friends, and political allies in neighboring states. Thus, any conflicts between majority and minority populations within a particular state were quickly externalized. Attempts to consolidate majority rule typically provoked protest not only by indigenous minority populations but also by populations and officials in neighboring states. Such protests were regarded by state officials as unwarranted intrusions into their sovereignty.

Because political relations *within* divided states tended to become the subject of controversy *between* divided states, officials came to regard indigenous protest as synonymous with "foreign" meddling, and they began to treat minority populations as disloyal aliens who owed their allegiance to a foreign power. Ben-Gurion, for example, described the Arab minority in the Jewish state as a potential "Fifth Column,"[30] and Harry Midgley, minister of education in Northern Ireland, once said of the Catholic population there, "All the minority are traitors and always have been traitors to the government of Northern Ireland."[31] Because it was seen as inspired or manipulated by outsiders, the indigenous opposition to majority rule was considered illegitimate. As a result, internal conflict was externalized and external conflict internalized. Partition drove a wedge not only between states, but also within states. To secure and maintain political power, empowered majorities restricted or qualified the citizenship of minorities, whose "loyalty" to the majority-ruled state was suspect. By enacting laws that restricted minority citizenship, state officials defined *majority* and *minority* in terms of a legalistic analogy. In the law, "minors" are considered incapable of fully exercising their legal rights until they reach the age of "majority." After partition, numerical minorities were assigned the status of minors, a group prevented from participating as equal members of civil society. Unlike children, however, who would attain equal rights upon reaching majority, the divided states' minorities were to be treated as minors permanently.[32] Thus, citizenship was divided, and civic rights and responsibilities were parceled out on an unequal basis. Denied the citizenship given others, minority populations were effectively disenfranchised, their freedom curtailed. As a further affront, state officials frequently awarded automatic citizenship to their ethnic group living in other states, while denying citizenship to some of their own residents. These developments led, in many divided states, to the creation of "civic apartheid," the permanent division of the populace along ethnic or ideological lines.

Such wholesale disenfranchisement has been an ongoing process. During the decades that followed partition, citizenship rights were lost, regained, and lost again. The character and meaning of citizenship for minorities (and majorities) were frequently altered by changes of government. The history of the divided states is marked by military coups and the imposition of martial law, as well as by the dissolution of military juntas and the installation of civilian government. Because these developments were uneven and differed from country to country, it would be difficult to attempt a single, chronological history. Nevertheless, it is possible to describe how certain general rights, usually associated with citizenship, were curtailed in the divided states during the years following partition. In nearly all cases, political officials qualified the right to vote, limited participation in the electoral process, restricted the right to bear arms, imposed military law over civilian populations, and curtailed individual liberties, including the right to exercise religious beliefs or to practice social customs (regarding language, education, marriage, divorce, travel, and property ownership).

Although various "rights" were restricted, they were not restricted vis-à-vis some universally accepted standard. No such standard exists, except perhaps in the abstract. Nor should these rights be understood simply in U.S. constitutional terms. Rather, the electoral, martial, and personal rights—as defined by the divided-state governments themselves—were allocated unequally. This uneven allocation has generally followed ethnic or secular lines.

To secure their political power, state officials attempted first to shape and control the electoral process. During partition itself, elections sometimes played a key role in the selection of officials for devolved states. U.S.-sponsored and UN-supervised elections in South Korea assigned representatives of various political parties to specific offices, as was the case in India and West Germany. But treaty and war served to designate the first generation of governmental officials in divided states, where the superpowers simply turned power over to existing political parties, which then styled themselves "representatives of the people." This was the case in North Korea, North and South Vietnam, Pakistan, East Germany, and Northern Ireland. In China, Taiwan, and Israel, dominant political parties created a government and designated themselves as officials in the devolved state. (In Israel, the UN partition plan had provided for a state in a given territory, but it did not specify the character of the government or identify its rulers.)

Whether they assumed state power by election, treaty, war, or self-designation, government officials had to decide how their successors would be chosen. Officials in most of the divided states provided for electoral mechanisms, ranging from the truly representative to the unduly restrictive.

In Ireland, West Germany, and India, the movements and political parties that took power were relatively strong, and the majorities they represented were sizable. Although West Germany and India placed some restrictions on minority participation in the electoral process, significant minority participation in the selection of government officials was permitted, and regularly scheduled elections have been held.

After a period of martial law during the civil war of 1920–1922, Irish officials permitted unfettered electoral participation. Eamon De Valera, who had led the opposition to partition and had fought unsuccessfully to prevent its implementation, was eventually permitted to participate in the electoral process. He stood for parliament and served as prime minister for many years. Participation by De Valera and his defeated minority party as well as participation by Protestants in the South attests to the relatively unrestricted character of the Irish Republic's electoral system.

West German officials established a parliamentary system dominated by Konrad Adenauer's Christian Democrats. During the 1950s and 1960s, opposition parties, including the Socialists, participated in the electoral process, but the Communist Party was harassed and then banned in 1956. The Federal Constitutional Court ruled that the basic elements of any communist program—their description of wage labor as "exploitation," their rejection of capitalism—were unconstitutional.[33] To some extent, the banning of the Communist Party limited participation of the Socialist Party, which wanted to avoid being excluded from the electoral process.[34]

Throughout most of the postpartition period, government officials in India conducted regular elections and encouraged widespread participation. Between 1975 and 1977, however, Prime Minister Indira Gandhi (Nehru's daughter) declared a state of emergency and suspended the normal electoral and parliamentary process. Her successor, her son Rajiv, declared martial law in some Indian states—he did so in 1987 in the Punjab as a result of secessionist Sikh violence—and instituted direct government rule, much as the British did in Northern Ireland following sectarian violence in 1972. Indian politics throughout much of the postpartition period has been dominated by the Nehru-Gandhi family, who have created a kind of informal, hereditary democracy.

Politics in South Korea, Pakistan, Israel, and Northern Ireland have been much more restrictive. In South Korea and Pakistan, electoral systems have been regularly disrupted by military intervention and popular revolt. In Israel and Northern Ireland, state officials have generally adhered to democratic, electoral conventions, but participation by minority populations has been formally or informally barred. And in Northern Ireland the electoral process was suspended following the imposition of direct British rule in 1972.

Politics in South Korea have oscillated between civilian and military rule. In the fallout from military coups and popular revolt, the constitution has been overhauled no less than eight times in the last forty years.[35] Syngman Rhee, who took office as a result of U.S.-sponsored elections, attempted to consolidate his hold on power by restricting opposition parties and amending the constitution to preserve his party's power in the assembly and in the executive branch of government. His party strong-armed voters during elections. In 1949 and again in 1952, he had opposition assembly members arrested. In 1952, when his reelection by the assembly was in jeopardy, Rhee arrested forty-five assembly members and released them only on condition that they vote for amendments that took presidential elections out of the assembly and made them direct, so that he could more easily control them.[36]

Widespread opposition to Rhee's autocratic control of the government and to widespread corruption by its officials prompted a student revolt in 1960. The constitution was rewritten, civil and political rights were strengthened, and presidential prerogatives were diminished. But a year later, a small group of army officers led by Maj. Gen. Park Chung Hee staged a coup and established a military junta that dissolved the assembly and banned political parties.[37] Leaders of the coup objected to official corruption and to the chaotic political situation created by the previous constitutional reform. Park ruled until he was assassinated in 1979 during an abortive coup attempt and was succeeded by Lt. Gen. Chun Doo Hwan. During the 1970s and early 1980s, the military regime conducted elections, but participation by opposition political parties was carefully circumscribed.[38] Indeed, government agents attempted to abduct opposition leader Kim Dae Jung when he was living abroad and placed him under house arrest when he returned to Korea in 1987. However, in response to widespread opposition to continued military rule, Chun agreed in 1987 to return the government to civilian rule. In the 1988 elections, Gen. Roh Tae Woo, Chun's chosen lieutenant, emerged the victor when the nonmilitary opposition split between two candidates. Roh then eased restrictions on political participation, a development that contributed to democratization there.

Like South Korea, Pakistan has also oscillated between civilian and military rule, with the military predominating. During the first decade after partition, an electoral system created by Jinnah and his designated successor Liaquat Ali Khan provided for widespread participation. But in 1958, Gen. Muhammed Ayub Khan led a military coup that toppled the government. As in Korea three years later, the junta claimed the coup was necessary to destroy official corruption. Ayub dissolved the constitution and imposed martial law, but he permitted the electoral process to continue under close military supervision. Ayub restricted participation by opposition parties, particularly those in East Pakistan, where Bengali parties could claim to represent a countrywide majority. (A majority of the country's population lived in East Pakistan.) Under pressure from Bengali and student protest in 1969, Ayub devolved power to a military successor, Muhammad Yahya Khan, who reimposed martial law to contain opposition parties but reformed the electoral process and permitted general elections in December 1970 and January 1971. But after the East Pakistani Awami League, which sought to create a more autonomous Bengal, won a majority of seats in the assembly, Yahya refused to convene the assembly and recognize Bengali participation in government. The Awami League responded by declaring its independence and seeking international recognition for Bangladesh. Civil war ensued (see chapter 8).[39]

After the civil war resulted in independence for Bangladesh, the discredited military regime returned the government to civilians and Zulfikar Ali Bhutto became president. But a 1977 coup led by Muhammad Zia Ul-Haq reestablished military rule. Zia arrested, tried, and hanged Bhutto. Since then, political participation has been curbed for majority and minority alike. In a manner typical of the kind of restrictions placed on electoral participation in Pakistan, Zia announced in 1988 that he would hold elections but he stipulated that candidates could not affiliate with parties.[40] Bhutto's daughter, Benazir, emerged as the leader of the opposition to continued military rule in spite of Zia's restrictions. After Zia was killed in a September 1988 plane crash, Benazir Bhutto won election as prime minister in relatively unfettered elections and reestablished civilian rule.

In Israel, a vigorous electoral system was created in which diverse parties compete for political power and representation in the Knesset, or parliament. Military leaders regularly participate in civilian governments, but they do so as elected officials, not as representatives of a military junta. The Israeli system of selecting government officials, moreover, has not been disrupted in the postpartition period by military coups. But whereas Jews can participate freely in the electoral process, Arab-Palestinians cannot. Arab Palestinian participation is restricted by the Absentee Property Law and, indirectly, by the Law of Return. In the Absentee Property Law, passed in 1950, the Knesset ruled that any person who was away from his home on or after November 29, 1947, would be regarded as an absentee and could not claim their property or citizenship in Israel.[41] The great majority of Arab Palestinian refugees, and even a large number of Arab Palestinians who continued to reside in Israel during the bitter war of 1948–1949, were denied citizenship and the right to participate in the Israeli electoral process. Children born of Arab Palestinians who *can* claim Israeli citizenship do not automatically become citizens. Arabs who become Israeli citizens can vote, and they usually do so for the Labor or Communist Parties, but they frequently practice an abstentionist politics—refusing to participate in elections—because they do not have effective representation.[42] Indeed, it is difficult for Arabs to form their own political parties in Israel. One attempt in 1964 to form an Arab Israeli political party—Al-Ard—was blocked by the Supreme Court. Al-Ard had sought "to find a just solution for the Palestinian problem as a whole, and as an indivisible unit . . . [and] work for peace in the Middle East and the world in general."[43] In a ruling that was similar to West Germany's ban on communist parties, the Israeli high court ruled that Al-Ard was illegal because its objectives were "utterly destructive of the existence of the state of Israel in general and of its existence within the present frontiers in particular."[44] (Jewish political parties have also been banned for similar reasons. In 1988, the Central Election Committee banned Rabbi Meir Kahane's Kach Party from parliamentary elections because it was "racist" and "undemocratic."[45])

Arab Palestinian participation in the electoral process is restricted in another, albeit indirect, way. The state provides Jews with electoral rights that Arab Israelis and Arab Palestinians generally cannot possess. The Knesset in 1950 passed the Law of Return, which awards Israeli citizenship to any Jew, living anywhere in the world, and grants the right to immigrate freely.[46] During the 1988 parliamentary elections, a number of Jews living in Brooklyn, New York, who were residents and citizens of the United States, flew to Israel and cast ballots for orthodox religious parties in the election.[47] Arab Palestinians who reside in or are citizens of another country cannot participate in Israeli elections. This right is reserved for Jews alone.

In Northern Ireland, for the first fifty years after partition, a functioning though restrictive electoral system encouraged participation by the Protestant majority while discouraging it by the substantial Catholic minority. Shortly after partition, in 1923, the Protestant-dominated parliament at Stormont abolished proportional representation and began gerrymandering electoral districts.[48] Whereas opposition Catholic parties controlled twenty-five of eighty local councils in the country in 1920, they controlled only two after the 1924 elections. For example, on the Omagh Rural council, which was 61.5 percent Catholic, Catholics had controlled twenty-six of thirty-nine seats in 1920. But after Protestant gerrymandering, Protestant parties controlled twenty-one seats, a majority.[49]

In the decades that followed, the Stormont parliament continued to adjust electoral boundaries to ensure continued Protestant rule. Gerrymandering was most egregious in Londonderry, a city that in 1968 had 14,325 Catholic and 9,235 Protestant voters.[50] By gerrymandering ward boundaries, the Protestant minority managed to obtain a twelve to eight majority on the council.[51]

Catholic participation in the electoral process was restricted in other ways as well. A 1946 "Representation of the People Bill" denied the right to vote to servants, subtenants, children over twenty-one living at home, and non-taxpaying lodgers.[52] The government gave limited companies the right to appoint votes on their behalf and required loyalty oaths from elected officials. Not surprisingly, the rallying cry of the 1968 Catholic-led civil rights movement was "one man, one vote," a demand for a return to proportional representation and a widening of the franchise.

In the decades after partition, Catholic political parties participated reluctantly in the electoral process. In the 1930s, when Catholic representatives rose to speak in Stormont, many Protestant ministers and representatives would leave the chamber for the smoke room.[53] Disenfranchised on the stump and humiliated in parliament, Catholic political parties frequently boycotted elections or, if they did participate in elections, absented themselves from parliament for years at a time. At a convention in 1938, for example, Catholic politicians voted not to run a candidate for office because, they said, "We affirm that attendance at the [Stormont] parliament by loyal Irishmen is harmful to the cause of Irish unity since it bolsters up this alien institution and misrepresents the state of Northern opinion."[54] The political conflict between Protestants and Catholics grew increasingly violent in the late 1960s and early 1970s, leading the British to dissolve the Stormont parliament in 1972, imposing direct rule from Westminster.

In the remaining divided states, democratic electoral conventions have been rarely observed. Government representatives in North Korea, China, Taiwan, North Vietnam, South Vietnam, and East Germany were chosen by the single political parties that had assumed power after partition. Instead of creating *electoral* systems to choose government officials, communist parties in North Korea, China, North Vietnam, and East Germany practiced what they called "democratic centralism." The collective party leadership assigned party members to positions in the party and in government, and in time the party and the government became more or less synonymous. Although communist parties in these states do not permit other political parties to participate in government, this does not make them wholly unrepresentative. Some of them could, at times, legitimately claim to represent a majority of the population, much as majority parties in Northern Ireland or Israel claim to represent majority opinion. By most accounts, the populations in North Korea, North Vietnam, and China pulled together behind the communist parties during the long revolutionary and interstate wars that preceded partition. The Viet Minh and the Chinese Communist Party rallied much of the population by their opposition to imperialist rule. They enjoyed widespread support (though this is hard to quantify) before and after partition. In fact, communist parties enjoyed much greater popular support than did their erstwhile rivals in South Vietnam and Taiwan. By contrast, the East German Communist Party was not able to rally the same kind of support, in part because it could not claim the same kind of wartime record. Moreover, neither East German officials nor their Soviet allies put much stock in the electoral process. As Khrushchev said in 1955, when asked why he rejected free elections, "The German people have not yet had time to be educated in the great advantages of communism."[55] Elections were occasionally held, but they were pro forma.

Just as electoral systems played almost no role in selecting government officials in communist-run states, they also played little or no role in non-communist Taiwan and South Vietnam. In Taiwan, government officials were "elected," but their election had taken place on the mainland during the civil war of 1947–1948. Until 1992, the ruling Kuomintang did not permit a general election on Taiwan itself, and legislators in the *Yuan* or National Assembly were said to represent their original constituencies in Peking or Shanghai. This assembly selected the president and ratified changes in the constitution. In 1988, half of the legislators were more than eighty years old; some Taiwanese derisively refered to aged legislators as *zou rou*, or "walking dead."[56] Because, on average, fourteen of these representatives died every year between 1980 and 1986, the government held supplementary elections to replace them. Supplementary elections began only in 1969, twenty years after the Kuomintang takeover.[57] Until 1974, only a handful of legislators were indigenous Taiwanese (the vast majority of the island's populace), and in 1988 only 73 of 312 representatives were from the island.[58]

Upon succeeding his father as president, Chiang Ching-kuo instituted modest reforms, permitting the formation of an opposition political party in 1977. Many of its leaders were arrested in 1979, but the opposition carried about 25 percent of the vote in supplementary elections in 1980 and 1983.[59] Despite reform, however, elections in the 1980s were marked by vote buying (the going price in 1986 was said to have been $5 to $10 a vote)[60] and by restrictions on opposition parties, which are prohibited from advertising their campaigns on radio, TV, or in the newspapers. Most of the island's media, in fact, is owned or controlled by the ruling Kuomintang.[61]

Elections also played little or no role in the selection of government officials in South Vietnam. The French-sponsored emperor Bao Dai designated Ngo

Dinh Diem as his successor on the eve of partition in 1954, and although the Geneva Accords had provided for general reunification elections in both the North and South, Diem announced in February 1956 that his government did not "consider itself bound by their provisions" and refused to hold such elections.[62] The French withdrew their forces in 1956, abdicating their responsibility as the "competent representative authority" for supervising elections in the South.[63]

After surviving several coup attempts, Diem was deposed by a military coup in 1963. A succession of military governments followed until Nyugen Van Thieu was elected president in 1967 and reelected in 1971 as a result of U.S. pressure. But these elections, conducted in the midst of an intense war, were extremely restrictive and could hardly claim to be "representative," because large sections of the population were under arms and the opposition—the National Liberation Front (NLF)—boycotted them.

In many divided states, government officials frequently hold rigged or uncompetitive elections. But if they are going to defraud democracy in this way, why bother to hold them at all? Pressure to observe democratic conventions—elections being viewed around the world as one of the most important political conventions—comes from two sources. Before assuming power, the independence movements themselves had held congresses, elected delegates, and passed real or symbolic resolutions. Once they assumed power, leaders of these movements could not easily discard these practices without calling into question their legitimacy. Elections could also provide the opportunity for factions within ruling parties to maneuver for power, even where this process is closed to the population at large. So government leaders have frequently held elections, which they have attempted to defraud, as a response to pressure from within their own ranks and from opposition groups, which have demanded adherence to global political norms.

The superpowers have also pressured state officials to hold elections. The United States, mindful of criticism that it supports dictators, frequently has insisted that elections be held so that it could claim that the governments of its allies were legitimate. Thus, at various times, it persuaded military leaders in South Korea, South Vietnam, and Pakistan to put their regimes to electoral tests.

Citizenship in the divided states was compromised in other ways as well. To maintain political power, officials in many divided states forcibly disenfranchised the citizenry by monopolizing control of the army and the police, restricting the right of opposition populations to bear arms, deploying irregular

police forces and militias to control minority populations, and subjecting the
country to martial law and military rule. These measures were commonly introduced to prevent disenfranchised populations from seeking redress and, if they
mounted effective political opposition, to crush protest by force.

In South Korea, South Vietnam, and Pakistan, military leaders organized
coups, seized power, and established military regimes that ruled for most of
the postpartition period. It is worth noting that the initial coups in these three
states occurred roughly one decade after partition: Pakistan in 1958, South
Korea in 1961, and South Vietnam in 1963. The assertion of military authority
after a decade of civilian rule probably attests to the fact that partition created
weak political formations in these countries. The leaders of military coups at-
tributed the weakness of civilian authority to corruption—a major complaint
of military insurgents in South Korea, South Vietnam, and Pakistan. In these
countries and in Taiwan, where the Kuomintang government was installed by
the army prior to partition, martial law was imposed much of the time. Under
martial law, representative parliaments were dissolved, political parties banned,
elections suspended, and the citizenry was subjected to arbitrary arrest and
prosecution under punitive security laws. Although martial law was occasionally
lifted in the other countries, in Taiwan the military government stuck to its
guns: the martial law imposed in 1949 was not lifted for thirty-eight years.

The situation was somewhat different in Israel and Northern Ireland, where
martial law existed alongside civilian authority. There, state officials directed
martial law provisions against minority populations and subjected them to rule
by regular and irregular forces. At the same time, majority populations were
provided with arms, allowed to form irregular militias, and permitted to remain
under civilian jurisdiction.

During the war of partition in Palestine, Israeli forces seized Arab Palestinian villages, disarmed the population, and evicted many of the residents. Those
who remained were disarmed and subjected to military laws, which were
adapted from British policies.[64] The British had passed an extensive set of laws
in 1945 that were designed to curb the activities of Jewish and Arab irregulars.
The laws restricted movement, controlled the press, regulated the possession
of arms, and gave military commanders vast powers to establish martial law.
Military authorities could search, seize, and destroy property; detain and expel
persons; impose curfews; and try the inhabitants in military courts.[65] The Israeli
government adopted and modified these laws in 1948 so that military authorities could deploy martial law provisions against non-Jewish populations. Military commanders were given wide discretion to "close" extensive areas of Israel

and impose military rule within them. When the Israeli Supreme Court ruled that the village of Kafr Bar'am should not be closed by military authorities and that its inhabitants be permitted to return to it in 1953, the Israeli Defense Force destroyed the empty village.[66] The closure of areas was widely practiced to control the *intifada* uprising that began in 1987. Moreover, the Israeli civilian authorities and the courts generally do not challenge the exercise of military authority over non-Jewish minorities.

Israeli military authorities need not disclose which areas are closed, and where martial law applies, inhabitants of closed areas may be prosecuted for violating the provisions of martial law even if they do not know that the area is under military control.[67] Areas within Israel can be treated in the same way that military authorities administer the occupied territories on the West Bank and Gaza. In the occupied territories, Arab and Christian inhabitants are subject to military rule, whereas Jewish settlers remain under the jurisdiction of civilian authorities.

Whereas the possession of arms by Arab Palestinians is severely restricted—whole villages have been destroyed and their inhabitants expelled for possessing "illegal" arms—Israeli authorities provide arms to much of the Jewish population. For Israeli Jews, guns are ubiquitous, and many Israelis are permitted to carry arms, in public, on a daily basis. Most are members of the armed forces or in the reserves, in which most Jewish men and women are enrolled. But some are settlers, residents of urban and rural *kibbutzim* who are permitted to carry weapons and use them in self-defense. Although legal restrictions apply to the use of force, the legal definition and social conventions regarding Jewish self-defense are broad, and settlers can use their weapons to intimidate non-Jewish populations with relative impunity.

Authorities in Northern Ireland also borrowed martial law provisions from wartime British law and used them to control indigenous minorities. In 1922, they adopted Special Powers legislation that modified the Restoration of Order Act, which the British had used against republican insurgency prior to partition. The Special Powers Act "provided for search, arrest, and detention without warrant; flogging and the death penalty for arms and explosives offenses; and allowed for the total suspension of civil liberties."[68] The act was selectively deployed intermittently against the minority Catholic population until the British reasserted their authority in 1972 and imposed their own version of martial law, the Emergency Powers Act, in 1973.[69] For instance, the government often used the Special Powers Act to intern, or jail indefinitely, people defined as political or military threats.[70] After 1972, British martial law was sometimes used to prosecute Protestant Irish irregulars, but in the main, it was directed at Catholic irregulars.

In addition to martial law, government officials in Northern Ireland also deployed Protestant militias and irregulars to maintain Protestant rule. The Ulster Special Constabulary, whose members were drawn from the prepartition Protestant militia, was established in 1920 as an armed auxiliary to the regular police.[71] In Northern Ireland, as in Israel, those who possessed the right to bear arms acquired rights that those who did not could not. Irregular police forces and militias used their privileges to extend majority rule over minority civilian populations.

Besides restricting participation in the selection of government officials and the ability to possess arms on an equal basis, officials in many of the divided states imposed differential restrictions based on language, religion, and social custom. Restrictions on these activities are commonplace throughout the interstate system. Indeed, they are so common as to be unremarkable. Human rights organizations such as Amnesty International dutifully catalog the restrictions imposed by states on the rights of its citizenry, not just in the divided states but in countries around the world. But a brief survey of the kinds of linguistic, religious, and customary restrictions imposed by officials of divided states illustrates two points. First, restrictions tend to be differential or unequally applied. They preserve the rights of some at the expense of others, usually minority populations. Second, their imposition antagonizes disadvantaged groups, which object to discriminatory practices. As a consequence, linguistics, religious, and customary issues frequently foster social conflict within and between divided states.

In some of these divided states, language poses no social problems. The fact that government officials conduct their business in German in both East and West Germany, where most of the inhabitants speak German, does not present problems, except for immigrants from non-German-speaking countries (e.g., Turkish and Yugoslavian guest workers). Koreans, North and South, speak Korean; Vietnamese, for the most part, speak Vietnamese.

Where affairs of state are conducted in a language that is not universally spoken, the ability to participate in government and politics is restricted. China conducts its official business in Mandarin, though regional dialects proliferate. English is the language of state in India, though it is not even an indigenous language, and the indigenous population speaks a number of heterogeneous languages and dialects. The use of standard languages in these countries acts as a de facto restriction on political participation for much of the citizenry, even though people who speak other languages and dialects are not formally penalized for doing so.

But language is more of a problem in divided states that elevate a particular language as the official medium of discourse and suppress others. These countries frequently establish de jure restrictions on political participation by those who speak other languages. The Kuomintang government in Taiwan, for example, insists on the use of Mandarin as the language of state, despite the fact that 80 percent of the population speak a different dialect. Indeed, local officials are sometimes brought to task for not conducting official business in Mandarin.[72] Because most residents in Taiwan do not speak Mandarin, their ability to participate as citizens is curtailed.

In Pakistan, Urdu-speaking state officials in the western half of the country attempted soon after partition to make Urdu the official and only language of state. Prime Minister Liaquat Ali Khan insisted, "It is necessary for a nation to have one language and that language can only be Urdu and no other language."[73] But because Urdu was spoken by only 7 percent of the population and hardly used at all in Bengali-speaking East Pakistan, this policy sparked violent Bengali opposition.[74] When Jinnah traveled to East Pakistan and reaffirmed his support for Urdu, the country's founding father was heckled and shouted down by students at Dacca University, and "angry students tore down his portraits in school and colleges."[75]

Movements opposing Urdu as the official language were organized in 1948, 1950, and 1952.[76] One Bengali leader in the Constituent Assembly complained that the

> attitude of the [ruling] Muslim League here was of contempt towards East Bengal, towards its culture, its language, its literature and everything concerning East Bengal. . . . Far from considering East Bengal as an equal partner, the leaders of the Muslim League thought that we were a subject race and they belonged to a race of conquerors.[77]

After tumultuous political struggles, Bengali was finally given equal status in the Constitution in 1956.[78]

Interestingly, after partition in Israel and southern Ireland, government representatives designated as "official" languages that were not widely spoken by Jews or Catholics. Hebrew, a language spoken only by biblical scholars and as part of Jewish religious services, was resuscitated and promoted over more widely spoken languages, such as Yiddish, as *the* Jewish language. The adoption of Hebrew helped exclude participation by Arabic speakers. The ascension of

Hebrew was followed by steps to suppress other languages in daily life. Road signs were changed from Arabic to Hebrew and villages renamed. Walter Eytan had said that returning Arabs might not find their villages because they had been razed. But within a few years, it would also be difficult to locate on a map those villages still standing or to find the way to them on the road.

The effort by Irish officials to revive Gaelic was less successful, but they did make some headway. Political parties adopted Gaelic nomenclature, in 1937 changing the name of the state from Ireland to Eire, a development that restricted political participation by Catholic majority and Protestant minority alike.

Religion has likewise been a divisive force in most of the divided states. State officials have promoted some religions and derogated others, especially in countries ostensibly divided along "religious" lines—India, Palestine, Ireland. The extension of religious authority and ascent of particular religions—the "Islamization" of Pakistan, the "Judaization" of Israel, the "Catholicization" of Ireland—have proceeded unevenly. But generally speaking, religious authority has increased over time.

Before partition, members of religious minorities in India, Palestine, and Ireland believed they could not practice their faiths in a unitary state dominated by adherents of a hostile majoritarian religion. But they turned the tables upon assuming political power. In Pakistan, Israel, and Northern Ireland, government officials promoted their own religion over others, adopted it as the official religion of state, and devolved some governmental responsibilities to religious authorities. This "confessionalization" of nominally secular states has resulted in the derogation of other religions and has further compromised the citizenship of those who profess different faiths.

Although the Muslim League wanted to create a separate state for Indian Moslems, Pakistan was intended to be a *secular* Moslem state. At the Constitutent Assembly meeting in Karachi on the eve of independence, Jinnah rejected the idea that the new country should be a confessional state and said:

> You are free; you are free to go to your mosques or to any other place of worship in this State of Pakistan. You may belong to any religion or caste or creed—that has nothing to do with the business of the State . . . We are starting with this fundamental principle that we are all citizens and equal citizens of one State. . . . [Y]ou will find that in the course of time Hindus would cease to be Hindus and Muslims would cease to be Muslims, not in the religious sense, because that is the personal faith of each individual, but in the political sense as citizens of the State.[79]

But Jinnah's views did not long survive his death in 1948. Some found it disingenuous to create a state based on religious claims and then deny that the state was religious. Others thought that Islam should become the state religion and be used to cement the "nationality" of a diverse population that consisted of people with different ethnic identities and separate languages. Religious groups organized in the early 1950s to make Pakistan into an Islamic state that they could control.[80] They forced the government to convene a second Constituent Assembly in 1955, which declared the next year that Islam was to be the state's official religion and that only a Moslem could serve as head of state. Pakistan officially became an "Islamic Republic."

Religious authorities, the mullahs, demanded that they be given a role in determining what makes the republic "Islamic." And over the years, during the course of revolts and coups that shaped Pakistani politics, government officials have devolved some of their responsibilities to religious authorities and have applied Islamic religious law to all its citizens, regardless of faith. In 1979, for example, the military government decreed that thieves should have their hands cut off and adulterers should be stoned to death according to Islamic law. (The government says it has not applied these laws, in part because doctors have refused to perform amputations.[81]) The government also created a federal Shariat Court (Shariat is the body of Islamic law) composed of religious jurists who have been given authority to review Pakistani laws that deal with financial affairs, marriage and divorce, inheritance, and family matters.[82] In October 1988, Acting President Ghulan Ishaq Khan decreed that *all* Pakistani laws would be subject to Islamic Shariat code.[83]

The Islamization of Pakistan has adversely affected the standing of many of its citizens. Women, certain Moslem sects, and non-Moslems have all lost ground during this process. For example, Pakistani law derogates the testimony of women in court: the testimony of two women is necessary to equal that of one man in financial cases, and four men must testify to obtain the conviction of a man charged with sexual offenses, no matter how many women have given testimony.[84] "Women have always been the greatest sufferers in the enforcement of their rights in this country," Hina Jilani, a feminist, said of Islamic laws in Pakistan.[85] Some Moslem sects, such as the Ahmadiya, who believe that Mohammed was not the "last" prophet, have been denied recognition by the government, which has ruled that they are "non-Moslem." Members of this sect, many of them professionals and scientists, have lost their jobs and had their property and mosques seized.[86] In addition, non-Moslems have found themselves subject to Moslem religious law, even thought they profess different faiths.

The Zionist founders of Israel, like the Islamic founders of Pakistan, were not particularly "religious," even though they argued that Israel would be the state of the Jewish people throughout the world. Like Jinnah, Ben-Gurion and Weizmann believed in creating a secular state in which all Jews—belonging to Orthodox, Conservative, and Reform denominations—could practice their faith. Many Orthodox Jewish sects, however, argued that the attempt to create a state, as opposed to creating an exemplary religious practice, was blasphemous. Some Orthodox Jews refused to accept identity papers, observe Israeli Independence Day, or serve in the army.[87] In their view, the government did not have the right to compel people who observed sacred law to follow secular law. Rabbi Menachem Porush, the leader of one Orthodox political party in Israel, has said, Zionists have "carried two flags, one of nationalism and another of Torah. They are always torn between the two. We have one flag: the Torah."[88]

Israeli government officials have also ceded responsibility for some civil matters to religious authorities, but to a lesser extent than in Pakistan. A Chief Rabbinate and Chief Rabbinical Council decide on the interpretation and application of Jewish law in some civil matters—the certification of food, instruction in the state's religious schools, and matters relating to marriage and divorce.[89] The 1953 Marriage and Divorce Law prohibited civil marriage and assigned jurisdiction over marriage and divorce to Orthodox rabbinical courts.[90] The Orthodox clergy has since extended its jurisdiction, pushing for the right to determine who is a Jew and therefore who can claim the rights to full Israeli citizenship. Although the Knesset in 1988 narrowly rejected a measure that would have given Orthodox courts the *exclusive* right to decide who is Jewish under the Law of Return, the courts have been able to narrow the definition over the years.[91] They have derogated not only non-Jews but also Conservative and Reform Jews in this process. One Orthodox rabbi justified this development by contemptuously saying, "Reform is a bridge for Jews to take to assimilation [non-Jewishness]."[92]

As in Pakistan, a variety of groups have been disenfranchised in this process, and others threaten to be. Moslem and Christian Arabs in Israel have found it difficult to observe their faiths in a Jewish state. Practicing Jews who are not born of Jewish mothers, some converts to Judaism, and people who cannot produce acceptable documentation of their conversion to Judaism cannot claim the full benefits of Israeli citizenship. One decorated army veteran had his Jewish identity established when he immigrated but then had it revoked. Because he was no longer "Jewish," he could not marry unless he converted under Orthodox supervision. (Jews are not permitted to marry non-Jews in Israel.) When called up for military service, he was told by his superiors that if he were killed in battle, he would not be buried in a Jewish cemetery.[93]

Secular Zionists and Reform and Conservative Jews also stand to lose if government authority of civil affairs is further devolved to Orthodox clergy, who have campaigned for strict observance of the Sabbath and other religious strictures. The November 1988 elections in Israel gave Orthodox religious authorities a potentially important role in the formation of a government, and they announced that they would use any power they acquired to expand and enforce Jewish religious law. Secular and non-Orthodox Jews petitioned the leaders of the two major political parties—Likud and Labor—not to allow Orthodox parties into the government. The leader of one Orthodox party, Rabbi Itzak Peretz, responded by attacking non-Orthodox Jews, saying, "They don't have any right to settle in Israel if they are willing to throw away the religious heritage passed on from our ancestors. Israel was given to the Jewish people for one overwhelming reason. That is, to live life as described in the Torah."[94] After failing in an attempt to bring Orthodox parties into a majority coalition, and after the United States agreed to hold talks with the PLO in December 1988, the Likud entered into a coalition government with the Labor Party, which excluded Orthodox religious parties.

The two Irish states were also divided along religious lines, but the process of confessionalization has not proceeded quite as far as it has in Pakistan or Israel. After partition, state officials in both states introduced religious instruction into their schools and provided special benefits to majoritarian religious schools. In southern Ireland, the constitution of 1937 recognized "the special position of the Catholic Church" but did not cede civil authority to the Church. Instead, the Dail passed legislation that censored films and books, prohibited divorce, and made the sale of contraceptives and, later, provision of abortions, illegal.[95] A 1986 referendum that would have permitted divorce was defeated by a margin of 63 to 37 percent.[96] But even though De Valera had described the South as "a Catholic Nation," Catholicism never became the official religion of the republic. As in the North, where Protestantism also occupied a "special position," the Catholic Church in the South remained a de facto, not a de jure, partner of the state.

In East Asian states and Germany, however, state officials have encouraged or discouraged religious practices, but they have not tried to elevate particular religions over others, recognize certain faiths as official, or turn government offices or the courts over to religious authorities. Whereas government officials in North Korea, China, North Vietnam, and East Germany actively suppressed religious practices and attempted to establish wholly secular communist states, their counterparts in South Korea, Taiwan, South Vietnam, and West Germany encouraged religious observances. Although these leaders did not elevate any particular religion to the status of an official religion, they did favor those religions that they practiced themselves. Such favoritism would lead to difficulties for these Asian leaders (Syngman Rhee, Chiang Kai-shek, Ngo Dinh Diem) who all practiced "exogenous" Christian faiths shared by only a small minority of their compatriots.

This situation proved particularly troublesome for Diem, who discriminated against South Vietnam's Buddhist population while rewarding Catholics, many of whom had fled the North, with influential posts in the military and civilian government, as well as lucrative economic privileges.[97] On May 8, 1963, Catholic South Vietnamese officials banned the flying of Buddhist flags during a march in Hue commemorating the birth of Buddha—this after having permitted Catholics to display papal banners during a march a week earlier. When Buddhists gathered for the march, the army opened fire on the crowd. Nine people were shot or trampled to death.[98] Buddhists then began organizing opposition to Diem throughout the country, and on June 11, Quang Duc, a sixty-six-year-old Buddhist monk, immolated himself on a busy street in Saigon. After the government blamed the Vietnamese communists for the troubles, more monks burned themselves in protest. Diem's sister-in-law, Madam Nhu, added fuel to the political fire by saying that these self-immolations were a "barbeque." "Let them burn," she said, "and we shall clap our hands."[99] The religious opposition soon ignited a political struggle, setting the stage for a military coup that toppled the Diem regime and murdered Diem and his brother on November 1.

Rhee, Chiang, and West Germany's Konrad Adenauer never attempted to promote their faiths as vigorously as Diem. They encouraged it as a personal matter, not as a matter of state. In addition, they did not institutionalize or codify the derogation of other religions as in the other divided states.

Government officials in the divided states also split their citizenry through restrictions on property. In some states, for example, property rights were differentiated on the basis of ethnicity; in others, on the basis of class. Both served to establish citizenship distinctions between majority and minority populations. Two examples illustrate this point.

In Israel, state officials used the 1950 Absentee Property Law to "national-ize" or expropriate the property of many Arab Palestinians. Before 1947, Jew-ish individuals or corporations owned just 7 percent of the land, but the law reclassified 70 percent of the land in the country as "absentee property."[100] This land then passed into the custody of the state or to parastatal Zionist agencies, which administered it, sometimes leasing it back to Jewish settlers and some-times back to Arab Palestinian renters. By 1954, one-third of the Jewish popu-lation lived on absentee property.[101] Land owned by Jews or the state cannot be sold or transferred to non-Jews under Israeli law, and absentees cannot claim, use, or profit from the property seized, because they possess no legal standing in Israel. When Israel occupied the West Bank and Gaza during the 1967 war, government officials designated 36 percent of the Jordan valley as absentee property and made it available to Jewish settlers.[102]

Officials in other divided states likewise expropriated land and confiscated property held by minority groups. In both North and South Vietnam, commu-nist *and* capitalist government officials expropriated property and used class to distinguish between the right of its citizens to hold and use land. In the North, as in other communist Asian states, officials practiced large-scale land reform, distributing land held by "bourgeois" and "feudal" landlords to the rural popu-lace. For a time after partition, officials in North Vietnam defined anyone who hired labor as a landlord and expropriated their land, transferring nearly two million acres to 2,220,000 families.[103] The "bourgeois" minority, many of whom where killed, was barred from buying or selling land or profiting from land worked by others. In South Vietnam, by contrast, Diem's government re-claimed the two million hectares expropriated from the French and redistrib-uted by the Viet Minh during the prepartition war.[104] To deprive the Viet Minh of its rural support, Diem's regime dispossessed rural inhabitants of their land and moved them into *agrovilles*, later known as "strategic hamlets" by the Americans, which were administered by state officials.[105] Hundreds of thou-sands of rural inhabitants lost their homes, ancestral graves, and land as a result of massive rural relocation projects.

There is another, further dehumanizing dimension to the practice of differ-entiating between the inhabitants of divided states. When equal citizenship is denied to large groups or classes of people, a tendency arises to treat them as a collective, not as individuals. The group itself is thus held responsible for the actions of its individual members. State officials regularly mete out collective punishment and hold individuals liable for actions that they did not themselves commit.

One common form of collective punishment is to make the restrictions imposed on one generation heritable. In Israel, the children of an Arab Palestinian classified as an absentee are themselves designated as absentees and are thus deprived of citizenship, even if they were born in Israel.[106] In North Korea, government officials classify individuals according to their *songbun*, or family class background. Children of families whose relatives fought against the Japanese receive preferential treatment—bigger housing allotments, larger food rations—over descendants of families with "bourgeois" class backgrounds. Landlords, capitalists, rich peasants, collaborators with the Japanese, and members of religious groups as well as the families of persons who fled to South Korea are denied access to good schools and government jobs, and they receive smaller housing allotments and smaller food rations.[107]

In the divided states it is not always children who are punished for the sins of their fathers. Sometimes parents are punished for their children's errant behavior. Israeli defense minister Ariel Sharon has recalled how he found a way to stop Arab Palestinian children from stoning Israeli soldiers patroling Gaza in 1973: he instructed his soldiers to meet with parents of Palestinian youths and explain that they would be held responsible for their children's behavior. If their children were caught throwing stones, Sharon recalled, "well, we took their father or their older brother. We gave them a canteen full of water, a piece of bread, a Jordanian dinar and a white flag. We took them up to the Jordanian police station at the border and marched them across." Sharon said that after a few dozen parents and siblings had been expelled, "instead of soldiers beating the students, fathers were beating their own sons and daughters. You could hear the screams all across Gaza. And the stonings stopped."[108]

Partition drives people apart, not only by creating separate states but by dividing people within these states. Partition separates people from their homes and families and deprives them of their rights. Minority populations are effectively disenfranchised by state-sponsored measures. Electoral participation is curbed, military service is barred, and languages and religions derogated by law. The meaning of citizenship is compromised, stunted, and deformed. The result of this process is the creation of political systems that divide and disenfranchise citizens, what might be called systems of apartheid.

Those laws and social practices that assign different rights to different groups, which effectively disenfranchise large numbers of individuals and ethnic or secular groups, create systems of apartheid. And apartheid reinforces and maintains social divisions and unequal citizenship over time. State officials do not distribute citizenship on an unequal basis simply to be punitive, though some measures are clearly retributive, but as part of an effort to create a unified, homogeneous nation-state that can participate equally in the interstate system. Yet this attempt to create a strong, homogeneous nation-state (sometimes called "nation building") is a utopian project. Partition created states where both majorities and minorities could exercise power over particular geographic areas. But it failed to create homogeneous states, where one group of people could exercise their power without constraint or complaint.

The attempt to create a state based on a socially and ethnically homogeneous population is accompanied by measures designed to strengthen majority rule, and these measures tend to result in the diminution of rights for minority populations, who resent and resist them. Indeed, the effort to create a unified nation-state in the divided states produces only greater division and dissension.

One of the most emblematic features of divided states is the walls they erect. Some of these walls are concrete, some psychological. They fortify and cement the political, social, and economic divisions between and within states. The wall erected by the Soviets and East Germans in Berlin is the most visible, notorious symbol of such division. Construction of the wall began on the night of August 13, 1961, when the Soviets and East Germans decided to stop emigration to the West from East Berlin and sealed the border between occupation zones in the city. The wall stood about ten to thirteen feet tall and had a smooth concrete finish and a rounded top, to prevent anyone from grasping it and pulling him- or herself over. The wall completely encircled West Berlin; if straightened, its serpentine route would have measured one hundred miles long—the distance from New York to Philadelphia.[109]

The wall also had a psychological dimension, which was harder to measure but no less real. This dimension can be gauged by the space the wall occupied in newspapers and in literature. Newspaper stories about it appeared every August, on the anniversary of its construction; it was been used as backdrop for speeches by U.S. presidents and as a staple setting for spy novels. Peter Schneider, author of *The Wall Jumper*, a collection of fictionalized tales or fables about the wall, described it as "a concrete symbol of the divided self." He observed, "The dialog between East and West German authors has made it particularly clear that the cement and barbed-wire Wall corresponds to a mental one. . . . It will probably take longer to tear down the Wall in our heads than the one made of concrete."[110]

The wall in Berlin was not the only barrier separating divided states and peoples. There are others. The inter-Korean border is also heavily fortified. The 17th parallel, which divided Vietnam for many years, suggests a neat line on the map, though the actual demarcation line was more tortuously drawn. A sea wall—the Taiwan Strait—divides the two Chinas. The frontiers between India and Pakistan were drawn by military forces. In the disputed Kashmir region, the boundaries have never been fixed, and Himalayan ranges serve as a mountainous wall between opposing forces.

A line on a map, which is sometimes secret, divides Arab and Jew in Palestine. Military authorities can close an area inside Israel proper, "walling" it off and preventing entry and exit. They need not publicly specify where these walls are; one discovers its existence by bumping into it. There is also the "Green Line," another permeable sort of wall separating Israel and its occupied territories, which are also under military jurisdiction.

Informal walls divide people as well. As Meron Benevisti, a former deputy mayor of Jerusalem, wrote:

> Late one afternoon in March, I was driving to the Hebrew University campus on Mount Scopus. Suddenly, as I was waiting near Damascus Gate for the traffic light to change, I made a decision: Instead of driving directly, as usual, through the Arab section, I turned left, taking the "Jewish way"—through the safe Jewish neighborhoods. It was at this moment, I realized with astonishment, that I had succumbed to the geography of fear. For the first time in 21 years I allowed my tribal affiliation to determine my psychological space in my own hometown.[111]

The walls Benevisti describes may be hard to locate on a map, but inhabitants of divided cities and divided states know instinctively where they are.

And finally, there is a wall that acts as a symbol of division in Jerusalem: the Wailing Wall. Jews venerate the Wailing Wall because it is the exposed, western part of a foundation on which the Jewish Second Temple was built. (The Romans destroyed it in A.D. 70.) Islamic shrines, including the Dome of the Rock mosque—the site of Mohammed's ascension to heaven—were subsequently built there. Moslems call it Haram al-Sharif; Jews call it the Temple Mount. These piggybacking shrines have been the site of repeated confrontations. Jewish excavations around the wall's foundations have led to Moslem rioting, as did a court decision permitting Jews to pray there. Jewish religious militants have twice plotted (in 1981 and 1984) to dynamite the Dome of the Rock and thereby remove it from sacred Jewish ground.[112]

The same sort of invisible yet tangible walls divide Catholic and Protestant in Northern Ireland. Although there is no single Berlin-style wall in Belfast, a series of fifteen-foot-high "peacekeeper" walls run through the yards, alleys, and streets between Catholic and Protestant neighborhoods. The British and Belfast city planners erected these corrugated iron barriers to prevent sniper fire and rock throwing incidents across "the line." Demolished, burnt, or boarded-up houses between neighborhoods also serve as barriers, much as unoccupied buildings did in Berlin before they were torn down and replaced by a wall that could be more easily patrolled. When one city planner suggested demolishing a row of abandoned and derelict houses and using the strip as park land, people on both sides of the proposed park objected, saying it would permit sniping and rock throwing at the border.[113] In its place, both sides approved a plan for a twenty-foot-high wall trimmed with thorny shrubs. The planner in charge of the project said:

> It is a serious plan, but everyone is holding off because no one wants to build it. The cost of construction of a brick wall, coupled with the feeling that you'd be dividing the city off with a Berlin-type wall, is just too much for people *outside* the community to take.[114]

A Department of the Environment official agreed: "One argument against putting up a permanent wall is that it is far easier to put them up than it is to take them down. By and large, it looks like we have build a psychological barrier, and it's the psychological barrier which is hard to take away."[115]

Psychological barriers are more difficult to describe, though one writer discovered a set of rules that enables one to identify religious divisions in Northern Ireland:

> In Belfast . . . the most segregated city in the North, one can quickly determine a man's religion just by asking him where he lives or what school he went to. Often one can tell from a person's name what church he or she holds dear: anyone named Sean, Seamus, Kieran, Patrick, Damien, Eamonn, Malachy, Theresa, Bernadette, Deirdre, Finnoula, or Colette is Catholic. William, Sammy, Ian, Hope, Joy and Grace are all Protestant.[116]

Residents of Belfast are provided with a whole series of clues to identify "the other." Once identified, a psychological wall can quickly be erected. As in Benevisti's Jerusalem, the walls individuals carry around in their heads can be deployed in an instant and guide their behavior as surely as a series of traffic diverters.

Walls between states, within states, and within individuals divide people

127
from each other and from themselves. The construction of real, social, and psychological barriers results in what might be called "schizophrenic states." In psychological terms, schizophrenia refers to psychotic reactions characterized by the withdrawal from reality with highly variable accompanying affective behavioral and intellectual disturbances. In the divided states, partition and its consequences have created conditions from which people recoil. States refuse to recognize sibling states, majorities disenfranchise minorities, and individuals discriminate against their neighbors. The refusal to recognize the sovereignty and citizenship of other states and minority peoples represents a withdrawal from reality. The denial of political reality leads to governmental and individual behavior that tends to deepen social divisions and to exacerbate social conflict within and between states.

NOTES

1. A. Jeyartnam Wilson and D. Dalton, *The States of South Asia* (Honolulu: University of Hawaii Press, 1982), 20.

2. Gregory Henderson, R. N. Lebow, and J. G. Stoessinger, *Divided Nations in a Divided World* (New York: McKay, 1974), 208; Sarah Nelson, *Ulster's Uncertain Defenders* (Syracuse, N.Y.: Syracuse University Press, 1984), 31.

3. John Sullivan, *Two Koreas— One Future?* (Lanham, Md.: University Press of America, 1987), 100; Henderson, Lebow, and Sroesslnger, *Divided Nations*, 60–61.

4. Henderson, Lebow, and Stoessinger, *Divided Nations*, 61.

5. Henderson, Lebow, and Stoessinger, *Divided Nations*, 100.

6. Henderson, Lebow, and Stoessinger, *Divided Nations*, 138.

7. Henderson, Lebow, and Stoessinger, *Divided Nations*, 28. See Frank Ninkovich, *Germany and the United States* (Boston: Twayne, 1988), 123; Henry Ashby Turner Jr., *The Two Germanies Since 1945* (New Haven, Conn.: Yale University Press, 1987), 130.

8. Ninkovich, *Germany and the United States*, 108.

9. Turner, *Two Germanies*, 130.

10. R. F. Holland, *European Decolonization, 1918–1981* (New York: St. Martin's, 1985), 80.

11. H. V. Hodson, *The Great Divide* (Oxford: Oxford University Press, 1985), 411.

12. Holland, *European Decolonization*, 80.

13. Hodson, *Great Divide*, 404.

14. Hodson, *Great Divide*, 404.

15. Edward Said and Christopher Hitchens, *Blaming the Victims* (London: Verso, 1988), 213, 236.

16. Said and Hitchens, *Blaming the Victims*, 4; Holland, *European Decolonization*,

120; Benny Morris, *The Birth of the Palestinian Refugee Problem, 1947–1949* (Cambridge: Cambridge University Press, 1988), 8.

17. Morris, *Palestinian Refugee Problem*, 297–98.

18. Milton J. Esman and Itamar Rabinovich, *Ethnicity, Pluralism and the State in the Middle East* (Ithaca, N.Y.: Cornell University Press, 1988), 97; J. C. Hurewitz, *The Struggle for Palestine* (New York: Schocken, 1976), 321; Said and Hitchens, *Blaming the Victims*, 266.

19. Said and Hitchens, *Blaming the Victims*, 74.

20. Said and Hitchens, *Blaming the Victims*, 75.

21. Morris, *Palestinian Refugee Problem*, 155–69.

22. Morris, *Palestinian Refugee Problem*, 141.

23. Morris, *Palestinian Refugee Problem*, 174.

24. Morris, *Palestinian Refugee Problem*, 240.

25. Morris, *Palestinian Refugee Problem*, 255.

26. Holland, *European Decolonization*, 121; Ritchie Ovendale, *The Origins of the Arab-Israeli Wars* (London: Longmans, 1984), 124.

27. Said and Hitchens, *Blaming the Victims*, 268, 252.

28. Said and Hitchens, *Blaming the Victims*, 261.

29. Said and Hitchens, *Blaming the Victims*, 261.

30. Morris, *Palestinian Refugee Problem*, 28, 280.

31. Michael Farrell, *Northern Ireland: The Orange State* (London: Pluto, 1980) 221.

32. Esman and Rabinovich, *Ethnicity, Pluralism and the State*, 27.

33. Werner Hulsberg, *The German Greens* (London: Verso, 1988), 19.

34. Hulsberg, *German Greens*, 20–21.

35. Henderson, Lebow, and Stoessinger, *Divided Nations*, 66.

36. Henderson, Lebow, and Stoessinger, *Divided Nations*, 64.

37. Ralph B. Clough, *Embattled Korea* (Boulder, Colo.: Westview, 1987), 33; Henderson, Lebow, and Stoessinger, *Divided Nations*, 65–66.

38. Sullivan, *Two Koreas*, 110–11.

39. Henderson, Lebow, and Stoessinger, *Divided Nations*, 304–05.

40. *New York Times*, October 3, 1988; *Washington Post*, June 22, 1988.

41. Uri Davis, *Israel* (London: Zed, 1987), 34–35.

42. Geoffrey Aronson, *Creating Facts* (Washington, D.C.: Institute for Palestine Studies, 1987), 12.

43. Aronson, *Creating Facts*, 12.

44. Sabri Jiryis, *The Arabs in Israel, 1948–1966* (Beirut: Institute for Palestine Studies, 1967), 133–34.

45. *New York Times*, October 6, 1988.

46. Davis, *Israel*, 9.

47. Reported on the *CBS Evening News*, November 2, 1988.

48. Farrell, *Northern Ireland*, 83.

49. Farrell, *Northern Ireland*, 84.

50. Farrell, *Northern Ireland*, 211–12.

51. Henderson, Lebow, and Stoessinger, *Divided Nations*, 212; See also Farrell, *Northern Ireland*, 84; Belinda Probert, *Beyond Orange and Green* (Dublin: Academy Press, 1978), 60.

52. Henderson, Lebow, and Stoessinger, *Divided Nations*, 211; Farrell, *Northern Ireland*, 85.

53. Farrell, *Northern Ireland*, 120.

54. Farrell, *Northern Ireland*, 145. Sinn Fein, the political wing of the illegal Irish Republican Army, ended a twenty-five-year electoral boycott in Northern Ireland in 1986. *Bangor [Maine] Daily News*, November 3, 1986.

55. Ninkovich, *Germany and the United States*, 113.

56. Thomas Omestad, "Dateline Taiwan: A Dynasty Ends," *Foreign Policy* 71 (Summer 1988): 184.

57. Omestad, "Dateline Taiwan," 179.

58. Selig S. Harrison, "Taiwan after Chiang Ching-Kuo," *Foreign Affairs* 66, no. 4 (Spring 1988): 794.

59. Omestad, "Dateline Taiwan," 181.

60. Omestad, "Dateline Taiwan," 185.

61. Omestad, "Dateline Taiwan," 186.

62. Gabriel Kolko, *The Roots of American Foreign Policy* (Boston: Beacon, 1969), 112.

63. Henderson, Lebow, and Stoessinger, *Divided Nations*, 145.

64. Jiryis, *Arabs in Israel*, 2.

65. Jiryis, *Arabs in Israel*, 7–9.

66. Jiryis, *Arabs in Israel*, 67.

67. Jiryis, *Arabs in Israel*, 15.

68. Farrell, *Northern Ireland*, 50.

69. Lynne Shivers and D. Bowman, *More Than the Troubles* (Philadelphia: New Society, 1984), 81.

70. Farrell, *Northern Ireland*, 94–95.

71. Probert, *Beyond Orange and Green*, 126; Farrell, *Northern Ireland*, 96.

72. Douglas Mendel, *The Politics of Formosan Nationalism* (Berkeley: University of California Press, 1970), 46.

73. Tariq Ali, *Can Pakistan Survive?* (London: New Left Books, 1983), 45.

74. Henderson, Lebow, and Stoessinger, *Divided Nations*, 303. "Bengali was spoken by 56 percent of Pakistan's population, Punjabi by 37 percent, and the remainder spoke Pustu, Sindhi, Baluchi and Urdu." Ali, *Can Pakistan Survive?* 44–45.

75. Ali, *Can Pakistan Survive?* 45.

76. Henderson, Lebow, and Stoessinger, *Divided Nations*, 303.

77. Ali, *Can Pakistan Survive?* 47.

78. M. J. Akbar, *India: The Seige Within* (New York: Penguin, 1985), 44; Henderson, Lebow, and Stoessinger, *Divided Nations*, 303.

79. Ali, *Can Pakistan Survive?* 42.

80. Akbar, *India*, 42.

81. *New York Times*, August 10, 1986.

82. *New York Times*, August 10, 1986.

83. *Washington Post*, October 17, 1988.

84. *New York Times*, August 10, 1988.

85. *New York Times*, August 10, 1988.

86. *New York Times*, August 10, 1988.

87. *New York Times*, November 11, 1988.

88. *New York Times*, June 29, 1987.

89. Norman Zucker, *The Coming Crisis in Israel* (Cambridge, Mass.: MIT Press, 1973), 79, 108.

90. Zucker, *Coming Crisis in Israel*, 108.

91. *New York Times*, June 15, 1988.

92. *New York Times*, November 8, 1988.

93. *Village Voice*, May 2, 1986.

94. *New York Times*, November 11, 1988.

95. O'Malley, *Uncivil Wars*, 62–63.

96. *New York Times*, June 28, 1986.

97. Stanley Karnow, *Vietnam: A History* (New York: Viking, 1983), 278.

98. Karnow, *Vietnam*, 279.

99. Karnow, *Vietnam*, 281. Diem's older brother, the archibishop of Hue at the time, was later excommunicated by the Vatican for religious extremism. Karnow, *Vietnam*, 691.

100. Davis, *Israel*, 18.

101. Davis, *Israel*, 19, 20.

102. Aronson, *Creating Facts*, 88.

103. Gerard Chaliand, *Revolution in the Third World* (New York: Penguin, 1977), 139.

104. Chaliand, *Revolution in the Third World*, 95.

105. Karnow, *Vietnam*, 231.

106. Davis, *Israel*, 35.

107. Clough, *Embattled Korea*, 58; *The New York Times*, December 3, 1988.

108. *New York Times*, November 9, 1988.

109. See Norman Gelb, *The Berlin Wall* (New York: Times Books, 1986), 4; *New York Times*, November 13, 1987.

110. Peter Schnieder, "Is There a Europe?" *Harpers*, September 1988, 56.

111. *San Francisco Chronicle*, October 19, 1988.

112. *New York Times*, August 13, 1988; Aronson, *Creating Facts*, 53.

113. John Conroy, *Belfast Diaries: War as a Way of Life* (Boston: Beacon, 1987), 113.

114. Conroy, *Belfast Diaries*, 114.

115. Conroy, *Belfast Diaries*, 117.

116. Conroy, *Belfast Diaries*, 108.

S I X

SOVEREIGNTY DENIED

In the years following partition, disenfranchised groups within the divided states began to resist the derogation of their rights and the restrictions on their citizenship imposed by state officials and dominant social groups. A second generation of independence movements soon emerged to reassert the rights of disenfranchised groups and to bid for state power of their own.

Second-generation movements share a common desire for independence. In the postpartition context, however, independence acquired a new meaning. Before partition, independence movements had sought to secede from colonial empires and acquire state power in a single, devolved territory. But after partition, when devolution resulted in the creation of two states, independence took on two possible meanings. For the National Liberation Front (NFL) in South Vietnam and the Irish Republican Army (IRA) in Northern Ireland, independence meant the *reunification* of two separate states. They believed that independence could only be realized in a single, united nation-state, in which the overall majority would rule. South Korean students in the early 1960s and late 1980s demanded democratization and reunification with the North as a means of promoting Korean independence. Other movements, such as the Awami League in East Pakistan and Sikhs in India, defined independence as *secession*, the further division of a divided state and the creation of a new nation-state in which they could exercise majority rule on their own terms.

Some movements argue for reunification as a means of achieving their independence, but they practice a form of separatism. Reunification has long been the ostensible goal of the Kuomintang in Taiwan, but the party clings to de facto separatism to survive and has made no real attempt to reunify China. The indigenous Taiwanese are more consistent. When they have asserted demands for independence, they have urged the creation of a separate Taiwanese state that is free from both mainland Communist and Kuomintang rule.

Until 1988, the Palestine Liberation Organization (PLO) rejected the UN-sponsored partition of Palestine and argued that Palestinians would secure their independence in a unified, secular Palestine. Arab Palestinians would make up a majority in such a unified state, and some Jews would be permitted to remain as a minority. But in November 1988, in the wake of the Arab-Palestinian uprising in the Israeli-occupied territories (the *intifada*), the PLO redefined its goals and demanded the creation of a separate, independent Palestinian state along lines suggested by the United Nations in 1947. So while they have long urged reunification, the PLO has now adopted a separatist definition of independence.

Postpartition independence movements sought to realize their goals by various means. Student movements in South Korea, Buddhists in South Vietnam, the Awami League in East Pakistan, Arab Palestinians in Israeli Palestine, East German workers, and Catholic civil rights activists in Northern Ireland all attempted to redress their grievances by legal means. They used elections, protest marches, and demonstrations to press for independence. But where "civil" means failed or were subjected to attack by military and paramilitary forces (often resulting in the deaths of nonviolent protesters), civil protest gave way to martial resistance. Whether by choice or necessity, the NLF, the Awami League, Sikhs in India, Pathans in Pakistan, the PLO, and the IRA all organized irregular, guerrilla forces to resist the derogation of their rights and to press for state power and independence.

Naturally, the government officials and military leaders and representatives of dominant communities viewed the development of second-generation independence movements with alarm. Moreover, the development of civil and martial resistance to partition and discrimination created a backlash in the majority populations. To a large extent, the coups that established military regimes and the imposition of martial law in many of the divided states (South Korea, Taiwan, South Vietnam, Pakistan, Israel, East Germany, and Northern Ireland) were a direct response to the challenge presented by the resistance of indigenous minority groups. In tightening control of subject populations, the dominant communities and state officials further derogated their political and legal standing.

State officials view second-generation independence movements with alarm because they advocate ideas such as self-determination that challenge the rule of dominant groups, and they draw support from friendly populations in neighboring states. When communists in South Vietnam enlisted the support of communists living in the North, when Catholics in Northern Ireland appealed to their compatriots in the South and the United States for assistance, the social conflict within divided states became externalized. Instead of confronting simply an indigenous insurrection, state officials also faced the prospect of foreign intervention. And the prospect of such intervention in their internal affairs triggered a visceral reaction by officials bent on maintaining their own sovereignty. Thus, Indian officials denounce Pakistan for supporting Sikh insurgency, while Pakistani officials accused India of assisting Bengali separatism. The foreign or cosmopolitan dimension of second-generation independence movements thus represents a far more serious challenge to state officials than they would if their efforts were strictly parochial. Leaders of independence movements understand this and seek to broaden or "internationalize" their struggle. The dramatic airplane hijackings of the 1970s and 1980s is symptomatic of efforts to publicize independence movements on a global scale.

Just as the meaning of citizenship was compromised by postpartition developments in the divided states, the meaning of sovereignty has also been abridged. Just as the derogation of citizenship led to political and social conflict within and between divided states, the derogation of sovereignty has contributed to conflict between divided states and their superpower allies.

Although partition was supposed to result in the creation of separate but sovereign nation-states that could participate as equals in the interstate system, state officials have discovered that partition crippled their sovereignty from the outset and would handicap their efforts to conduct normal diplomatic relations with other states. For the independence movements that took state power, this development was extremely disillusioning. Frustrated officials sought to remove the restrictions imposed on them by partition, sibling states, and superpower states and to recover their sovereignty by force. Whereas the derogation of citizenship created second-generation independence movements that sought to take state power by force, the derogation of sovereignty contributed to the willingness of state officials to undo the limitations imposed on their power by force.

As noted in chapter 1, the United States and Soviet Union together created an interstate system that was theoretically egalitarian but in practice hierarchical. No state would be allowed to exercise its independence without restraint, and some would be permitted greater power in the system than others. Nation-states could pass laws, levy taxes, and raise armies, but they could not easily pass laws that offended superpower propriety, levy taxes that expropriated foreign property, or deploy armies against foreign countries without risking sanction by the superpowers and the other members of the interstate system. The superpowers could act with greater freedom than smaller and weaker states, but even at the height of its power, neither the United States nor the Soviet Union could act with disregard for the other or its allies.

When governmental power was devolved, officials in the divided states expected to acquire the kind of sovereignty enjoyed by most other, nonsuperpower states. Being realists, few expected that they would obtain the freedom of action enjoyed by the superpowers (China is the notable exception). Eamon De Valera, for instance, did not expect that Ireland would be able to act as Great Britain did in international affairs. But officials did expect to enjoy the sovereign rights accorded to lesser states and to be treated as equals in the diplomatic protocols.

They soon found, however, that these rights were difficult to obtain because partition had diminished their standing, because the divided states themselves took actions that resulted in the diminution of sovereignty, and because other states obstructed their rights.

Except in Palestine, where a separate Israeli state was created and some of the land assigned to an Arab Palestinian state devolved to Jordan, and in Ireland, where Northern Ireland became a semiautonomous province of Great Britain, partition resulted in the creation of two new states. From the outset, the status of these states was ambiguous. Because many partition agreements—in Korea, Vietnam, India, and Ireland—provided for reunification elections within a few years, it was unclear whether the states created would be temporary or permanent members of the interstate system. It was also unclear how much territory each state could legitimately claim as its own. Such ambiguity about the status of the divided states arose because they were anomalies in a system based on permanent nation-states with coherent populations and definitive borders. The divided states themselves reinforced this ambiguity by making claims inconsistent with the accepted behavior of separate, sovereign states. Many of the divided states, for example, had prepared constitutions that claimed territories not assigned to them and derogated the sovereignty of sibling states, which resulted in the derogation of sovereignty for both.

The preamble of the 1960 constitution of North Vietnam began, "Viet Nam is a single entity from Lang-Son [on the northern border with China] to Camau [the southernmost tip of the country]."[1] The 1956 South Vietnamese constitution made the same claim, asserting jurisdiction over all of Vietnam, not just half of it. Article 1 read, "Viet-Nam is an independent, unified, territorial indivisible republic."[2] Similar repudiations of partition appear in the constitutions of southern Ireland, North Korea, South Korea, China, and Taiwan; in Germany, the two states for many years considered each other's claim as illegal. The Basic Law, West Germany's de facto constitution, treats itself as provisional: according to Article 146, "This Basic Law shall cease to be in force on the day on which a constitution adopted by a free decision of the German people [East and West] comes into force."[3]

India and Pakistan recognize each other's existence but dispute large territories in the Kashmir and areas that have changed hands as a result of three wars.

The unwillingness of government officials to accept assigned territories and their determination to claim territories held by others violates the principles on which sovereignty in the interstate system is based. As the historian Immanuel Wallerstein has noted, "What is conceptually impermissible in the modern state-system was an explicit recognition of permanent overlapping jurisdictions. Sovereignty as a concept was based on the Aristotelian law of the excluded middle."[4] Overlapping territorial claims has prompted objections by sibling states, which view these claims as a direct attempt to infringe their sovereignty, and has antagonized other states, which doubt the commitment of these states to act as responsible members of the interstate system.

The divided states have also tried to limit the sovereignty of sibling states by insisting that recognition of one state *precluded* recognition of the other. In 1955, the West German government adopted the Hallstein Doctrine, which made either/or recognition the government's official policy. The government refused to establish diplomatic relations with any country that established relations with East Germany. When nonaligned Yugoslavia established diplomatic relations with East Germany, the West German government described the move as "an unfriendly act" and severed its existing relations with Yugoslavia.[5] (Curiously, the West Germans did not apply this doctrine to the Soviet Union, which established and eventually recognized East Germany. The West Germans did not because they could not get rid of residual Soviet occupation authority without first signing a peace treaty with the Soviets, a treaty that partition had deferred.) The East German government reciprocated in 1967, promulgating the "Ulbricht Doctrine," which threatened sanctions against countries that made contacts with West Germany.[6] The two Germanies finally abandoned their either/or recognition policies in 1969; mutual recognition came four years later.[7] It was only after they abandoned their exclusionary recognition policies that they were admitted to the United Nations.

Although the Hallstein approach allows one state to derogate the sovereignty of another, however, its effect is to derogate the rights of both. In 1957, the Soviets tried to obtain UN membership for North and South Vietnam and North and South Korea, but U.S. officials led the fight against admission in the General Assembly and the proposal was defeated.[8] Like West Germany, the United States preferred that only one state—its ally—be admitted and recognized. Failing that, U.S. officials preferred that neither be recognized. This was the downside of Hallstein Doctrines everywhere. And as the West Germans discovered, some countries even used the Hallstein Doctrine to extract economic concessions from them by threatening to recognize East Germany.

Such developments have made it difficult for states to secure and maintain recognition in the interstate system. The controversy admitting a delegation from mainland China or Taiwan into the United Nations illustrates the problematic nature of sovereignty for divided states. While the Soviets and Americans locked horns over this issue for more than twenty years, the governments in mainland China and Taiwan also attached considerable importance to this question. Aside from the practical difficulties that result from nonrecognition—it is more difficult to obtain foreign aid and participate in international organizations such as the International Monetary Fund, the World Health Organization, or the Olympics—it undermines one's position in a conflict. When the Soviets absented themselves from the United Nations just prior to the Korean War (which they had done to protest the U.S. refusal to admit China), U.S. representatives were able to persuade the United Nations to commit troops to the conflict and to condemn China's entrance into the war as an illegal act of an aggressor. With some reason, then, the Kuomintang government in Taiwan now fears the same kind of treatment.[9] Should they become embroiled in a conflict with China, the Nationalists might find it difficult to obtain outside assistance without access to the United Nations.

The sovereignty of divided states is also abridged by the actions of other states, particularly the superpowers. After helping to engineer partition, the superpower states continued to take an active interest in the internal and external affairs of these countries. Frequently this interest has been expressed by military intervention and diplomatic meddling, which has infringed divided states' ability to exercise their full sovereignty.

In Germany, for many years, both superpowers reserved their rights as occupation authorities. They did not permit either state to conduct a fully independent foreign and military policy. Until 1990, the superpowers maintained control over even relatively minor matters. When East German leader Erich

Honecker made plans in the early 1980s to visit West Germany and meet with officials there, the Soviets repeatedly canceled his trips, a humiliating experience for a head of state.[10] Likewise, after a group of NATO jets crashed into a large crowd during an air show at a U.S. base in West Germany, killing sixty-five spectators, West German defense minister Rupert Scholz's decision to ban acrobatic flying touched off a controversy because he did not have the authority to dictate such prohibitions to the United States and NATO. After the incident, *Stern* magazine editorialized, "The time has come to ask the question of who really governs this country. Almost half a century after the end of the war, West Germany continues to be a nation with only limited sovereignty."[11]

In South Korea, as in West Germany, the United States maintains control of the armed forces, which were placed under United Nations command during the Korean War. In 1960, the *New York Times* reported that "Koreans cheered U.S. Ambassador Walter McConaughy's automobile, with its U.S. flags flying, as he proceeded slowly down a main avenue in Seoul" to tell Syngman Rhee that it was time to step down.[12] When the South Korean government sent South Korean troops to crush the 1979 uprising in the city of Kwangju, they first had to obtain permission of the U.S. commander to redeploy their troops. When President Chun Doo Hwan was faced with massive demonstrations protesting his attempt to designate a successor without elections, U.S. diplomats in 1987 told Chun to reconsider his decision. He did. And a year later, elections were held to choose a successor, and Roh Tae Woo, the commander of the forces that had crushed the Kwangju rebellion, was elected president. The United States played a similar role in South Vietnam, where for twenty years it chose political leaders, sanctioned coups, and controlled, directly or indirectly, the country's foreign and military policy.

U.S. aid is an important lever in its relations with many divided states. A 1957 report of the U.S. Senate's Foreign Relations Committee concluded:

> Technical Assistance is not something to be done, as a Government enterprise, for its own sake or for the sake of others. The U.S. Government is not a charitable institution, nor is it an appropriate outlet for the charitable spirit of the American people. . . . Technical Assistance is only one of a number of instruments available to the United States to carry out its foreign policy and promote its national interests abroad.[13]

Recipients of U.S. aid thus found that aid gave U.S. officials a hand in shaping their foreign and military policy. Because divided states are typically immersed in conflict with their neighbors and desperately seek military assistance, they often surrender a great deal of control over their foreign and domestic policy to obtain U.S. assistance, which can make them vulnerable to attacks by domestic opponents.

Prior to partition, Jinnah announced that Pakistan would pursue a nonaligned foreign policy. But after its first war with India, General Ayub in 1953 negotiated with the United States to obtain military aid. Pakistan was then quickly enrolled in the U.S. sphere of influence. U.S. officials first urged Pakistan to join an alliance with Turkey in April 1954 to form a bulwark against Soviet expansion and, later that year, to join SEATO to "contain Chinese aggression."[14] In 1955, the United States persuaded Pakistan to sign the Baghdad Pact with Britain, Iran, Iraq, and Turkey to forestall radical nationalist revolution in the Middle East. Naturally, these developments made it difficult for Pakistan to conduct the kind of independent, nonaligned foreign policy foreseen by Jinnah. The domestic consequences of this were quickly felt in 1956, when President Gamal Abdel Nasser of Egypt expropriated the Suez Canal from the British and French, a move extremely popular among Moslems and nationalists throughout the Middle East and South Asia. But because of its treaty commitments, Pakistan backed the anti-Islamic British, whereas neighboring India backed Moslem Egypt. Demonstrations against the Pakistani government's policy broke out across the country, and opponents of the government's pro-Western foreign policy formed a political party that would subsequently make considerable trouble for the government.[15]

This does not mean that Pakistan's foreign and military policy was wholly controlled by its superpower ally. Pakistan, like other divided states, could and did take unilateral foreign policy initiatives. State officials in Pakistan three times initiated wars with India in the postpartition period, a fact that attests to their capacity and determination to use military force to exercise their sovereignty. But although Pakistan could begin these wars, it could not conclude them on its own terms, which suggests that even its capacity to wage war was restricted in important ways.

Israeli state officials also found that although they enjoyed the capacity to make war on their own initiative, they could not always conclude them on their own terms. During the first three Arab-Israeli wars—1948–1949, 1956, and 1967—the Israelis seized the initiative and quickly crushed Arab military opposition. But military victory did not force Israel's opponents to sue for peace, to sign treaties recognizing Israel's territorial claims, or to agree to restrict the size and character of their armies. The only time Israel was able to conclude a favorable peace was five years after the largely unfavorable 1973 war (which had been launched at Egyptian initiative). Even then, the United States pressured Israel and Egypt to sign the Camp David Accords. Israel had not been able to conclude its previous or subsequent wars on favorable terms because in each case the United States, Israel's foremost ally and economic benefactor, insisted that the Israelis limit their military and political objectives and agree to cease-fires that preserved intact their neighbors' armies and governments. U.S. officials restricted Israeli action in part because it wanted to prevent the Soviet Union from intervening on behalf of threatened Arab states and in part because the United States itself wanted to preserve the integrity of certain Arab states, which were important political and economic allies.

The United States has also intervened in Israeli domestic affairs, though not as vigorously as in other divided states. U.S. officials have been reluctant to use massive economic and military aid to Israel as a means of forcing changes in Israeli policy and have not attempted to overthrow or push aside the civilian government, as they have done in some of the other divided states. But during the recent Arab Palestinian uprising in the Israeli-occupied territories, U.S. officials have condemned the shooting of demonstrators by Israeli forces and have refused to veto a UN Security Council resolution condemning Israel.[16] But although the United States places fewer restrictions on Israel's sovereignty than on some of the other divided states, it abridges, in some way, the sovereign rights of all.

The Soviet Union did much the same thing. It intervened militarily in East Germany and used economic and military aid to shape its allies foreign and military policy. Ironically, though, the Soviet Union was less effective than the United States at restricting the sovereignty of its allies. This may at first seem counterintuitive. One would expect the Soviets to exercise greater control over states ruled by like-minded communist parties than the United States could over states ruled by democratic, nationalist parties or military regimes. But although the Soviet Union *did* influence directly the domestic, foreign, and military policy of East Germany, it was not able to establish that kind of influence in Asia because China was able to forge a relatively independent foreign and domestic policy there. China's ability to assert its sovereignty set an example for other divided states to obtain greater rights than they could have otherwise. In the U.S. sphere of influence, no state (except perhaps France) has been able to obtain rights vis-à-vis the United States that China was able to exercise vis-à-vis the Soviet Union.

Government officials in China were able to initiate and conclude several wars—the 1947–1949 civil war, the Korean War, the war with India in 1962, the border clashes with Vietnam in 1979, and a conflict with the Soviet Union itself in 1969–1970—on their own terms. The assertion of China's independence from Soviet policy dictates led in the late 1950s to a split between the two countries, making it possible for North Korea and North Vietnam to assert their own, though more modest, rights by playing the Soviets and the Chinese against each other. The Sino-Soviet split thus gave smaller divided states greater room in which to maneuver.

During the 1950s, North Korea maintained close ties with both countries, avoided taking sides in the Sino-Soviet disputes, and adopted a policy of studied neutrality in 1961. As the Sino-Soviet dispute sharpened, the Soviet Union practiced its own de facto version of the either/or Hallstein Doctrine and withdrew all aid from North Korea because the North Koreans refused to break with China. North Korean officials then sided with China, though they continued to press for Soviet and Chinese aid and insisted on North Korean independence. Tensions between China and North Korea rose during the Chinese Cultural Revolution (1965–1969) when Red Guards attacked North Korean premier Kim Il Sung as a "fat revisionist" and the "Khrushchev of Korea."[17]

Although they were offended by Chinese behavior during the Cultural Revolution, the North Koreans were also offended by the Soviets' Brezhnev Doctrine, under which the Soviets claimed they had a right to invade Czechoslovakia "to preserve socialism" in 1968. (North Korea, like Czechoslovakia, borders the Soviet Union.) So in the 1970s, they returned to their neutralist position, attempting to keep both China and the Soviet Union at arm's length and pursuing independent contacts with nonaligned and third world countries.[18]

The North Vietnamese maintained more consistent relations with the Soviet Union and developed more antagonistic relations with China than the North Koreans, but they too preserved a great deal of autonomy during their long war with France, the United States, and various South Vietnamese regimes. North Vietnam was able to conduct a relatively independent foreign and military policy, initiate and conclude the war on its own terms, play the Soviets and Chinese against each other, and keep some distance from both for the duration of the war. But after the war's conclusion in 1975, the Chinese attempted to assert greater control over the Vietnamese: they initiated a border war with Vietnam but were rebuffed, and they sided with the ousted Khmer Rouge after the Vietnamese invaded Cambodia in 1979. Although the Chinese have not been able to bring Vietnamese policy into line with their own, they have in recent years been able to confine Vietnamese initiatives and prevent them from concluding the war in Kampuchea on their own terms.

Still, the Vietnamese communists, like the North Koreans and Chinese, have exercised control over domestic and foreign policy that communist regimes in Eastern Europe could not. For the most part, they have also been able to exercise greater control than their sibling-state counterparts. South Korea and South Vietnam ceded control over their armed forces to the United States and Taiwan was beholden to U.S. naval forces for its very survival. None of these states was able to launch any wars of its own, and regimes in South Korea and South Vietnam survived only with massive U.S. assistance. By contrast, China, North Korea, and Vietnam maintained effective control over state power (the Soviets did not attempt to organize coups to topple them) and over their armed forces, deploying them effectively and independently throughout this period.

However, the greater sovereignty enjoyed by communist divided states in Asia did not mean that the superpowers failed to restrict their sovereignty in important ways. It was the superpowers, after all, that prevented the North Koreans and Chinese from reuniting their countries in the postpartition period and delayed, at great cost, the reunification of Vietnam. Superpower activity also prevented these states from gaining admission to the United Nations and exercising the rights enjoyed by full-fledged members of the interstate system. The abridgement of these rights continues to be a source of continuing frustration and anger for government officials in these states.

India has charted a middle course and has thereby found greater freedom to conduct its foreign and domestic policy than Pakistan and most other divided states. By playing off the U.S.–Soviet and Sino-Soviet disputes, Indian officials have been able to acquire control of their domestic and foreign policy, but the desire of Indian state officials to conduct a nonaligned foreign policy has been frustrated by superpower alignments on issues affecting India and Pakistan.[19] India reluctantly aligned itself with the Soviet Union, in large part because the United States (and later China) found Pakistan a useful ally. India has been able to conclude one war with Pakistan on its own terms (1971), but was unable to do so in previous wars with Pakistan (1947–1949, 1965) or China (1962).

Ireland is the only partitioned country that has not been affected by superpower rivalry. After shaking off the last British restrictions on its sovereignty in 1949, the Irish Republic acquired sovereign rights enjoyed by most members of the interstate system. In Northern Ireland, by contrast, local officials enjoyed considerable autonomy, though not sovereignty (they remained part of Great Britain), for many years. But when they were unable to contain civil and martial

Catholic protest and Protestant reaction in the early 1970s, they found their autonomy quickly abridged by British authorities. In 1972, the British dissolved the provincial parliament and took over direct responsibility for civilian and military administration. This legal coup from above severely restricted the autonomy that Protestant officials and political parties had come to expect, and the derogation of Protestant autonomy in Northern Ireland has since deepened. In 1985, the British took a symbolic step that spoke volumes about the derogation of sovereign rights in Northern Ireland: they repealed a thirty-two-year-old Flags and Emblems law, which had made it illegal for residents to display the tricolored flag of the Irish Republic. Protestant groups had long marched through Catholic neighborhoods beating drums, singing marching songs, and waving the Union Jack as a means of asserting their domination. This law and Protestant practice had long angered Catholics, and the British repealed the measure to reduce tension. But Protestants viewed the British move as further evidence that their rights were being abridged and that by permitting the tricolor to be raised meant that the Union Jack was symbolically lowered. Ulster Defense Association leader John McMichael defended the old law, saying, "Symbols are most important to people not involved in the niceties of Governments."[20]

Officials in many of the divided states regulate or ban the display of flags representing sibling states or sometimes even the wearing of colors represented on their flags. China submitted an official protest to the Soviet Union after a Soviet magazine appeared with the Kuomintang flag printed on the cover. The Chinese took this as a back-door attempt by the Soviets to recognize Taiwan and derogate the mainland's sovereignty.

The use of flags and emblems by state officials and citizens is full of meaning. A country's flag, its currency, and its stamps are used to assert sovereign rights and make claims about the character of its inhabitants. U.S. currency, for instance, is full of totemic symbols (the eye above the pyramid), slogans ("In God We Trust," "Annuit Coeptis"), representations of founding fathers, and endorsements by contemporary officials. This is no less true of the practice of government officials in the divided states. Flags, currency, and stamps are used as the coin of sovereignty. (Traditionally, British gold coins impressed with the monarch's image have been called "sovereigns.")

Officials in some of the divided states use stamps to complain of partition. The West Germans, for example, issued a stamp commemorating the 1948–1949 Berlin airlift. The stamp features a tall, arching concrete hurdle, displays the flags of the occupying countries that assisted in the relief of West Berlin—

the United States, Great Britain, and France (a usage that also hints at the derogated sovereignty of West Germany)—and notes *"Luftbrücke Berlin"* and the dates 1948–1949 to remind contemporary Germans of past events. Not to be outdone, the East German government issued a stamp commemorating the twenty-fifth anniversary of the *"Antifaschistischer Schutzwall"* ("Antifascist Bulwark"), elsewhere known as the Berlin Wall. It depicts the Brandenburg Gate, not the pedestrian cement barrier that circles West Berlin, in the background and a smiling woman handing red carnations to three smiling, heavily armed soldiers in the foreground.

But it is a South Korean stamp that perhaps best expresses official frustration with partition and the derogation of sovereignty. The red-and-blue stamp depicts an outline map of the Korean peninsula. A heavy link chain stretches across the 38th parallel. But the chain is severed midway by a flaming, Olympic-like torch held by three muscular fists and arms. The dramatic imagery is plain: the torch of freedom, held by South Korean "arms," will cut the chain that both divides and enslaves the country.[21]

Just as the disenfranchisement of "minority" populations creates resistance by indigenous movements, the derogation of sovereign rights stimulates official determination to remove the obstacles that constrain independence. As a result, government officials of divided states have frequently used force of arms to claim their rights as sovereign states.

NOTES

1. Bernard Fall, *Two Vietnams* (New York: Praeger, 1964), 409.

2. Fall, *Two Vietnams*, 428.

3. Gregory Henderson, R. N. Lebow, and J. G. Stroessinger, *Divided Nations in a Divided World* (New York: McKay, 1974), 35.

4. Immanuel Wallerstein, *Historical Capitalism* (London: Verso, 1983), 49.

5. Henderson, Lebow, and Stroessinger, *Divided Nations*, 36; Henry Ashby Turner, Jr., *The Two Germanies since 1945* (New Haven, Conn.: Yale University Press, 1987), 87.

6. Edwina Moreton, *Germany between East and West* (Cambridge: Cambridge University Press, 1987), 110.

7. Moreton, *Germany between East and West*, 164.

8. Henderson, Lebow, and Stroessinger, *Divided Nations*, 147.

9. In 1989, only twenty-three countries recognized Taiwan. *Washington Post*, April 7, 1989.

10. Honecker finally made the trip in 1987. *New York Times*, July 19, 1987.

11. *New York Times*, September 19, 1988.

12. *Washington Post*, July 5, 1987.

13. Tariq Ali, *Can Pakistan Survive?* (London: New Left Books, 1983), 51.

14. Ali, *Can Pakistan Survive?* 51–52.

15. Ali, *Can Pakistan Survive?* 52.

16. *New York Times*, December 23, 1987.

17. Bong-youn Choy, *A History of the Korean Reunification Movement* (Peoria, Ill.: Institute of International Studies, Bradley University, 1984), 123.

18. Choy, *Korean Reunification Movement*, 123–24.

19. See Eisenhower's and Dulles's critical views of Indian "neutralism" and their attempt to undermine the nonaligned movement and India's leadership role in it. Joann Krieg, *Dwight D. Eisenhower* (New York: Greenwood, 1987), 200–04.

20. *New York Times*, December 2, 1985.

21. The Greek Cypriots have a similar set of stamps. One depicts the island set in a blue sea, with the northern, Turkish-occupied half of the island engulfed in flames. Above it, the 1984 stamp notes, "Ten years of Occupation of Cyprus Territory by Turkey." Other Cypriot stamps feature children or groups of men encircled by rolls of barbed wire.

SEVEN

STATES OF WAR

In a speech at the University of Virginia in early 1947, George Kennan said of the Soviets:

I sometimes think they have created something [communism] more powerful than themselves . . . that they have sown their dragon's teeth and now they find themselves, willy-nilly, for better or for worse, the masters and the servants of the weird and terrifying warriors who have grown up in their pasture.[1]

Fifty years later, Kennan's prophetic warning applies not only to Soviet communism, but to the partition policies of all the great and superpower states. Partition prepared the ground for the development of "weird and terrifying warriors" who would wage destructive irregular and conventional wars in the divided states and in neighboring countries.

It is commonplace today to describe irregular warriors—sword-carrying Sikh secessionists, scarf-wearing Palestinian militia, and ski-masked IRA gunmen—as "terrorists." This term, however, does not adequately describe their social origins, contemporary politics, or future goals. As Christopher Hitchens notes, *terrorist* as it is commonly defined—"the use of violence for political ends"—is vague. The term's meaning could theoretically "cover any state, party, movement or system not explicitly committed to pacifism or [be] simply a synonym for 'swarthy opponent of U.S. foreign policy.' "[2]

Despite the inherent inexactitude in labeling the irregular forces in the divided states as "terrorists," they may certainly be described as "weird and terrifying." It would be difficult, for instance, to describe the Khmer Rouge in Cambodia except as both weird and terrifying. Its national anthem, "Glorious April 17," named for the day in 1975 when the Khmer Rouge seized the Cambodian capital, celebrated a sanguine identity:

Bright red blood that covers the towns and plains of Kampuchea, our mother-land/Sublime blood of workers and peasants/Sublime blood of revolutionary men and women fighters/The blood changing into unrelenting hatred.[3]

It is hard to imagine a tune that could carry these stanzas.

The movements that wage irregular wars are not, of course, the only weird and terrifying warriors in the divided states. Government officials who massacre peaceful demonstrators, who adopt "Iron Fist" policies (which include breaking the hands of rock-throwing demonstrators), who subject minority populations to military and paramilitary rule, or who launch surprise attacks on neighboring states might also be described in this fashion.

The superpowers came to regard some of their own allies in the divided states as weird and terrifying. Soviet Premier Nikita Khrushchev was appalled at Mao Tse-tung's belief that nuclear war was like conventional conflict. "War is war," Mao told Khrushchev. "The years will pass and we'll get to work producing more babies than ever before." Or, "If worse came to worse and half of mankind died, the other half would remain while imperialism would be razed to the ground."[4] Khrushchev believed that Mao's views revealed him as one who might take catastrophic risks. In 1959, he warned China's leaders not to "test the stability of the capitalist system by employing armed force" and accused China of being "keen on war like a bellicose cock."[5] Across the Taiwan Strait, U.S. officials believed that Chiang Kai-shek was an unreliable ally who might start a war he couldn't finish. In 1950, for example, Kuomintang officials expressed the hope that a third world war would give them the opportunity to recover the mainland, and they urged a widening of the Korean War to provoke a global war.

Allies such as Mao and Chiang, who were willing to take potentially catastrophic risks regardless of the consequences, might justifiably be seen as weird and terrifying by U.S. and Soviet officials. But sometimes the shoe was on the other foot: during the course of conflicts in the divided states, U.S. and Soviet leaders many times threatened to use nuclear weapons. During a 1955 crisis in the Taiwan Strait, President Eisenhower said he might use "new and powerful weapons" to prevent "armed aggression" by the Chinese and claimed that tactical nuclear weapons could be used without massacring civilians.[6] From the Chinese perspective, U.S. officials—who had once used nuclear weapons to destroy heavily populated cities in Japan and who now threatened to use them in another densely populated country—might also be regarded as weird and terrifying. Conflicts in the divided states tend to unleash forces and produce consequences that the participants do not intend, fail to anticipate, and often cannot control. Indeed, the distinction among irregular, conventional, and nuclear war easily blurs.

Kennan was prophetic in another respect. Partition and the derogation of citizenship and sovereignty would make great and superpower states become "the masters *and* the servants" of other movements and states. Great and superpower states might have mastered these countries during the process of devolution and division, but they could not easily control the developments that followed. Movements and officials in the divided states frequently took matters into their own hands and initiated wars without the consent or approval of their superpower allies, frequently forcing the superpowers to intervene militarily on their behalf. Both the United States and the Soviet Union have often found themselves acting at the behest of allies who have initiated civil and conventional wars of their own, serving their own interests.

Partition, displacement, and the derogation of citizenship and sovereignty in the divided states prepared the ground for the emergence of irregular, conventional, and nuclear warriors. To understand these conflicts and their consequences, which have had a dramatic impact on both divided and superpower states, it is useful to distinguish the three forms that such conflict take. Although violence occurs across a continuum that makes it difficult to draw sharp distinctions among irregular, conventional, and nuclear war, the actors involved—independence movements, divided states, and superpowers—tend to specialize in particular forms of war.

Displaced and disenfranchised peoples in many of the divided states have adopted irregular war as a means to achieve their secessionist or reunificationist ends. Historically, irregular war has taken many forms: assassination, bombing, booby-trapping, hostage taking, sabotage, arms-gathering assaults on military posts and police stations, rebellion, insurrection, civil war, revolution. These practices are "irregular" because their adherents are not in the employ of a state and because they challenge both civilian and military authority. There are no established "rules of engagement" (such as the Geneva conventions), and the practitioners do not usually wear uniforms identifying themselves as soldiers who can be distinguished from the civilian population at large. Various mufti—pajamas, burnooses, ski masks, camouflage fatigues, baseball caps— have become identified with some irregulars by the popular press, but these accoutrements are typically donned to *conceal* the wearer's identity.

Depending on the circumstances, political movements also blur the distinction between irregular and legal means of achieving their ends. In Northern Ireland, for instance, the Catholic reunificationist movement supports the IRA irregulars, but it also runs candidates for elected office through legal parties. The decision to participate or abstain from provincial elections has frequently split the movement. In 1969, the Provisional IRA, or "Provos," split from the main body of the IRA over this issue, rejecting the majority decision to participate in elections and pressing ahead with its own paramilitary campaign.[7] Most resistance movements, however, practice an abstentionist politics, though they may also maintain legal front organizations.

Straddling the border of legality, the movements that conduct irregular wars make it difficult for state officials to use force against them. By threatening civilian as well as military personnel, these movements can spread out a state's defenses, making it easier for small irregular forces to attack successfully. By concealing their identity, submerging themselves in the civilian population, movements make it more difficult for state officials to use force against them. The state risks attacking the "wrong" people, which can alienate them and encourage them to support the insurgents. And by maintaining a legal presence, movements can act as legitimate participants in the political process. Attempts to suppress legal participation, moreover, often arouse the opposition of other legal parties and organizations that fear that their own, nonrevolutionary activity will be jeopardized by the state.

To be effective, movements that wage irregular wars must be able to develop mass-based organizations that will support and protect the clandestine forces, while maintaining discipline among the irregular soldiers. Without disciplined troops who are able to distinguish friend from foe, irregular forces can lose popular support. Movements must also obtain and maintain support from *external* sources, from sympathetic populations and state officials in neighboring states. It is much easier for state officials to isolate and destroy irregular forces if they do not receive money, arms, and diplomatic support from abroad.

In the divided states, conditions generally permit movements to obtain indigenous support, maintain discipline, and secure outside assistance. The disenfranchisement of indigenous minorities tends to create communities that are willing to support legal and clandestine resistance to majority rule. But sometimes it takes a dramatic turn of events to energize these communities. In Northern Ireland, for example, the Catholic minority refused to support or assist IRA bombing campaigns in the late 1930s or in the late 1950s and early 1960s. These campaigns were ineffective, and most of the irregulars were captured. But after Protestant irregulars and the Royal Ulster Constabulary attacked peaceful mass demonstrations and Catholic neighborhoods in 1968–1969, the Catholic population threw its support behind the irregular forces. A significant percentage has maintained this support to this day. In Israel, the Arab Palestinian population was generally unsupportive of irregular *fedayeen* attacks until after the 1967 Arab-Israeli war and the Israeli occupation of the West Bank and Gaza—and then its support was muted. It was only in the late 1980s, after Israel's unsuccessful war in Lebanon, that the indigenous population demonstrated widespread support for the PLO, its irregular forces, and the creation of a separate Palestinian state.

First-generation movements that conducted irregular war to win independence in devolved states provide a model of discipline for second-generation movements. There is no copyright on the methods of irregular war. Its practice has been freely copied by groups professing very different ideologies: capitalist or communist, ethnic or secular, secessionist or reunificationist. So, for instance, the PLO's conduct of its irregular campaigns owes as much to Zionist irregulars—Menachem Begin's Irgun, the Stern Gang—as it does to Arab irregulars such as the Green Hand gang that operated during the British mandate period.

To be successful, movements that practice irregular war must conduct themselves in a manner that does not alienate their supporters. This means that the violence they employ must be selective, not random. Context is important. The press often describes the incidents that accompany irregular war as indiscriminate acts of violence and terror. The bombing of Irish pubs, car bomb attacks in crowded markets, and the massacre of passengers traveling on buses, trains, or planes are usually treated as indiscriminate terrors because they are attacks on civilians. But on closer inspection, these attacks are usually more selective. The IRA bombed Protestant pubs, Christian irregulars in Lebanon attacked markets in Moslem districts, and in one case, Sikh militants separated Sikh from Hindu before slaughtering the Hindu passengers on a bus in the Punjab. Irregular forces attempt to distinguish between friend and foe and convey these distinctions to their supporters and enemies. This is why the ubiquitous claiming of responsibility for acts of violence is so important to irregular movements. These claims are part of an ongoing political effort to demonstrate that their use of violence is selective rather than indiscriminate. If violence is seen by potential supporters as random, irregulars will be treated as thugs, hoodlums, or madmen. In this context, an irregular movement's "discipline" is measured by its ability to employ violence selectively and to persuade its supporters that discriminate violence is a legitimate, necessary, and effective means of self-defense. This, however, is very difficult to do, for inevitably friends as well as foes are killed.

The successful conduct of irregular war also depends heavily on a movement's ability to obtain external support. Because partition led to massive migration across newly created borders, minority populations found they could rely on sympathetic populations and officials in neighboring states to provide financial, military, and political assistance. IRA representatives from Northern Ireland raise money from Catholics in Ireland and the United States and use this money to purchase arms,[8] while the Irish Republic pressures the British to eliminate discriminatory measures against Northern Catholics, restore human rights, and end martial law. Likewise, the PLO for many years subsisted on the support of Arab Palestinian populations and sympathetic state officials in Egypt, Jordan, Syria, and Lebanon before wearing out its welcome in each of these states. Sikhs in India rely on Sikh neighbors in Pakistan and depend on state officials there to treat their activities—raising money and acquiring arms—with a wink and a nod. Without the financial, military, and political assistance from external supporters, many movements that conduct irregular war would be more easily isolated and destroyed.

Some movements are more successful than others at indigenous organization, discipline, and external support. In the postpartition period, however, only *two* movements that have waged irregular war have been ultimately successful. The NLF in Vietnam was the only successful reunificationist movement, and the Mukti Bahini, the armed wing of the Awami League in East Pakistan, was the only successful secessionist movement. Of the two, the NLF demonstrated a greater capacity to enlist popular support; wage an effective, disciplined irregular war; secure the support of sympathetic populations in neighboring states (North Vietnam, Laos, Cambodia) and around the world as well (even, to some extent in the United States); and survive a protracted and determined effort by officials in South Vietnam and the United States to crush it. As Douglas Pike, a Rand Corporation analyst, said of the NLF:

> If the essence of the Chinese revolution was strategy and the essence of the Viet Minh was spirit, the essence of the third generation revolutionary guerrilla warfare in South Vietnam was organization. . . . The National Liberation Front was a Sputnik in the political sphere of the Cold War.[9]

The Mukti Bahini was not as well organized as the NLF, but it was equally succsessful because it received Indian army intervention on its behalf.

Movements that conduct irregular war are extremely difficult to defeat once they can develop internal and external support. The South Vietnamese found it impossible to defeat the NLF, even with massive U.S. assistance. The Israelis have never been able to subdue the PLO; they have only succeeded in chasing it from one country to the next, in 1970 from Jordan and in 1982 from Lebanon. And the British have found it impossible to defeat the IRA so long as it obtains support from sympathetic populations in and outside Northern Ireland. As a result, irregular war has thus become an obdurate feature of conflict in many of the divided states.

Moreover, because movements actively seek to drag outside people and states into war, irregular war frequently contributes to the outbreak of conventional war. In the five years preceding the outbreak of the 1950 Korean War, North Korea had supported the irregular guerrilla movement and civilian uprisings in the South; South Korean troops had also made forays across the 38th parallel to attack guerrilla bases in the North.[10] The irregular war increased tensions, contributed to attempts by both sides to build up conventional armies, and spurred South Korean officials to advocate war as a way to eliminate North Korean support for irregulars in the South. And when conventional North Korean troops marched across the 38th parallel in 1950, they evidently believed that their invasion would trigger a popular uprising and assist the beleaguered irregular forces that remained in the South.

The irregular war in Vietnam, which began in 1956–1960 as a result of Diem's efforts to destroy the residual Viet Minh infrastructure, contributed to the U.S. decision to send military advisers and then conventional troops to assist the South Vietnamese. The U.S. escalation in 1964–1965, quadrupling the number of U.S. troops, led in turn to the introduction of North Vietnamese troops.[11] These developments contributed to large-scale conventional interstate war, with Cambodia and Laos eventually drawn into the conflict.

During the 1947 partition of India, civilian uprisings and irregular war resulted in the deployment of conventional troops and war between Pakistan and India. Although the British determined the general outline of partition, the particulars were not nailed down. Ruling princes possessed nominal authority over as much as one-third of the subcontinent as a result of separate treaties made with British administrators in the eighteenth and nineteenth centuries, and although the partition agreement did not automatically assign these states to either India or Pakistan, the independence movements in both countries made it clear that they would not permit princes to retain any autonomous authority within the devolved states. For instance, the Moslem ruler of Hyderabad (a large central state with a predominantly Hindu population) tried to establish authority separate from the Indian government that would be joined with the British Commonwealth. When demonstrations broke out protesting this move, Indian troops entered the principality and forced the ruler to surrender all his authority to the newly created central government.[12] But it was in Kashmir, a predominantly Moslem province in the northwest that is wedged between India and Pakistan, where the outbreak of popular revolt and irregular war provoked conventional conflict.

The Hindu maharaja of Kashmir favored joining India after partition; the 80 percent Moslem majority preferred Pakistan. Armed rebellion broke out in late 1947 and was suppressed by provincial forces loyal to the maharaja. Moslem tribesmen, with the approval of the Pakistani government, then invaded Kashmir to support Moslem insurgency and force the maharaja to devolve power to Pakistan. As these irregular forces advanced on the Kashmiri capital, the maharaja appealed to India for military assistance. Indian officials agreed to send troops provided the maharaja agreed to devolve power to India. The irregular war developed into a wider, interstate war as Pakistani troops joined the fighting to assist the Moslem irregulars. Not until January 1, 1949, after fourteen months of war, did a UN cease-fire take effect, along with the de facto division of Kashmir between India and Pakistan.[13] In short order, this division created the geographic basis for revanchist claims and further conflicts. India and Pakistan would clash again over Kashmir in August 1965 and 1971.

Irregular war in Palestine, which broke out sporadically between 1945 and 1947 and intensified prior to the devolution of British power, contributed to the outbreak of conventional interstate war in 1948, when Arab states joined the fighting. In this regard, the first Arab-Israeli war most closely resembles the Korean conflict, in which protracted irregular warfare prior to partition escalated into a wider conventional war.

In Northern Ireland, irregular war did not lead to conventional interstate war, but it did lead to the introduction of conventional British forces into the province in 1969. The movement of British troops into Northern Ireland resembles the Indian government's intervention in the princely states, which possessed some autonomy though not sovereignty vis-à-vis the central government. In Northern Ireland, as in Hyderabad, the introduction of central government regulars did not provoke a wider interstate conflict with neighboring states, even though the central governments' military intervention supported the ethnic majority against minority claims.

Irregular indigenous war and conventional interstate war have a reciprocating effect, making it difficult to establish whether they are "civil" or "international" conflicts. The interstate system is structured so that "aggression" is condemned and punished and "self-defense" is thought legitimate and supported, but this distinction is largely irrelevant in divided-state conflicts. Because partition results in a problematic definition of states, borders, and relations, it is difficult and usually meaningless to try to determine who violated whose frontiers first.

In the postpartition period, large-scale, conventional, interstate war has erupted between most of the divided states. The conflicts in Korea, Vietnam, and India have claimed more lives—civilian and military—than any other wars since 1945.[14] And conventional war in India and Palestine has broken out repeatedly. India and Pakistan have waged three major wars; Israel and its Arab neighbors have fought five times, once in every decade since partition. Fortunately, conventional interstate war did not brake out between China and Taiwan, between East and West Germany, or between Northern Ireland and the Irish Republic. Conflict between these pairs of states took other forms.

Government officials wage war to resolve social and political problems that were created by partition. By waging a successful war, government officials hope to suppress indigenous insurgencies, remove external threats, settle refugees, define permanent borders, undo the results of previous wars, or improve their standing in the interstate system. But whatever the proximate cause of conventional war between divided states, almost all of their wars are initiated by officials in the divided states, not by great and superpower states.

Although great and superpower states helped create conditions that led to war, they did not license their allies to wage war on their behalf. Partition was supposed to *reduce* conflict between indigenous movements. It did not. Instead, the conflicts between indigenous movements, which were contained within single states prior to partition, developed into interstate conflicts to be settled by large armies.

Government officials in the divided states do not wage war at their allies' request, nor do they agree to be surrogates for cold war superpower conflicts. They initiate war because they have their own scores to settle. Sometimes they receive superpower permission to do so, as the North Koreans evidently did prior to their 1950 invasion of the South, but for the most part they wage war unilaterally. Of the ten major conventional wars in the divided states since partition—the Korean War, the Vietnam War, three Indo-Pakistani wars, and five Arab-Israeli wars—only one was initiated by officials outside the region: the 1956 Suez or second Arab-Israeli war.

After Egyptian president Nasser nationalized the Suez Canal in 1956, the French and British asked the Israelis to precipitate a war with Egypt that could be used as a pretext for French and British military intervention. The French and British would then send troops into Egypt and seize the canal to "protect" it from the Israeli advance. The Israelis agreed to act as a great power surrogate because they hoped to achieve military objectives of their own: to reopen the Straits of Tiran, which the Egyptians had closed to Israeli shipping, and to drive the Egyptian army from the Sinai and thus create an expansive buffer between Israel and its most powerful Arab opponent.[15] But the great powers neglected to obtain U.S. approval; when they put their plan into operation, the United States condemned it and forced the French, British, and Israelis to halt their largely successful military campaign and withdraw from territory gained. This experience discouraged the Israelis from playing a surrogate role in the future; they conducted three subsequent wars on their own initiative. (The 1956 war proved to be a rehearsal for the Israelis' 1967 campaign in the Sinai, except that in 1967 they conquered the peninsula on their own.) The Israelis did not seek or secure superpower approval for their conduct in subsequent wars and frequently concealed their moves from their allies as well as from their opponents.

Officials in divided states are not inclined to act as superpower surrogates, because they must live with the consequences of war. The nine other major conventional wars were started by government officials in the divided states. Once under way, however, each of these wars prompted superpower intervention, though the character of such involvement varied widely. In Korea and Vietnam, the United States committed large numbers of troops to the fighting and conducted massive aerial and naval campaigns against their opponents. Although the Soviets did not introduce troops into these conflicts (apart from some advisers), they did provide significant material and financial assistance.

The superpowers have been less inclined to introduce troops into the Israeli-Arab conflicts, though they both have supplied advisers, technicians, and large amounts of military and financial assistance. The United States has sent small troop contingents to serve as partisan "peacekeeping" forces, either in combination with UN forces or on their own, as they did during the 1982 war in Lebanon. The Soviets placed more than twenty thousand military personnel in Egypt to provide air defense against Israel between 1967 and 1973.[16]

Superpower intervention in the three Indo-Pakistani wars, however, has been even less tangible. Both superpowers have tried to mediate between the parties and bring these wars to a speedy conclusion, primarily through their role as permanent members of the UN Security Council. They have also provided advanced military assistance to their respective allies—the United States to Pakistan, the Soviet Union to India. (During the 1971 war, the United States used a formidable display of naval power in an unsuccessful attempt to conclude the war on terms favorable to its ally.) The fact that the Indo-Pakistani wars are far removed from the center of both U.S. and Soviet power bases in Europe, Asia, and the Americas, and the fact that neither superpower played a role in the subcontinental partition, helps to explain why their intervention in these conflicts has been less pronounced. (Much the same is true of conflict in Ireland; neither superpower has intervened in postpartition conflicts there.)

Although government officials in the divided states can start conventional wars, they cannot finish them. And although the superpowers do not start them, they can stop them, at least for a time. The North Korean invasion in 1950, which initially routed South Korean forces, ground to a halt after U.S. and United Nations forces joined the war. And the U.S.–UN advance in the North, which nearly reached Chinese and Soviet borders, failed to retake the North after China intervened on North Korea's behalf. Intervention by U.S.–UN and Chinese forces thus prevented Korean armies from conducting war on their own terms. The war ended essentially where it began, with armies drawn up on either side of a demilitarized zone near the 38th parallel. Likewise, when war has broken out between India and Pakistan or between Israel and its neighbors, the superpowers have immediately called for an end to the conflict. The participants conduct military blitzkriegs in part to capitalize on the element of surprise and in part to achieve military objectives before superpower cease-fires take hold.

Partition also forged alliances between indigenous regimes and superpower states and grouped divided states into collective security regimes organized by the United States and the Soviet Union. Because both parties to conventional war have superpower allies, the attack by one will trigger superpower intervention on behalf of the other. And intervention by one superpower prompts intervention by the other. But while this chain of events, of action and reaction, tends to widen the conflict and turn regional conflicts into global superpower contests, conventional wars in the divided states have never resulted in the introduction of troops by *both* superpowers or direct military conflict between them. Given the fact that their allies have ten times gone to war, it is remarkable that U.S. and Soviet troops did not meet in battle.

Regional conventional wars in the divided states did not escalate into direct superpower confrontation because the superpowers acted to stop or limit them in important ways. Soon after war breaks out, the superpowers begin calling for a cease-fire. After the outbreak of the 1956 Suez war, for instance, President Eisenhower told Secretary of State Dulles to send a scathing message to Prime Minister Ben-Gurion of Israel: "You'll tell'em, goddamn it, we're going to apply sanctions, we're going to the United Nations, we're going to do everything that there is so we can stop this thing."[17] At the United Nations, U.S. officials told members that the United States would introduce a resolution calling for a cease-fire, the withdrawal of Israeli forces from the Sinai, and called on UN members—Great Britain and France—to refrain from the use of force and participate in an embargo against Israel until it withdrew from the Sinai.[18] The Soviet Union, Egypt's ally, threatened to intervene on its behalf and joined the United States in a UN resolution calling for an immediate cease-fire and the withdrawal of Israeli, French, and British forces.

The effect of U.S. and Soviet moves was to impose a cease-fire before French and British troops could wrest the Suez Canal from Egyptian control. In subsequent Arab-Israeli wars, superpower intervention brought the fighting to a halt before one side could completely destroy its opponents. As Stephan Kaplan has noted:

> Within hours of the [1973] Arab attack, Soviet representatives began asking Egypt and Syria (the Soviet Union's own allies) to halt their offensive. Although Cairo and Damascus would not do this, Moscow continued to press for a cease-fire, thus antagonizing President Sadat and straining Soviet-Egyptian relations.[19]

The superpowers also acted quickly to halt the fighting in Indo-Pakistani wars. During their second war in 1965, the United States and the Soviet Union

> joined forces in the U.N. security council to press for a cease-fire, while the United States cut off all military assistance to both parties during the conflict, a step that proved far more damaging to [its ally] Pakistan than to India, as [Pakistan] was almost wholly dependent on U.S. military assistance.[20]

Soviet mediation of the conflict resulted in the Tashkent Declaration, an armistice that ended hostilities.[21]

When the superpowers did not take action to stop conventional wars, they still attempted to limit and confine them in important ways. This was true even in Korea and Vietnam, where the United States participated directly in intense, large-scale wars.

The 1950 war between the two Koreas triggered massive U.S. military intervention on behalf of its South Korean ally. The introduction of U.S. ground troops and naval and air forces naturally intensified and widened the war, yet the Korean conflict remained "limited," as both the United States and the Soviet Union took steps to contain the fighting to the peninsula. The Soviet Union helped to contain the fighting by not reintroducing troops that had been withdrawn from Korea prior to the outbreak of war. Although the United Nations took a partisan role in the conflict, the Soviet Union did not withdraw from the United Nations (calling instead for a return to the status quo ante), nor did it create a new crisis in Berlin, attack Yugoslavia, or invade Iran during the war.[22] The United States, in turn, did not accept Chiang Kai-shek's offer to send troops to Korea, because it would have antagonized the Chinese and possibly widened the war even further. After U.S. forces failed to reunify the country on their own terms, U.S. officials scaled back their military and political objectives. As Secretary of State Acheson told Ernest Bevin in 1951:

> Our purposes in Korea remain the same, namely to resist aggression, to *localize* hostilities, and to wind up the Korean problem on a satisfactory U.N. basis and in such a way as *not* to commit U.S. forces in large numbers indefinitely in that operation [emphasis added].[23]

As in Korea, U.S. military intervention in Vietnam greatly intensified the war and helped spread it to Laos and Cambodia. But the great and superpower states, including the United States, also took steps to limit the war's scope.

During the course of the war in Vietnam, U.S. officials did not request UN intervention; they did not send the navy into the Taiwan Strait, as they had in Korea (in fact, they withdrew residual U.S. naval forces from the strait in 1969); they did not conduct an Inchon-type landing on the North Vietnamese coast; and they did not cross the Demilitarized Zone at the 17th parallel in an attempt to overrun the North. The United States never challenged North Vietnam's right to exist as a sovereign state or tried to reunify the country on U.S. terms. After the bulk of U.S. forces were withdrawn in 1973, following the 1973 armistice that recognized the 1954 partition as the status quo, U.S. officials did not attempt to reintroduce troops that had been withdrawn (as they had done in Korea in 1950) or renew the air war when North Vietnamese and NLF forces overran the South and captured Saigon in 1975.

The Soviets provided military assistance and financial aid to their North Vietnamese allies. The provision of antiaircraft weapons, planes, and missiles made a significant contribution to the North's war effort—much as the subsequent provision of U.S. antiaircraft weapons would greatly assist Afghan rebels during their war against the Soviets.[24] But the Soviets did not send troops to

participate in the war or challenge the United States elsewhere in the world—
quite the contrary. In the late 1960s and early 1970s, the Soviets sought to reduce tensions in U.S.–Soviet relations by pursuing detente, even while the war
in Vietnam raged.

The Chinese also acted to confine the war. They did not send troops to assist
their ally, as they had in Korea, or take the opportunity to threaten an invasion
of Taiwan, even after U.S. naval forces had quietly been withdrawn from the
strait. The Chinese opening to the United States, and President Nixon's visit to
Beijing in 1972, occurred during the latter stages of the war in Vietnam.

These developments effectively limited the war and also constrained the
North Vietnamese war effort, which may have preferred a wider war that
would have involved the North's allies. North Vietnamese general Vo Nguyen
Giap claims that the Chinese collaborated with the Soviet Union to limit the
conflict throughout much of the war:

> The Chinese government told the United States that if the latter did not threaten
> or touch China, then China would do nothing to prevent the [U.S.] attacks [on
> Vietnam]. It was really like telling the United States that it could bomb Vietnam
> at will, as long as there was no threat to the Chinese border. . . . We felt that we
> had been stabbed in the back.[25]

The superpowers have consistently acted to limit conventional wars in the
divided states for a variety of reasons: to punish or dissuade minor power states
from waging war on their own initiative; to defend their spheres of influence,
which emerged out of the partition process; to avoid direct confrontation,
which despite occasional talk of containment and cold war neither superpower
actively sought; and to protect the general integrity of the interstate system,
which they jointly developed and which was undermined by regional wars. As
a consequence, it was very difficult for government officials in the divided
states to conduct decisive military campaigns or wage conclusive wars. The
World War II concept of "total victory," which results in the "unconditional
surrender" of opposing forces, proved elusive. With the exception of Vietnam,
where the North Vietnamese were able to defeat their opponents and reunify
the country on their own terms, none of the major conventional wars has been
conclusive. Even where military campaigns have inflicted decisive defeats on
enemy forces, they have been inconclusive over the long term. Israeli forces
have twice conquered the Sinai and many times destroyed Arab armies wholesale, but neither the 1956 nor 1967 campaigns brought their enemies to terms.
It was only after the Egyptians managed a partially successful attack on Israeli

forces during the 1973 Yom Kippur War that a partial settlement—the Camp David Accords—could be reached. (Camp David marked an agreement between only two of the Middle East's many combatants.) The blitzkrieg campaigns launched by North Koreans, Indians, Pakistanis, Israelis, and Arabs have all failed to achieve decisive results.

Because conventional wars are indecisive, because they cannot or are not permitted to resolve the issues that gave rise to war, they simply provide the pretext for subsequent wars. Successful efforts to limit conventional wars stops the fighting inconclusively, making the recurrence of armed conflict more likely. This is why conventional war, like irregular war, is an obdurate and seemingly irremediable expression of conflict in the divided states.

Ever since they were first developed in 1945, nuclear weapons have been used to achieve political ends. Nations have frequently threatened their use during the course of conflict in the divided states, with profound consequences for the superpowers and the divided states alike.

It is commonplace to say that nuclear weapons have been "used" only on two occasions: when the United States exploded atomic bombs over two heavily populated cities in Japan—Hiroshima and Nagasaki—during surprise attacks on August 6 and 9, 1945. This use of nuclear weapons was explicit, dramatic, and catastrophic. Hundreds of thousands lost their lives in an instant. Many thousands more died from the bombs' lingering effects.

But it is important to recognize that nuclear weapons have been "used" in a variety of other ways as well. States have used the explosion of nuclear weapons at remote desert or island test sites to demonstrate their capacity to develop and perfect complex nuclear weapons technologies. The expansion of nuclear arsenals and the development of tactical and strategic delivery systems have been used to reduce great and superpower states' reliance on conventional military forces. States that possess nuclear weapons have threatened to attack others with them as a way to compel nonnuclear states to change their behavior. In addition, nuclear weapons have been used to deter other nuclear weapons-possessing states from using their own weapons. As Daniel Ellsberg points out, states can use nuclear weapons without firing them: "When you point a gun at someone's head in a confrontation, you are using the gun, whether or not you pull the trigger."[26] In the eyes of the law, a gun is "used" when it is brandished during the commission of a crime. In the same way, nuclear weapons can be used without being exploded over populous cities.

Although the use of nuclear weapons to destroy cities is rare, the practice of using nuclear weapons to compel states to change their behavior is fairly common. According to the Brookings Institution, the United States has issued nuclear threats on some twenty occasions since it destroyed Hiroshima and Nagasaki.[27] (It is hard to be exact about the number because few of these threats were publicly announced.) Some threats were conveyed though third parties, some were deliberately ambiguous, and some were made in rapid succession, which makes them difficult to distinguish. Some of these threats became known only years later, which means that the number may be greater yet. Certainly U.S. officials considered using nuclear weapons—and drew up contingency plays for doing so—more often than they actually used them to make threats. But whatever the exact number, a general pattern of partition-related threats can be discerned.

Although U.S. officials have used nuclear weapons to threaten Yugoslavia, Uruguay, Guatemala, Lebanon, and Jordan in the late 1940s and 1950s and threatened to use nuclear weapons against the Soviet Union during the Cuban Missile Crisis of 1962, the majority of U.S. threats have been directed at or motivated by events in the divided states. The United States threatened East Germany and the Soviet Union several times during the conflicts over Berlin, repeatedly threatened the North Koreans and their Chinese allies during the Korean War, threatened the Chinese in separate conflicts over Taiwan, issued a number of nuclear threats against the North Vietnamese during the later stages of the Vietnam War, used naval nuclear forces to threaten India during the third Indo-Pakistani war, and issued threats against Arab states and their Soviet ally during various Arab-Israeli conflicts.[28]

The use of nuclear weapons by the United States against opponents in the divided states may seem surprising. But nuclear weapons were developed with the intention of dropping them on Germany or Japan, and U.S. officials sought to continue to wield them to achieve political goals in conflicts that emerged around the world.[29] In various ways these officials attempted to make plain to others their determination to use nuclear weapons. Secretary of State George Marshall said in 1948, after the U.S.-Soviet confrontation over Berlin had begun, "The Soviets are beginning to realize for the first time that the United States would really use the atomic bomb against them in the event of war."[30]

U.S. presidents have tended to be more prudent than their advisers regarding the use of nuclear weapons. Truman did not heed Churchill or MacArthur's advice to employ them widely, nor did he accept the proposals of Gen. Leslie Groves (the director of the Manhattan Project), who advised destroying the

atomic bomb-manufacturing capacity of other countries—particularly the Soviet Union—before they developed nuclear weapons.[31] Nevertheless, by 1953,
having already threatened its opponents with nuclear weapons, the United
States adopted their use as official U.S. policy: "In the event of hostilities, the
United States will consider nuclear weapons to be as available for use as other
munitions."[32] Since then, U.S. officials have adopted this policy in their conduct
of military diplomacy. As conventional wars and other conflicts in the divided
states prompted a U.S. response, nuclear threats often served to move these
conflicts toward an outcome favorable to the United States and its allies.

   The use of nuclear weapons since Hiroshima and Nagasaki has been constrained in one important way. Nuclear weapons are rarely used by U.S. officials to threaten states that possess nuclear weapons of their own. Typically,
U.S. officials threaten *non*nuclear opponents.[33] The United States threatened
the Soviets during the first Berlin crisis in 1948, but this was *before* the Soviets
acquired nuclear weapons. After the Soviets acquired the bomb, U.S. threats
increasingly took the form of a standing threat to use nuclear weapons in the
event of direct conflict with the Soviet Union, as was the case during subsequent Berlin, Middle East, and Cuban crises. And at least until the 1970s, U.S.
nuclear threats against the Soviet Union have to be understood in the context
of decisive nuclear superiority. In 1953, the United States possessed some
1,600 operational nuclear weapons; the Soviets had less than 100.[34] Nine years
later, during the Cuban Missile Crisis, Defense Secretary Robert McNamara
reported that the United States had a seventeen-to-one advantage.[35]

   More telling is the pattern of U.S. threats in Asia and the Middle East.
When U.S. officials threatened North Korea and China during the Korean War
and later threatened China separately during the Quemoy and Matsu crises,
neither country possessed nuclear weapons. (The Chinese did not obtain nuclear weapons until 1963.) When the United States threatened North Korea in
1968 and North Vietnam between 1969–1972, it was careful not to threaten
China or the Soviet Union directly. The United States threatened India in
1971, two years before that country acquired nuclear weapons. And in the Middle East, U.S. threats were typically directed at Arab states that did not themselves possess nuclear weapons. This kind of behavior should not be surprising;
it is obviously less risky to threaten a nonnuclear opponent than a nuclear one.

   The Soviet Union exploded its first atomic bomb in August 1949.[36] Since
then, Soviet officials, like their U.S. counterparts, have used nuclear weapons
to threaten others, though they have done so less frequently. Soviet officials
used nuclear weapons for the first time during the 1956 Suez war, when they

threatened Great Britain, France, and Israel, asked Eisenhower to take joint U.S.–Soviet military action to halt the fighting, and requested that the UN Security Council adopt a resolution calling for the dispatch of UN forces to assist Egypt.[37]

In this instance, Soviet threats were directed at two nonnuclear states (France and Israel) and one country with only a rudimentary nuclear force (Britain). Soviet threats were made only after U.S. officials had condemned their erstwhile allies' attack, were *not* directed at the United States, and were accompanied by a proposal for joint U.S.–Soviet measures to end the fighting. Although the Soviets threatened the British and French with "rocket attacks," they did not mobilize their strategic nuclear forces, as the United States frequently did when issuing its nuclear threats.

The Soviets subsequently threatened to use nuclear weapons against Israel during the 1973 Yom Kippur War, on behalf of its Egyptian and Syrian allies. As in 1956, Soviet nuclear threats were made to stop the fighting, and they were accompanied by proposals for joint superpower action to impose a cease-fire.

While the Soviets made vague nuclear threats on China's behalf when it was threatened by the United States in 1958, the Soviets used nuclear weapons to threaten China several times during 1969 and 1970.[38] It is significant that although the Chinese had some nuclear weapons, they possessed only relatively short-range missiles, and they could not yet count on support from a superpower ally to deter Soviet threats.[39]

More recently, in 1986, the Soviets conveyed ambiguous threats to Pakistan.[40] The Soviets may also have conveyed other secret threats, but the best available source suggests that they used nuclear threats on five or six occasions during the postwar period, about one-third as often as the United States.[41] Soviet threats were not accompanied by large-scale military moves or dramatic deployments, such as the movement of nuclear-capable forces to the point of regional conflict—as in the U.S. deployment of B-29s to Europe and Asia during the Berlin crisis and Korean War or the deployment of naval nuclear forces off the coast of Taiwan or India.[42] The Soviets did not put their nuclear forces on full-scale alert, as U.S. officials regularly have. This did not mean that Soviet threats were less real, only that they were perhaps more cautious or sensitive to world opinion on nuclear matters.

Soviet threats in divided-state conflicts have been much like U.S. threats in two important respects: first, they have been typically made against nonnuclear opponents (France and Israel in 1956) or nuclear states that possess only rudimentary nuclear capability (Great Britain in 1956, China in 1969, Pakistan in 1986). Second, where U.S. and Soviet nuclear threats have been exchanged, they have usually threatened third parties—Israel or China, for example—not the opposing superpower.[43]

Although the superpowers have at different times promised to deter any nuclear threat made against their allies who participate in collective security organization, they have not always done so. As a result, the credibility of superpower nuclear guarantees has been seriously eroded. Superpower allies have discovered through bitter experience that the United States and Soviet Union would not necessarily wage nuclear war on their behalf.

Soviet allies in Asia discovered that Soviet officials would not act to deter U.S. nuclear threats made during conflicts in Korea, China, and Vietnam during the 1950s and 1960s. For example, when U.S. forces crossed the 38th parallel into North Korea, the Soviets did not intervene. When China entered the war, the Soviets did not invoke the Sino-Soviet Treaty, which served as a mutual defense agreement, nor did they send troops to join the fighting. And when Presidents Truman and Eisenhower threatened North Korea and China with nuclear weapons, the Soviets did not counter these threats with warnings of their own, even though the Soviets possessed nuclear weapons and its allies did not.

When China was threatened by the United States during the first Quemoy-Matsu crisis in 1954–1955, the Soviet Union did not extend nuclear guarantees to China or deter U.S. threats, despite the fact that the Sino-Soviet Treaty contained an implied Soviet pledge to provide China with a nuclear umbrella.[44] U.S. threats demonstrated to the Chinese that they could not rely on the Soviets to protect them. In 1963, Chinese foreign minister Chen Yi said of Soviet nuclear guarantees, "How can any one nation say that they will defend another—these promises are easy to make, but they are worth nothing. Soviet protection is worth nothing to us."[45]

The North Vietnamese discovered much the same thing about nuclear-armed allies during its war with the United States. Neither the Soviet Union nor China sent troops to assist the North Vietnamese, as China had done during the Korean War—though the United States did not invade North Vietnam as it had North Korea. Afterward, neither moved to deter U.S. nuclear threats made between 1969 and 1972.

After reviewing Soviet behavior towards its Asian allies, a Brookings Institution report concluded:

In the Korean War, the Quemoy-Matsu missile crises, the Vietnam War and the Sino-Vietnamese conflict, Moscow was more concerned about avoiding conflict with the United States and China than it was about protecting the sovereignty and security of its allies, who, if they may not have expected the Soviet Union to go to war on its behalf, did seem to expect the Kremlin to do more than it did.[46]

In 1956, U.S. allies—Great Britain, France, and Israel—discovered what Soviet allies were learning: that their superpower ally would not necessarily act to deter nuclear threats. The Suez crisis signaled U.S. unwillingness to support its allies, particularly when they initiated war without U.S. approval. This lesson had a profound effect on each of the three U.S. allies. In the year after Suez, the British greatly increased spending for their rudimentary nuclear forces. In a 1957 Parliamentary debate, Denis Healey called the expanded program a "virility symbol to compensate for the exposure of . . . military impotence at Suez."[47] The French historian Bertrand Goldschmidt likewise observed that, in Paris, "the [Guy] Mollet government, which with the Israelis had prepared the Suez operation in utmost secrecy, felt the affront it had just suffered. Its previous hostility toward atomic weapons was transformed overnight into a determined and positive interest in national nuclear armament."[48] De Gaulle subsequently pursued the development of an independent French nuclear arsenal.

The Israelis were also troubled by U.S. behavior. Yaacov Herzog, Ben-Gurion's principal political adviser, wrote that Ben-Gurion was "entirely unprepared for the vehemence of President Eisenhower's backing of the General Assembly's call for immediate and unconditional Israeli withdrawal. *What the U.S. did then was to remove Israel's—as well as Britain's and France's— protective shield against possible retaliation, leaving them all exposed* [emphasis added]."[49] Like the French, the Israelis became determined not to rely solely on their superpower ally. This episode fueled their determination to acquire nuclear weapons of their own. With French assistance, they eventually did. The *force de frappe*, or independent nuclear force, became the common French and Israeli response to superpower behavior during the 1956 Suez war.

For a number of reasons, the superpowers did not always seek to deter each other's nuclear threats in every instance. In seeking to limit conflicts that erupted in the divided states and in using nuclear threats to confine these conflicts and conclude them on favorable terms, they hoped to preserve the integrity of the interstate system, which was designed to mitigate against the globalization of regional war. The whole notion of common security through the United Nations was promoted by the superpowers to prevent the escalation of Balkan-type conflicts into world war. The superpowers were thus unwilling to risk global nuclear war on behalf of the "Serbias" of the world. And for this reason, they tried to avoid direct superpower confrontation over regional conflicts. The de facto rule seems to have been that troops from one superpower could intervene in divided state conflicts, but not both. In addition, the superpowers were also unwilling to risk global nuclear war on behalf of allies who started their own wars, preferring to let these countries assume the risks attendant upon their actions.

In recent years, then, the superpowers have quietly folded up the nuclear umbrellas they once extended over their allies around the world. Although U.S. and Soviet officials insisted that they would use nuclear weapons to guarantee their allies' security, they in practice demonstrated an unwillingness to do so. Even some U.S. officials and commentators have questioned the reliability and durability of the U.S. nuclear umbrella. After he left office, Henry Kissinger told a group of Europeans in 1979, "Our European allies should not keep asking us to multiply strategic [nuclear] assurances that we cannot possibly mean, or if we do mean, we should not want to execute, because if we execute, we risk the destruction of civilization." He also said it was absurd in the 1980s "to base the strategy of the West on the credibility of the threat of mutual suicide."[50]

This has not been lost on the superpowers' allies. Based on their experience with nuclear threats and with the disappearance of superpower deterrence at crucial times, some of the divided states have decided not to rely on superpower guarantees but to develop nuclear weapons of their own.

In 1962, President John Kennedy said:

> We do not believe in a series of national deterrents. We believe that the NATO deterrent, to which the United States has committed itself so heavily provides adequate protection. Once you begin, nation after nation, beginning to develop its own deterrent, or rather feeling it's necessary as an element of its independence to develop its own deterrence, it seems to me you are moving into an increasingly dangerous situation.[51]

Yet this is precisely what has happened. The *force de frappe* has been the generic response; nuclear proliferation has been the result.

For the officials in these states, the acquisition of nuclear weapons has been a difficult process, requiring enormous human and material resources and a determination to proceed whatever the financial or political cost. As Pakistani leader Zulfikar Ali Bhutto is reputed to have said, "If India gets the bomb, we will eat leaves and grass to do the same."

China was the first of the divided states to possess this kind of determination. As early as 1951, Chinese officials argued that "only when we ourselves have the atomic bomb, and are fully prepared, is it possible for the frenzied warmongers to listen to our just and reasonable proposals."[52] But the decision to initiate a nuclear weapons program came after the Korean War, during the first Quemoy-Matsu crisis, when the Chinese were faced with both the U.S.–Taiwan treaty and increased American threats to use nuclear weapons against them.[53]

When they tested their first atomic bomb on October 16, 1964, Chinese officials announced that the weapons would not be used to launch a first strike but would instead be "for defense and for protecting the Chinese people from U.S. threats to launch a nuclear war." When the Chinese had developed long-range delivery systems, the Americans would "not be so haughty, their policy of nuclear blackmail and nuclear threats [would] not be so effective."[54] Mao was even more blunt. He said he hoped the nuclear program would "boost our courage and scare others."[55]

Initially the Chinese relied heavily on Soviet assistance, but as the Sino-Soviet split widened in the late 1950s, the Chinese pursued the project on their own. However, the social and economic cost of developing technically sophisticated weapons in a poor country was enormous. In the decade that the Chinese took to develop nuclear weapons, the government was struggling to recover from the costly Korean War, to feed its population, and to break free from the grip of poverty and backward industrial development. Yet despite these obstacles, Chinese leaders remained determined. As Foreign Minister Chen Yi said in 1961, the third straight year that harvests failed, the strategic nuclear weapons should continue "even if the Chinese had to pawn their trousers for the purpose."[56]

Lacking a sophisticated industrial infrastructure, the Chinese used rudimentary, seat-of-the-pants methods to build the bomb. Thousands of peasants combed the countryside for uranium ore, which they dug up by hand. One official sent to collect the mined radioactive ore found it stored in stalls at a village market. "What a place it was!" the cadre recalled. "Yellowcake . . . was piled at random and could be seen everywhere."[57] The head of the group developing the detonator for the bomb mixed high explosives in used army buckets over an open fire on the test range in Donghuayuan. When the bomb was trans-ferred to the test site, "two purplish-red long sofas" were used to cushion it.[58]

China's ability to develop nuclear weapons under these circumstances was, in the parlance of the day, a Great Leap Forward. The Chinese managed to build a bomb because they were determined to do so and because they ob-tained enough information from U.S.- and Soviet-trained Chinese scientists to figure out the best way to do it on the cheap. As Premier Chou En-lai had said during the program, "Spend less, get more."[59]

Mao may have had the United States in mind when he said that the Chinese bomb would "boost our courage and scare others." But it was another country that received a fright. India had just fought a brief, unsuccessful war with China over disputed boundaries in the Himalayas in 1962. The detonation of a Chinese bomb in 1964 had a profound impact on Indian officials. Within a few days, Homi Bhabha, head of India's atomic power program, said the only de-fense against nuclear attack "appears to be the capability and threat of retalia-tion,"[60] and one hundred members of parliament petitioned the government to develop nuclear weapons.[61]

Prime Minister Lal Bahadur Shastri, who had succeeded Nehru a few months earlier, initially opposed development of nuclear weapons. But as pres-sure mounted, he agreed to support its development for "peaceful" purposes, such as excavating and tunneling.[62] Supporters of nuclear weapons develop-ment, such as the diplomat Sisir Gupta, argued that "China may subject a non-nuclear India to periodic blackmail, weaken its spirit of resistance and self-con-fidence and thus without a war achieve its major political and military objec-tives in Asia."[63] The decision to work toward the development of an Indian bomb was taken despite British assurances that they would provide a British nuclear umbrella for India.

During the 1960s, the Indian nuclear program developed slowly, though pushed along by fear of Chinese weapons, Indian officials remained ambivalent about the program and did not rush to develop nuclear weapons, even though the Chinese developed and tested a hydrogen bomb in 1967. The impetus to develop nuclear weapons received a second push during the third Indo-Paki-stani war, in 1971. President Nixon's decision to send nuclear-capable naval forces into the Bay of Bengal to warn India against intervention in East Paki-stan/Bangladesh, and to prevent them from pursuing an all-out war against West Pakistan, spurred Indian efforts to acquire nuclear weapons. The decision to proceed with the manufacture and testing of a bomb was made in early 1972 (following the cessation of hostilities with Pakistan),[64] and two years later, on

May 18, 1974, the Indians detonated their first atomic bomb, which they described as a "peaceful nuclear explosion."

Like China, India's ostensible reason for developing nuclear weapons was to deter threats by the superpowers, but its program frightened not nuclear-capable powers but a nonnuclear neighbor—Pakistan. Pakistani prime minister Bhutto did not accept the Indians' assertion that theirs was a "peaceful explosion." Pakistan, which had been divided in half by the secession of Bangladesh in 1971, now confronted a sibling state that possessed superior conventional and nuclear forces. Although Pakistan had signed a 1955 mutual security treaty with the United States, it did not enjoy nuclear protection against India from the United States, the Chinese, or the British.[65] During Pakistan's war with India, the United States may have threatened India with nuclear weapons, but it had also slapped an arms embargo on Pakistan.[66]

The initial Pakistani decision to develop nuclear weapons came in 1972, when Prime Minister Bhutto announced his determination to do so at a secret meeting with Pakistan's top nuclear scientists.[67] The subsequent Indian test spurred Pakistani efforts. With assistance from the French and the Chinese, Pakistani officials pressed ahead with their own program.[68] In 1986, Dr. Abdul Quadir Khan, head of the Pakistani project, explained Pakistani thinking in a manner reminiscent of earlier Indian and Chinese proponents of weapons development:

> If India openly starts a weapons programme, the deep-rooted Pakistani fears of India, especially after its active role in the dismemberment of Pakistan in 1971, would put tremendous pressure on Pakistan to take appropriate measures to avoid a nuclear Munich at India's hands in the event of an actual conflict, which many Pakistanis think very real.[69]

A year later, Khan told an Indian journalist, "What the CIA has been saying about our possessing the bomb is correct. . . . They told us that Pakistan could never produce the bomb . . . now they know we had done it."[70] Pakistani president Zia ul-Haq confirmed this in March 1987: "You can virtually write today that Pakistan can build a bomb whenever it wishes. . . . Pakistan has the capability of building the bomb."[71]

Unlike China or India, Pakistan has not exploded a nuclear bomb. It prefers to retain some ambiguity about its capability and to avoid the risk of censure—and the cutoff of U.S. aid—that an explosion would provoke. But new "flash X-ray" technology makes it possible to test a nuclear weapon without actually exploding it.[72] In his 1987 speech, Zia attempted to play down Pakistani development, saying that U.S. officials should not be unduly alarmed by Pakistan's "tiddly-widdly nuclear program."[73]

But other countries do not view the acquisition of nuclear weapons as a "tiddly-widdly" development. Prime Minister Rajiv Gandhi of India told parliament, "If Pakistan gets a weapon, India will have to think very seriously about its own option."[74] U.S. officials also considered cutting off aid to Pakistan after Zia's announcement, but they were reluctant to do so while Pakistan was assisting insurgents fighting the Soviets in Afghanistan.[75]

Other countries were also reluctant to view Pakistan's nuclear program as unimportant. The Soviet Union warned that it could not be indifferent to such developments. Israel viewed this development with some concern, especially because Pakistani leaders referred to their weapon as an "Islamic Bomb."[76] Thus, like India and China before it, Pakistan antagonized countries that it had not intended to threaten when it decided to acquire nuclear weapons.

During this period, Israel also responded to nuclear threats by pursuing nuclear weaponry. The French helped Israel build its first nuclear research reactor and provided important technical and material assistance, including weapons-grade plutonium.[77] Although Israeli progress was slow, by 1975 Israeli president Katzir admitted that Israel had developed the capability of building nuclear weapons, and the CIA concluded that Israel had already done so.[78] According to U.S. analysts, Israel had more than ten weapons in 1975 and between one hundred and two hundred a decade later.[79] Like the Pakistanis, Israeli officials have kept their program under wraps, have not conducted a public test, and have adopted a deliberately ambiguous nuclear policy: "Israel will not be the first country to introduce nuclear weapons into the Middle East." As one Israeli military analyst argues, "Deliberate ambiguity maximizes our deterrence."[80]

The superpowers have not been happy with these developments and have tried to limit the spread of nuclear weapons. The 1968 Nuclear Non-Proliferation Treaty, which the superpowers negotiated and signed, attempted to limit the spread of nuclear technology by regulating nuclear power programs around the world and monitoring the production of materials—enriched uranium and plutonium—that could be used to manufacture bombs. But they have done nothing to control their own use of nuclear threats as an instrument of policy, which is probably the most significant factor in the decision by other countries to obtain nuclear weapons in the first place. The modest cuts in U.S.–Soviet arsenals (the 1988 INF Treaty cut superpower arsenals by only 5 percent) also make many countries suspicious of superpower claims that they want to control the spread of nuclear arms. After China took a seat in the United Nations in 1971, its delegates called superpower arms control efforts "a hoax."[81]

The United States failed to prevent its allies—Israel and Pakistan—from developing nuclear weapons; the Soviet Union could not prevent its allies—China and India—from doing the same. The two superpowers, however, successfully forestalled the development of nuclear weapons by other divided-state allies.

After the United States abandoned its effort to prevent the reunification of Vietnam by the North and withdrew completely in 1975, South Korean leaders became concerned that the United States might eventually withdraw, in a similar fashion, from Korea. Only a month after the fall of Saigon, President Park declared, "If the U.S. nuclear umbrella were to be removed, we [would] have to start developing our nuclear capability."[82] Intense U.S. diplomatic pressure persuaded the South Koreans not to begin a program, though they possessed complex nuclear power facilities. A South Korean agreement to purchase a French reprocessing plant was canceled in 1976 after the United States objected.[83]

President Carter's 1977 announcement that he planned to withdraw all U.S. ground forces from the peninsula over a four-to five-year period rekindled South Korean interest in nuclear development. Foreign Minister Tong-jin Park told the National Assembly that the government would proceed with weapons development "if it is necessary for national security interests and people's safety."[84] And the government subsequently released a report that expressed support for the idea of a South Korean nuclear deterrent.[85] The implicit threat to develop nuclear weapons if U.S. policy was not changed may have been the first time a nonnuclear state has used the prospect of atomic weapons to threaten a nuclear power. In 1979, President Carter suspended the plan to withdraw U.S. troops. It is not clear what role South Korea's threat to go nuclear played in this decision or whether there was a quid pro quo—the United States agreeing to stay if the South Koreans agreed not to develop nuclear arms—but both countries returned to the pre-1977 status quo.

In North Korea, the Soviets (at U.S. urging) pressured the communist government to ratify the nonproliferation treaty in 1985. The North Koreans had previously built a large research reactor at Yong Bong, which might have been used as the basis for a nuclear weapons program.[86] Vietnam, on the other hand, withdrew from the nonproliferation treaty in 1975,[87] but the Vietnamese do not possess any nuclear facilities that might be used for weapons development.

Taiwan, fearing U.S. abandonment (like South Korea), twice began developing an independent nuclear weapons program. The withdrawal of the U.S. fleet from the Taiwan Strait in 1969; U.S. recognition of China in 1971, which resulted in Taiwan's ouster from the United Nations and the seating of the Chinese Communist delegation; the alteration of U.S. security commitments and aid to Taiwan in the 1970s; the withdrawal of U.S. forces from Vietnam—these events undoubtedly played a role in the decision by Kuomintang officials to embark on covert attempts to develop nuclear arms in 1975–1977 and again in 1987.[88] When U.S. officials discovered these secret facilities, they successfully persuaded government officials to halt and dismantle their clandestine operations.

In Europe, despite the introduction of nuclear weapons into Germany by both superpowers, the superpowers have prevented either German state from acquiring nuclear weapons, though both possessed the means to do so. The United States has occasionally discussed providing nuclear weapons to German NATO forces, but neither superpower was eager to put nuclear arms in German hands.

The introduction of nuclear weapons in the divided states, where sibling states are prone to irregular and conventional war, where the acquisition of nuclear weapons is itself regarded as a threat, and where the norm of international behavior is to use them against nonnuclear opponents, is, in President Kennedy's prescient words, "an extremely dangerous development."

In this context the concept of "deterrence" acquires a different meaning. As Hans Spier wrote in 1957, "A government that is exposed to atomic threats in peacetime readily regards them as 'blackmail' whereas the threatening power is likely to call them 'deterrence.' "[89] Indeed, this was precisely how the Soviets used the term. Richard Betts has noted that in describing their own use of nuclear weapons to deter the West, "the Soviets most commonly use the term *sderzhivaniye* ("restraining")," but when they describe the West's use of nuclear weapons as a deterrent, "they use the word *ustrasheniye*, which comes very close to meaning 'intimidation.' "[90] In the divided states, nuclear weapons acquire both meanings. Because they are used both to restrain and to threaten, or as Mao said, "to boost our courage and scare others," the presence of nuclear weapons stimulates the acquisition of more nuclear weapons by others.

As it is employed by superpower strategists, deterrence—the use of massive nuclear arsenals to prevent the use of other massive nuclear arsenals—is supposed to keep the peace and prevent the outbreak of war. In the context of U.S.–Soviet relations, large arsenals generally deterred U.S. and Soviet officials from threatening or attacking each other. It is also true that the superpowers frequently shared a common interest in preserving the interstate system and were reluctant to depart from it.

But if deterrence can be said to "work" or have a restraining influence on superpower relations, it has had the *opposite* effect in the divided states. The acquisition of nuclear weapons by divided states, ostensibly to "deter" superpower nuclear threats, encourages their neighbors to develop their own nuclear weapons. This development promotes both regional and global insecurity and tension. It puts countries at odds with their neighbors and with their allies and superpower enemies. It permits countries that have regularly engaged in irregular and conventional wars to express their conflicts in nuclear terms.

Ironically, the superpowers, which attempted to use nuclear weapons to assert their mastery over others, have found themselves, "willy-nilly, for better or worse, the masters and the servants of the weird and terrifying warriors who have grown up in their pasture." The eruption of conflict in nuclear-capable divided states is today capable of turning local and regional conflicts into wider, nuclear conflicts. As Soviet general-secretary Mikhail Gorbachev admitted in his speech to the United Nations in December 1988, "The bell of regional conflict tolls for all of us."[91]

NOTES

1. John L. Gaddis, *The Long Peace* (New York: Oxford University Press, 1987), 151.

2. Christopher Hitchens, "Wanton Acts of Usage," *Harper's*, September 1987, 66.

3. "The Second Coming of Pol Pot," *World Press Review*, October 1988, 25.

4. John Lewis and L. Xue, *China Builds the Bomb* (Stanford, Calif.: Stanford University Press, 1988), 66.

5. Lewis and Xue, *China Builds the Bomb*, 72.

6. Lewis and Xue, *China Builds the Bomb*, 40.

7. Peter Merkl, *Political Violence and Terror* (Berkeley: University of California Press, 1986), 94–95.

8. One Irish minister was forced to resign in 1970 after his participation in an IRA gunrunning scheme was revealed. Michael Farrell, *Northern Ireland: The Orange State* (London: Pluto, 1980), 269.

9. Quoted in Frances FitzGerald, *Fire in the Lake* (Boston: Atlantic Monthly Press/ Little Brown, 1972), 176.

10. See Bruce Cumings, *Child of Conflict: The Korean-American Relationship* (Seattle: University of Washington Press, 1983), 3–56.

11. Tom Hartman and J. Mitchell, *A World Atlas of Military History, 1945–1984* (New York: Da Capo, 1985), 78.

12. Hartman and Mitchell, *Atlas of Military History*, 53.

13. Hartman and Mitchell, *Atlas of Military History*, 54.

14. The recent wars in Afghanistan and the Persian Gulf killed a fraction as many. Only the Nigerian-Biafran war killed people on the same scale with wars in Korea, Vietnam, and India, in which more than two million people died. Ruth Sivard, *World Military and Social Expenditures, 1987* (Washington, D.C.: World Priorities, 1987), 31.

15. Hartman and Mitchell, *Atlas of Military History*, 11.

16. Stephen Kaplan, *Diplomacy of Power* (Washington, D.C.: Brookings Institution, 1981), 1.

17. Yaacov Bar-Siman-Tov, *Israel, the Superpowers and the War in the Middle East* (New York: Praeger, 1987), 50.

18. Stephen Ambrose, *Eisenhower: The President* (New York: Simon & Schuster, 1984), 361.

19. Kaplan, *Diplomacy of Power*, 187.

20. Carnegie Task Force on Non-Proliferation and South Asian Security, *Nuclear Weapons and South Asian Security* (Washington, D.C.: Carnegie Endowment for International Peace, 1988), 30; hereafter cited as Carnegie Report.

21. Carnegie Report, 30.

22. Marc Trachtenberg, "A Wasting Asset," *International Security* 13, no. 3 (1988/89): 28.

23. Gaddis, *Long Peace*, 100. General MacArthur's unwillingness to accept these more limited objectives led Truman to dismiss him in April 1951. MacArthur had expressed a desire to abandon the UN's "tolerant effort" to limit the fighting to Korea. Trachtenberg, "A Wasting Asset," 70.

24. Kaplan, *Diplomacy of Power*, 652.

25. Douglas Pike, *Vietnam and the Soviet Union* (Boulder, Colo.: Westview, 1987), 87–88.

26. Keenen Peck, "First Strike You're Out," *The Progressive*, July 1985, 32.

27. Barry Blechman and S. Kaplan, *Force without War* (Washington, D.C.: Brookings Institution, 1981), 48, 51, 100; Morton Halperin, *Nuclear Fallacy* (Cambridge, Mass.: Ballinger, 1987), 24; Richard K. Betts, *Nuclear Blackmail and Nuclear Balance* (Washington, D.C.: Brookings Institution, 1987), 7–8.

28. Blechman and Kaplan, *Force Without War*, 48, 51, 100; Irving Kristol, "Does NATO Exist?" in Irving Kristol, *Reflections of a Neo-Conservative* (New York: Basic Books, 1983), 5–6.

29. Trachtenberg, "Wasting Asset," 49; Roger Dingman, "Atomic Diplomacy During the Korean War," *International Security* 13, no. 3 (1988/89): 51–53.

30. Betts, *Nuclear Blackmail*, 23.

31. Trachtenberg, "Wasting Asset," 5.

32. McGeorge Bundy, *Danger and Survival* (New York: Random House, 1988), 246; Gaddis, *Long Peace*, 124.

33. Stephen P. Cohen, *The Pakistani Army* (Berkeley: University of California Press, 1984), 153. As the Indians and Pakistanis have observed, the only time nuclear weapons were exploded over civilian populations was when the opponent (Japan) did not possess nuclear weapons.

34. Timothy Botti, *The Long Wait* (New York: Greenwood, 1987), 111.

35. McNamara, however, says the Soviets still possessed enough weapons to make nuclear war an unthinkable option. James Blight, "Interview with Robert S. McNamara," Washington, D.C., May 21, 1987, 22, 33–34.

36. Rosemary Foot, *The Wrong War* (Ithaca, N.Y.: Cornell University Press, 1985), 38.

37. Bar-Siman-Tov, *Israel*, 57.

38. Kaplan, *Diplomacy of Power*, 141.

39. Betts, *Nuclear Blackmail*, 79.

40. Leonard S. Spector, *Going Nuclear* (Cambridge, Mass.: Ballinger, 1987), 111.

41. Steve Weissman and H. Krosney, *The Islamic Bomb* (New York: Times Books, 1981), 57, say that the Soviets again threatened the Chinese during the 1971 Indo-Pakistani war. China was warned not to assist its ally, Pakistan.

42. Betts, *Nuclear Blackmail*, 132.

43. Examining the pattern of U.S.-Soviet nuclear confrontations, particularly in the Middle East, James McConnell and Ann Kelly note that it appears "permissible for one superpower to support a friend against the client of another superpower as long as the friend is on the defensive strategically; the object must be to avert decisive defeat and restore the balance, not assist the client to victory." James M. McConnell and Anne M. Kelley, "Superpower Naval Diplomacy in the Indo-Pakistani Crisis," in *Soviet Naval Developments: Capability and Context*, ed. Michael MccGuire (New York: Praeger, 1973), 449.

44. Lewis and Xue, *China Builds the Bomb*, 12.

45. William Kincade and C. Bertram, *Nuclear Proliferation in the 1980s* (London: Macmillan, 1982), 13.

46. Kaplan, *Diplomacy of Power*, 89–90.

47. Kincade and Bertram, *Nuclear Proliferation*, 18.

48. Bundy, *Danger and Survival*, 475. Diana Johnstone states that the development of an independent nuclear weapons program "forced a certain national consensus between right and left." Diana Johnstone, *The Politics of Euromissiles: Europe's Role in America's World* (London: Verso, 1984), 90.

49. Herzog went on to say, "How vulnerable this actually made Israel was something that could not be determined with certainty at that time. . . . The fact was that a regional conflict . . . escalated overnight into a potential global war." Bar-Siman-Tov, *Israel*, 60–61.

50. Johnstone, *Euromissiles*, 180, 181.

51. Bundy, *Danger and Survival*, 485–86.

52. Rosemary Foot, "Nuclear Coercion and the Ending of the Korean Conflict," *International Security* 13, no. 3 (1988/89): 99.

53. Bundy, *Danger and Survival*, 526; Lewis and Xue, *China Builds the Bomb*, 34. The Chinese program, like the Israeli program, was conducted in secret, at least until a bomb was tested.

54. Lewis and Xue, *China Builds the Bomb*, 215.

55. Lewis and Xue, *China Builds the Bomb*, 216.

56. Lewis and Xue, *China Builds the Bomb*, 130.

57. Lewis and Xue, *China Builds the Bomb*, 90.

58. Lewis and Xue, *China Builds the Bomb*, 154, 159.

59. Lewis and Xue, *China Builds the Bomb*, 107. Zhou announced the successful test at the musical performance of "The East Is Red." After telling the crowd the news, he told them, "You may celebrate all you like. But mind you don't damage the floor." Lewis and Xue, *China Builds the Bomb*, 189.

60. Mitchell Reiss, *Without the Bomb* (New York: Columbia University Press, 1988), 203.

61. Gerald Segal, *Arms Control in Asia* (New York: St. Martin's, 1987), 103.

62. Reiss, *Without the Bomb*, 215–16.

63. Sumit Ganguly, "Why India Joined the Nuclear Club," *Bulletin of the Atomic Scientists* 39, no. 4 (April 1983): 31.

64. Reiss, *Without the Bomb*, 226–27.

65. Kincade and Bertram, *Nuclear Proliferation*, 71.

66. Carnegie Report, 35.

67. Spector, *Going Nuclear*, 102.

68. Carnegie Report, 46; Walter Patterson, *The Plutonium Business* (San Francisco: Sierra Club Books, 1985), 86.

69. Spector, *Going Nuclear*, 108.

70. Carnegie Report, 19.

71. *Washington Post*, March 24, 1987; see also March 19, 1987.

72. Spector, *Going Nuclear*, 87.

73. *Washington Post*, March 24, 1987.

74. Spector, *Going Nuclear*, 83. The construction of new reactors in the mid-1980s greatly increased India's capacity to build bombs. Spector, *Going Nuclear*, 77.

75. U.S. officials reportedly considered a pre-emptive, covert attack on Pakistan's nuclear facilities. Weissman and Krosney, *Islamic Bomb*, 193.

76. Spector, *Going Nuclear*, 113.

77. Spector, *Going Nuclear*, 131; Reiss, *Without the Bomb*, 140, 148.

78. Reiss, *Without the Bomb*, 45–46.

79. Reiss, *Without the Bomb*, 146.

80. *New York Times*, November 9, 1986.

81. William Epstein and T. Toyoda, *A New Design for Nuclear Disarmament* (Bristol: Arrowsmith, 1977), 13.

82. Reiss, *Without the Bomb*, 93.

83. Kincade and Bertram, *Nuclear Proliferation*, 74; Patterson, *Plutonium Business*, 115.

84. Reiss, *Without the Bomb*, 94.

85. Reiss, *Without the Bomb*, 94–95.

86. Leonard S. Spector, *The Undeclared Bomb* (Cambridge, Mass.: Ballinger, 1988), 71.

87. William Walker and M. Lonnroth, *Nuclear Power Struggles* (Boston: Allen & Unwin, 1983), 119.

88. Patterson, *Plutonium Business*, 139; Spector, *Undeclared Bomb*, 75, 77–79.

89. Hans Spier, "Soviet Atomic Blackmail and the North Atlantic Alliance," *World Politics* 9, no. 3 (April 1957): 308. According to Jervis and Lebow, "deterrence has its etymological roots in the Latin term for 'terror.' " *Psychology and Deterrence* (Baltimore, Md.: Johns Hopkins University Press, 1985), 4.

90. Betts, *Nuclear Blackmail*, 5.

91. *New York Times*, December 8, 1988.

E I G H T

DICTATORSHIP AND DIVISION

Partition enabled Great Britain to shed its colonies in Ireland, India, and Palestine. It also provided a way for the United States and the Soviet Union to delineate spheres of influence and settle some of the disputes that had animated the cold war. But partition was never more than a partial solution, a temporary reprieve, because it typically created problems within and between divided states. After Vietnam was divided in 1954, partition fell into disuse. No country was partitioned in the late 1950s or during the 1960s, though ethnic movements in Burma, the Congo, Ethiopia, Nigeria, and Spain tried and failed to divide these countries. Then in the 1970s, Pakistan and Cyprus were divided. In both cases, dictatorships took steps that resulted in their partition by regional powers: India and Turkey. Partition had thus become a procedure practiced not only by great powers but also by lesser states.

Pakistan was created when India was divided in 1947. It would be subdivided twenty-four years later in 1971. In a geographic sense, it had been subdivided from the outset, because partition had created two Moslem territories (the Punjab in the West and Bengal in the East), separated by a thousand miles of Indian territory, and called them both Pakistan. But geography does not alone explain why people in the two territories waged a bloody civil war that resulted in the creation of an independent Bangladesh in the East.[1] Subdivision was more a product of disenfranchisement and dictatorship in the years after Pakistan was created as a separate state.[2]

When the British divided India, they devolved power in Pakistan to the Muslim League, whose power base was strongest in West Pakistan. Muhammad Ali Jinnah established Karachi (in the West) as the capital and declared that Urdu should become the country's official language, despite the fact that

Bengali was more widely spoken.[3] His successors filled civil service and army posts with candidates from the West (of 741 top civil servants in the mid-1950s, only 51 hailed from Bengal) and in 1952 formally adopted Urdu as the only national language.[4] Fearing that inability to speak Urdu would bar their entry into the university, civil service, and army, Bengalis rioted, and several were killed.[5] These events persuaded politicians in Bengal to break from the Muslim League in 1953 and found the Awami League. Its twenty-one-point program demanded a greater role for Bengal in Pakistan's affairs.[6]

In 1958, the military staged a coup and deposed the civilian government. Its leader, General Muhammed Ayub Khan, argued that he would root out "disruptionists, political opportunists, smugglers, black-marketeers and other such social vermin, sharks and leeches," and he promised eventually to restore democracy, "but of the type that people can understand and work."[7]

Opposition to the dictatorship emerged in both East and West during the 1960s, but parties in each region took rather different political forms. In the West, the Pakistan People's Party, organized and led by Zulfikar Ali Bhutto, pressed for an end to military rule but did so as a kind of loyal opposition, with Bhutto serving for a time as the junta's foreign minister. In the East, the Awami League, led in the 1960s by Sheik Mujibur Rahman, demanded both an end to military rule and greater autonomy for Bengal. The League's six-point program demanded greater control of government finances and the creation of a parliament that would more accurately reflect the country's demographic distribution.[8] Because Bengal was more populous than the West, the Awami League expected a new parliament to give Bengal a stronger voice.

Although the two major opposition parties shared a common antipathy to dictatorship and a common identity as Moslems in an Islamic state, they mobilized along different lines. Bhutto organized along populist, relatively secular class lines; Mujibur, along ethnic regional lines. The result was the creation of a relatively secular unificationist movement in the West and an ethnic movement demanding greater regional autonomy in the East. Although Bengalis constituted a majority of Pakistan's population, they organized as if they were a disenfranchised minority, objecting to their underrepresentation in the civil service and the military and their lack of economic progress, compared with the West. They believed that greater autonomy would increase their political power and assist economic growth. While Bhutto wanted to take power from the military without substantially changing the existing regional distribution of power, Mujibur sought to change the constitution and redistribute power.

In 1968, riots in both East and West forced General Ayub to step down.

Widespread protest persuaded his successor, Gen. Muhammed Yaya Khan, to schedule elections that would install a new parliament charged with drafting a new constitution and restoring civilian government.[9] As the elections approached, the political and economic differences between the two major opposition movements became apparent. Like the Muslim League and the Indian National Congress, which had split as the devolution of British power approached, the Awami League and People's Party parted company as the transfer of military authority neared.

The elections, originally scheduled for October 1970, were postponed until late December after heavy floods and a ferocious cyclone struck East Pakistan. The regime's weak response to the disaster undermined support for the government and assisted the Awami League in Bengal. The League captured almost the entire vote in Bengal and gained an absolute majority—160 of 300 seats—in the new constituent assembly.[10] While the People's Party won a majority of the vote in the West, it secured only half as many seats as the Awami League.[11] Because neither party contested elections in both regions, the elections widened the regional political divide.

When it became clear that the Awami League had won a majority and could therefore draft a new constitution, which would significantly redistribute power, without interference, the military authorities and civilian parties in the West balked. Arguing that "a majority alone doesn't count in national politics," Bhutto demanded that Mujibur treat the People's Party as one of "two majority parties," draft a new constitution as equals, and include Bhutto in the cabinet of the new government.[12] Of course, Mujibur refused to surrender his electoral majority. Bhutto then persuaded the military to postpone the opening of the constituent assembly, to give him time to rally other political parties in the West behind his leadership, and force Mujibur to make concessions and depart from strict adherence to the League's six-point program.[13]

But by postponing the assembly and pressuring the League to surrender its political advantage, military and civilian leaders in the West antagonized the Bengal majority. Mujibur argued that General Yaya and Bhutto were trying to "sabotage the making of a constitution by the elected representatives of the people and the transfer of power to them" and warned, "if the ruling coteries seek to frustrate these aspirations, the people are ready for a long and sustained struggle for independence."[14] Massive demonstrations, strikes, and widespread civil disobedience in Bengal convinced the military that negotiations were useless and that they would have to "sort this bastard [Mujibur] out" and crush the Awami League to preserve their power and national unity.[15]

On March 25, 1971, military forces, which had been built up in Bengal following the election, seized Mujibur, arrested Awami League leaders, attacked students, civil servants, and civilians, and fought with police and soldiers who defected en masse from government service. Tens of thousands were slaughtered, Moslems and Hindus alike. The dictatorship imposed martial law, banned all political activity, and set out to destroy all opposition to West Pakistani rule.[16]

The regime's assault ignited civil war. Bengali police officers and soldiers who escaped the army dragnet formed an irregular army—the Mukti Bahini—and began waging guerilla war against the dictatorship. A provisional government was established in India, and on April 17 it issued a declaration of independence, announcing the creation of the "Sovereign People's Republic" of Bangladesh.[17] Bengalis were no longer campaigning for regional autonomy, they were fighting for independence in a separate state.

The outbreak of civil war forced millions of Bengalis to seek refuge in India. Some four million fled to India by May, eight million by August, and nearly ten million by mid-November.[18] The massive influx of refugees created serious problems for Prime Minister Indira Gandhi's government. Cholera swept through the more than one thousand refugee camps, killing six thousand in September alone.[19] Burgeoning refugee populations taxed local and central government resources and competed for jobs on badly overcrowded local labor markets. This situation depressed wages, fueled resentment among poor Indian residents of provinces adjacent to Bengal, and threatened to rekindle a Naxalite insurgency that had only recently been suppressed.[20] Early on, Gandhi warned that "if the world does not take heed" of these problems, "we shall be constrained to take all measures as may be necessary to insure our own security and the . . . structure of our social and economic life."[21]

As the civil war intensified and refugee flow accelerated, Gandhi directed the Indian army first to arm and train Bengali irregulars and then, in late November, to invade Bengal to restore peace and return refugees.[22] Indian incursions across the border and then air strikes on India by Pakistan on December 3 triggered interstate war between divided and dividing states, not only in Bengal but also across the Punjab and Kashmir.[23]

The Indian army, accompanied by Mukti Bahini irregulars, defeated the isolated West Pakistani army in Bengal within a few weeks, while making modest gains on the western front.[24] While the dictatorship in Pakistan ignited conflict between West and East, India divided Pakistan and created an independent Bangladesh.

Pakistan was divided by a regional power, but both superpowers allowed partition to occur. The Soviets signed a security treaty with India in August 1971 and used their UN Security Council veto to block efforts to impose a cease-fire before the Indian army and insurgent forces could defeat West Pakistani forces in Bengal. Although U.S. officials sided with West Pakistan—President Nixon sent nuclear-capable naval forces into the Bay of Bengal in an attempt to dissuade India from widening the war—they also imposed an arms embargo on both sides, which hurt West Pakistan more than India (which continued receiving military aid from the Soviet Union under the new security agreement). This led many in Pakistan to criticize the United States as an "unreliable ally."[25] For a time, Pakistan adopted it own version of the Hallstein Doctrine and severed diplomatic ties with states that recognized Bangladesh. But it was forced to abandon this policy after the United States recognized Bangladesh and admitted it to the United Nations in 1974.[26] So although the United States did not support India's partition of Pakistan, it treated partition as a fait accompli and allowed it to stand. Humanitarian concerns, aroused by natural disaster, widespread starvation, and attacks on an unarmed civilian population by the West Pakistani army, together with the fact that neither the Awami League nor its Indian ally was communist, made it easier for the United States to accept the partition of its own ally.

Although partition ended the civil war and brought the Awami League to power, it contributed to ongoing social and political problems. Some ten million Bengalis fled the country, and fifteen million more were displaced within the country.[27] Many refugees returned to their homes after the war, but many also stayed in India, leading to social conflict in Indian provinces during the years that followed. Some Indian leaders have called for the expulsion of Bengali refugees. In Tripura, an Indian state east of Bangladesh, indigenous movements have alternatively demanded the repatriation of Bengali refugees and the creation of a separate state, which would presumably expel Bengalis on their own authority.[28]

The advance of the Mukti Bahini insurgents during the war also created a second, though much smaller, wave of migration—that of Bihari loyalists who had supported the West Pakistani government and then had fled into India as the Mukti Bahini and Indian army approached. Other Biharis remained in Bengal. But many were killed when the Awami League returned to power, and hundreds of thousands were rounded up and herded into refugee camps inside Bangladesh, where they remained for years.[29] These various displacements and migrations continue to strain governments in India and Bangladesh.

Awami League officials believed that independence would promote regional economic development. But war, migration, and partition, which severed economic aid from West Pakistan, made economic recovery and self-sufficiency difficult to achieve.[30] Postpartition Bangladesh is one of the poorest countries in the world. A telling measure of its poverty was the government's 1986 announcement that it would award a bounty for every rat killed by its citizenry, offering 50 poish per rat, or the equivalent of 20 cents per dozen. Rats consume as much as twenty million tons of grain per year, or one-tenth of the country's annual crop. Agricultural Minister Abdul Munim said that "this is almost the quantity we need to import annually to meet our food shortage."[31]

Political developments in postpartition Bangladesh have also been disappointing. Sheik Mujibur Rahman assumed power after the war, but his attempts to strenghten the League's monopoly on power and widespread nepotism antagonized opposition parties and the army.[32] Mujibur was murdered along with eighteen family members in a military coup in 1975. His oldest daughter, Hasina Wajed, was studying abroad at the time and escaped the massacre. She returned to lead the Awami League, which became an opposition party under successive dictatorships.[33]

A second coup brought Gen. Ziaur Rahman to power three months after Mujibur's death. He led a military junta for three years, then reintroduced "civilian rule" with himself as president. He survived twenty coup attempts before he was assassinated in a coup in 1981. His widow, Khaled Zia Rahman, now heads the Bangladesh National Party.

For many years, Wajed and Rahman collaborated against the military regime headed by Hussain Muhammad Ershad, who came to power in a 1982 coup. But when demonstrations forced Ershad to call elections and surrender power in 1991, Wajed and Rahman disagreed over the constitutional form the government should take, and their relationship became extremely acrimonious. Rahman was elected prime minister in 1991, but her ability to govern was compromised because Wajid boycotted the 1996 elections and has since conducted paralyzing demonstrations and strikes. The conflict between them has divided Bangladesh politically, with the heirs of former rulers battling to establish their claims to a disputed patrimony.[34]

Political developments in Pakistan have followed similar lines, though coups have been less frequent. The defeat by India so discredited the dictatorship in Pakistan that it quickly transferred power to Bhutto, who, like Mujibur, attempted to consolidate power at the expense of other political parties and the army. As in Bangladesh, the army in Pakistan overthrew the civilian govern-

ment in 1977. Gen. Muhammad Zia ul-Haq arrested Bhutto and had him
hanged. Bhutto's daughter Benazir, like Mujibur's daughter Wajid, assumed
leadership of his party.

Zia ruled for the next decade. He pressed ahead with the Islamization of the
country and disenfranchised secular political parties and ethnic movements of
Pathans and Baluchis that opposed the ascent of Punjabis within the civil service and the army. After Zia was killed in an airplane crash in 1988, the military
authorities held elections that returned power to civilians. Benazir Bhutto's
party won an electoral majority, and she became prime minister in December
1988. But she was dismissed in a "constitutional coup" directed by the military
in 1990, returned to power in 1993, and removed again by the president at the
military's request in 1996.[35] The ongoing struggle between civilian politicians
and military authorities for control of the state has also been complicated by
conflict between different ethnic groups. In Karachi, fighting has erupted between Muhajirs (Urdu-speaking immigrants from India who allied themselves
with the military and received patronage in return) and local Sindhis (who resent the immigrants and have opposed their military sponsors). Fighting between them claimed nearly two thousand lives in 1995, and continues today.[36]

In Cyprus, partition advanced in waves, on a rising tide. Partition was first proposed by the British in the late 1950s, when they were negotiating the transfer
of power to indigenous independence movements. It gained a beachhead in
the mid-1960s, when the United States suggested dividing Cyprus and awarding parts to Greece and Turkey. It finally swamped the island in 1974, when a
coup sponsored by the dictatorship in Greece triggered an invasion by Turkey,
dividing Cyprus along lines first suggested by the British.

Cyprus had become a British colony in 1878. After World War II, the British
refused to surrender it, largely because their retreat from other colonies increased its strategic importance as a naval and military base in the Mediterranean. As Prime Minister Clement Atlee wrote in 1947, "[Our] position in
Palestine and Egypt has deteriorated and it is now more than ever necessary
from the strategic aspect to keep our foothold in the Eastern Mediterranean in
Cyprus."[37] As their military dependence on Cyprus increased, the British refused even to consider independence for the colony. In 1954, Henry Hopkin-
son, minister of state for colonial affairs, said of Cyprus, "It has always been
understood and agreed that there are certain territories in the Commonwealth
which, owing to their particular circumstances, can *never* expect to be fully
independent [emphasis added]."[38]

British intransigence stimulated the growth of three anti-colonial movements during the 1950s, each seeking power on their own terms. Two movements organized the Greek Cypriot majority, some 80 percent of the island's population, and one organized the Turkish Cypriot minority. The National Organization of Cypriot Fighters (EOKA), led by Col. George Grivas, pressed for devolution and unification, or *enosis* with Greece.[39] Grivas mobilized along right-wing, ethnic lines, based on the Greek Cypriots' linguistic and cultural identity as Greeks. He waged a violent guerilla war against both the British and the Turkish Cypriot minority, receiving money and arms from sympathetic officials and citizens in Greece, who supported *enosis*.

Archbishop Makarios III, head of the Greek Orthodox Church in Cyprus, organized a second, more secular movement in the Greek Cypriot community. In the early 1950s, he endorsed *enosis* and supported Grivas in the fight against British colonialism. But in 1958, as the British prepared to devolve power, Makarios began pushing for independence because he did not want to subordinate his movement to Greek authority or antagonize Turkey and the Turkish Cypriot minority.

A third movement arose in the Turkish Cypriot community. Within it, groups such as the Turkish Defense Organization (TMT) were much like the EOKA. They took up arms against British colonialism and pressed for union with Turkey, which would be achieved by dividing the island, what they called *taksim*. They were supported by Turkish state officials and sympathetic populations in mainland Turkey.[40]

The EOKA's guerilla war aginst British rule and Turkish Cypriots triggered British reprisals and intercommunal violence between 1955 and 1959.[41] The outbreak of war on the island, and Britain's humiliation during the Suez Canal crisis in 1956, persuaded the British to open negotiations with Greece and Turkey, and then with the different anticolonial movements. The British considered devolving and dividing power between separate movements, as they had done in India and Palestine. But they eventually abandoned partition as a solution because they wanted to keep large military bases on the island after devolving power, and this would be difficult to do if Greece and Turkey absorbed Cyprus. Instead the British decided to transfer power to Makarios, who led the largest and most moderate of the three movements. They believed that Makarios was not strong enough to challenge a continued British military presence on the island but was strong enough to defuse conflict between Greek and Turkish Cypriot militants. During the negotiations in 1958–1959, the British insisted that they be permitted to keep their bases and that the new republic provide

constitutional guarantees for the Turkish minority. The British then prepared
to devolve power to an anticolonial independence movement in a unified state,
and Makarios became its first president in 1960. Makarios reluctantly accepted
guarantees that the Turkish vice president could veto many presidential decisions and that Turkish-speaking citizens be given 30 percent of the positions in
the bureaucracy and 40 percent of the ranks in the army. As one observer
noted, "Cyprus was the first country in the world to be denied majority rule by
its own constitution."[42]

But independence on these terms frustrated the two other anticolonial
movements. Greek Cypriots who wanted to unify with Greece and Turkish
Cypriots who wanted to separate from Cyprus and unite with Turkey began
to clash violently in 1963. Makarios compounded the difficulty by introducing
proposals that would have amended the constitution, stripped the Turkish vice
president of his veto powers, and established the principle of majority rule.[43]
Widespread violence, however, forced Makarios to ask the British to restore
order. British troops intervened and inserted themselves between warring
communities, establishing a "Green Line" between Greek and Cypriot neighborhoods in Nicosia, the capital. But the British soon tired of a protracted
peacekeeping role and in 1964 asked the United Nations to assume this responsibility. However, fighting escalated despite UN intervention. Because the
Turkish Cypriots bore the brunt of violence, the Turkish government threatened to invade the island and intervene on their behalf.[44]

President Lyndon Johnson then ordered the Sixth Fleet into the area—
much as Truman had done with the Seventh Fleet in the Taiwan Strait in
1950—to block a Turkish invasion of the island, which is located only eighty
miles off Turkey's southern coast.[45] Johnson acted not because he wanted to
preserve an independent Cyprus (in fact, U.S. officials detested Makarios,
whom they regarded as a Communist) but because he did not want to risk war
between two NATO allies: Greece and Turkey. U.S. official therefore advanced
a plan that they thought would placate both parties—divide the island, awarding a chunk of the north to Turkey and the bulk of the south to Greece.[46] But
the Greek government and Makarios rejected this proposal: the Greeks, because it did not go far enough (it did not cede the whole island to Greece);
Makarios, because it went too far (it would have extinguished Cyprus as an
independent state). President Johnson then briefly threatened to withdraw
NATO aid from Greece and allow Turkey to invade the island if the Greeks did
not accept the U.S. plan. But he backed down. U.S. officials did not permit

Turkey to invade Cyprus in 1964, or again in 1967, after pro-*enosis* militants led by Colonel Grivas renewed their attacks on Turkish Cypriots.[47]

The outbreak of violence and threat of invasion persuaded Makarios and the Greek Cypriot majority to abandon *enosis* as a possible goal. In 1968, Makarios conceded that a solution to conflict in Cyprus "must necessarily be sought within the limits of what is *feasible*, which does not always coincide with the limits of what is *desirable* [emphasis added]," arguing that *enosis* was no longer a feasible political project.[48] Support for unification with Greece or partition and annexation by Turkey declined throughout Cyprus during the late 1960s, and Makarios was reelected by majorities in *both* Greek and Turkish communities. But while support for *enosis* declined in Cyprus, it found new enthusiasts in Greece, where a military junta had recently seized power.

In 1967, a group of Greek military officers launched a coup to preserve the monarchy and prevent republicans, led by George Papandreou, from coming to power.[49] The leader of the coup, George Papadopoulos, was adamantly opposed to electoral democracy. He argued that "responsible democracy . . . cannot be merely the democracy which is expressed by the casting and canvassing of votes. . . . There is no possibility of [this kind of] democracy ever returning to Greece. Democracy means the exercise of responsible authority . . . for the satisfaction of the public interest."[50]

By 1973, opposition to the dictatorship had regrouped, and students at the polytechnic in Athens demonstrated against the regime. The army sent in tanks to crush the rebellion, and soldiers were ordered to shoot their rifles and "slug the flesh" of unarmed demonstrators. Between forty-three and eighty students were killed.[51] Student protest tested the regime at a time when the country faced a deepening economic crisis, which was caused by the oil price shocks associated with the October 1973 Yom Kippur War in the Middle East.[52] Facing both a political and economic crisis, members of the regime deposed Papadopoulos on November 25, 1973, and installed Dimitrios Ioannidis in his place. Ioannidis had long supported *enosis* with Cyprus and detested Makarios, who had been a vocal and effective critic of the Greek dictatorship. Ioannidis immediately began planning a military coup in Cyprus that would depose Makarios and install Nicos Sampson, who had taken over the EOKA after Colonel Grivas died, paving the way for *enosis*. If successful, the unification of Greece and Cyprus would deflect the junta's growing political and economic crisis—*enosis* remained extremely popular in Greece—and help legitimate the Ioannides regime.

On July 15, 1974, just eight months after Ioannidis took power, pro-*enosis* military forces in Cyprus attacked the presidential palace, seized control of the island, and established a military government led by Sampson. But they failed to capture or kill Makarios, who escaped out the back, fled into the hills, and soon made his way to London.[53] With Makarios safely in exile, the new regime could not easily claim legitimacy or secure diplomatic recognition.[54] Fighting between Greek and Turkish Cypriots erupted. Four days later, Turkish paratroopers began landing on Cyprus in advance of a larger invasion fleet. This time, however, the United States did not block the Turkish invasion, and Great Britain did nothing to oppose Turkey's actions, despite its treaty obligations to maintain the "independence, territorial integrity and security [of Cyprus]."[55]

Sampson's new regime in Cyprus was not prepared to defend the island against Turkish invasion. After their Greek allies, who had a small contingent on the island, incurred heavy casualties during the initial assault, it became clear that Greece was in no position to help.[56] As the military situation for allied Greek and Cypriot regimes deteriorated, Ioannidis ordered the Greek army to mobilize its forces and prepare for general war with Turkey.[57] But the army balked, its frontline generals well aware that they could not win a war against superior Turkish forces, particularly because the United States had abandoned the Greek junta as a result of its provocative and uninvited actions. Frontline troops then demanded that the junta dissolve, that a "Council of National Salvation" be established, and that former prime minister Constantine Karamanlis be allowed to return from exile in Paris to head a new government in Greece.[58]

On July 23, 1973, the dictatorships in Greece and Cyprus both collapsed.[59] Karamanlis returned to head a civilian government in Greece; Makarios eventually returned to Cyprus in December. But in the interim, a Turkish invasion force occupied the northern half of the island, and independent republican government was restored only to the southern half of Cyprus.[60]

In many respects, the Greek junta's actions in Cyprus were similar to those of the Pakistani regime in Bangladesh. In Pakistan, the dictatorship tried to *maintain* unification by force; in Cyprus, the Greek junta tried to *obtain* unification by force. Both dictatorships tooks steps that led to intervention by neighboring states: India and Turkey. And in both cases, the attempt to maintain or obtain unity led to war and partition.

In Cyprus, neither the United States nor the Soviet Union opposed partition. The United States did not because the Greek-sponsored coup and Turkish invasion achieved what the United States had earlier proposed: the partition of the island and the diminution of Markarios's authority over it. The Soviet Union did not oppose partition because the conflict over Cyprus divided two

NATO allies and resulted in the collapse of an anticommunist dictatorship in Greece and the restoration of an independent, nonaligned government in Cyprus.[61]

In the end, partition did not result in "double *enosis*"—the unification of Turkish Cyprus with Turkey and Greek Cyprus with Greece—but it came close. Had Makarios been killed in the coup, Sampson could have established himself as Makarios's successor and then ceded his authority to Greece. But Makarios survived. Sampson could not quickly obtain the legitimacy he needed, and the unificationist putsch failed, toppling juntas in both Cyprus and Greece. The irony is that *enosis*, long advocated by many Greeks and Greek Cypriots, was instead realized by Turks and Turkish Cypriots. *Taksim* triumphed; *enosis* failed.

As in other divided states, partition had disruptive social and political consequences. Nearly 180,000 Greek Cypriots and 37,000 Turkish Cypriots fled their homes during the fighting. Five thousand people were killed. After the war, a massive population "swap" took place: twenty thousand Turkish Cypriots moved north; two hundred thousand Greek Cypriots headed south.[62] Some seventy-four thousand settlers from Turkey subsequently immigrated into the northern zone.[63]

The Greek Cypriot government has demanded that Turkish settlers and troops be withdrawn and the country reunited on the basis of "three freedoms"—freedom of movement, settlement, and property ownership for all indigenous Cypriots.[64] But the Turkish government has rejected these demands and moved instead to solidify Turkish rule in the north. In 1975, Turkish officials announced that northern Cyprus had become the Turkish Federated State of Cyprus. This placed Turkish-occupied Cyprus in an ambiguous legal position, because federation fell short of either annexation or independence.[65] The government attempted to clarify its status in 1983 by sponsoring elections that resulted in the creation of a government led by Rauf Denktash, a former prime minister of Turkey. This government then declared itself to be the independent Turkish Republic of North Kibris.[66] But as in many other divided states, sovereignty is a problematic thing. Prime Minister Turgut Ozal of Turkey said in 1986 that other states would eventually recognize North Kibris as an independent state, but so far only Turkey has done so.[67] This should not be surprising given the fact that North Kibris uses the Turkish currency, receives financial aid from Turkey, relies on troops from Turkey for its defense, and grants citizenship to migrants from Turkey.[68] In this sense, North Kibris is no more independent from Turkey than Northern Ireland is from the United Kingdom.

In southern Cyprus, Makarios (who died in 1977) and his successors pressed for reunification with the north.[69] But repeated efforts to negotiate a solution, mediated by U.S., Soviet, British, and UN diplomats, have failed.[70] Tension remains high along the "Green Line" dividing the island, and war between the two sides has frequently threatened, most recently in 1998, when the Cypriot government's purchase of Russian missiles raised the prospect of renewed war.[71]

In the years since partition, the country has become deeply divided. There is only one civilian crossing point along the 118-mile frontier, and separate currencies circulate in the north and south. They even use different standards of time. Clocks in the north have been set back one hour "so that the north of Cyprus beats time, literally as well as metaphorically, with Anatolia," not its island neighbors.[72] And the two communities stage rival rallies every year on July 20 to mark the anniversary of Turkey's 1974 invasion. People attending events in the north mark the occasion with celebrations; those in the south go into mourning.[73]

In Pakistan, the transfer of power from military dictatorship to civilian government, a process of "democratization," led to division. As we will see in the next chapter, democratization in Eastern Europe and the Soviet Union also contributed to partition there. This suggests that when political power is devolved, during periods of decolonization or democratization, partition can occur. In Cyprus, by contrast, the chain of events was reversed. The partition of Cyprus led to democratization in Greece, where civilian government was restored.

In both Pakistan and Cyprus, regional powers—India and Turkey—were largely responsible for partition, though of course the dictatorships that launched abortive coups deserve much of the blame. Unlike previous partitions, the superpowers played minor, reactive roles. They did not initiate or manage the partition process but rather allowed regional power to divide neighboring states. This suggests that partition had become institutionalized, an accepted diplomatic practice in the interstate system, not merely a policy unique to postwar, great-power politics.

Violence and war accompanied partition in both countries. In Cyprus, it contributed to the ongoing threat of conflict, which persists today. In Pakistan, by comparison, there has been no residual conflict between Pakistan and Bangladesh, probably because they are geographically separated. Although Pakistan and Bangladesh soon normalized relations, Pakistan and India have not. Indeed, the subdivision of Pakistan contributed to accumulated and persistent hostilities between Pakistan and India. Still, the fact that Pakistani-Bangladeshi relations are amicable suggests that partition does not always or inevitably lead to conflict between divided states.

NOTES

1. Richard Sisson and Leo E. Rose, *War and Secession: Pakistan, India, and the Creation of Bangladesh* (Berkeley: University of California Press, 1990), 15–16.

2. Lee Burcheit, *Secession: The Legitimacy of Self-Determination* (New Haven, Conn.: Yale University Press, 1978), 202–03.

3. Sisson and Rose, *War and Secession*, 9.

4. Sisson and Rose, *War and Secession*, 10.

5. Sisson and Rose, *War and Secession*, 9–10.

6. Sisson and Rose, *War and Secession*, 12.

7. Sisson and Rose, *War and Secession*, 16, 17.

8. Sisson and Rose, *War and Secession*, 19–20.

9. Sisson and Rose, *War and Secession*, 21–24.

10. Sisson and Rose, *War and Secession*, 33.

11. Sisson and Rose, *War and Secession*, 33.

12. Sisson and Rose, *War and Secession*, 60–61, 70.

13. Sisson and Rose, *War and Secession*, 72.

14. Sisson and Rose, *War and Secession*, 87, 101.

15. J. N. Saxena, *Self-Determination: From Biafra to Bangladesh* (Delhi: University of Delhi Press, 1978), 53; Sisson and Rose, *War and Secession*, 81, 93, 123, 132–33.

16. Burcheit, *Secession*, 206.

17. Burcheit, *Secession*, 206–07; Sisson and Rose, *War and Secession*, 4, 142–43.

18. Burcheit, *Secession*, 207; Sisson and Rose, *War and Secession*, 152.

19. Sisson and Rose, *War and Secession*, 152–53.

20. Sisson and Rose, *War and Secession*, 179–81.

21. Sisson and Rose, *War and Secession*, 188, 153.

22. Sisson and Rose, *War and Secession*, 213, 187.

23. Sisson and Rose, *War and Secession*, 214.

24. Sisson and Rose, *War and Secession*, 214–15.

25. Sisson and Rose, *War and Secession*, 264.

26. Gregory Henderson, R. N. Lebow, and J. G. Stoessinger, *Divided Nations in a Divided World* (New York: David McKay, 1974), 325–26.

27. Henderson, Lebow and Stoessinger, *Divided Nations*, 314.

28. *New York Times*, August 14, 1988.

29. *New York Times*, May 18, 1986.

30. M. G. Kabir, "Religion, Language and Nationalism in Bangladesh," in *Religion, Nationalism and Politics in Bangladesh*, ed. Rafiuddin Ahmed (New Delhi: South Asian Publishers, 1990), 28.

31. *Bangor* [Maine] *Daily News*, October 1, 1986.

32. Zillur R. Khan, "From Mujib to Zia: Elite Politics in Bangladesh," in Ahmed, *Religion, Nationalism and Politics*, 55.

33. *New York Times*, November 14, 1988.

34. Craig Baxter, "Can Democracy Survive?" *Current History* (April 1996): 182–83.

35. Samina Ahmed, "Pakistan at Fifty: A Tenuous Democracy," *Current History* (December 1997): 421.

36. Ahmed Rashid, "Pakistan: Trouble Ahead, Trouble Behind," *Current History* (April 1996), passim; Ahmed, "Pakistan at Fifty," passim.

37. William R. Louis, *The British Empire in the Middle East* (Oxford: Clarendon, 1984), 224.

38. Stanley Mayes, *Makarios: A Biography* (New York: St. Martin's, 1981), 54–55.

39. Mayes, *Makarios*, 159.

40. Kyriacos Markides, *The Rise and Fall of the Cyprus Republic* (New Haven, Conn.: Yale University Press, 1977), 23.

41. Robert Stephens, *Cyprus: A Place of Arms* (London: Pall Mall, 1966), 132.

42. Mayes, *Makarios*, 162–63. "The Greeks would have liked to describe the new Republic as 'democratic,' but, as the neutral advisor, M. Bridel, pointed out that 'democratic' implied majority rule, the Turks managed to get this word deleted." Mayes, *Makarios*, 141.

43. Mayes, *Makarios*, 164.

44. Mayes, *Makarios*, 164, vii.

45. Robert McDonald, *The Problem of Cyprus* (London: Brassey's, 1989), 13; Stephens, *Cyprus*, 180.

46. Christopher Hitchens, *Hostage to History: Cyprus from the Ottomans to Kissinger* (New York: Noonday, 1989), 57.

47. Markides, *Cyprus Republic*, 134.

48. Mayes, *Makarios*, 192, 223–24.

49. C. M. Woodhouse, *The Rise and Fall of the Greek Colonels* (London: Granada, 1985), 2; George Zaharopoulos, "Politics and the Army in Postwar Greece," in *Greece under Military Rule*, ed. Richard Clogg and George Yannopoulos (London: Secker & Warburg, 1972), 28; Constantine Tsoucalas, *The Greek Tragedy* (Harmondsworth, United Kingdom: Penguin, 1969), 192–93.

50. Woodhouse, *The Rise and Fall of the Greek Colonels*, 7.

51. Woodhouse, *The Rise and Fall of the Greek Colonels*, 134–40, 143–44; Thanos Veremis, "Greece: Veto and Impasse, 1967–74," in *The Political Dilemmas of Military Regimes*, ed. Christopher Clapham and George Philip (Totowa, N.J.: Barnes & Noble, 1985), 40; Constantine P. Danopoulos, *From Military to Civilian Rule* (London: Routledge, 1992), 47.

52. Robert K. Schaeffer, *Power to the People: Democratization around the World* (Boulder, Colo.: Westview, 1997), 69–71.

53. Woodhouse, *The Rise and Fall of the Greek Colonels*, 154- 55. In a transcript supplied by the Greek embassy to a journalist, Ioannidis and Sampson discuss Makarios's escape.

> "I see that the old shit has escaped. Where could he be now?" Ioannidis asked Sampson by phone the day after the coup. "On the mountains. . . . I hope to have him arrested within two or three hours," Sampson replied. At this point Ioannidis demanded, "Nicky, I want his head. You shall bring it to me yourself, OK Nicky?"

Christopher Hitchens, *Cyprus* (London: Quartet, 1984), 93–94.

54. Constantine P. Danopoulos, "Beating a Hasty Retreat: The Greek Military Withdraws from Power," in *The Decline of Military Regimes: The Civilian Influence*, ed. Constantine P. Danopoulos (Boulder, Colo.: Westview, 1988), 242.

55. Hitchens, *Cyprus*, 97–98; McDonald, *The Problem of Cyprus*, 10.

56. Woodhouse, *The Rise and Fall of the Greek Colonels*, 157–58.

57. Danopoulos argued that the mobilization brought into the army many soldiers who opposed the government. Danopoulos, "Beating a Hasty Retreat," 239.

58. Danopoulos, "Beating a Hasty Retreat," 239.

59. Taki Tehodoracopulos, *The Greek Upheaval: Kings, Demagogues and Bayonets* (New Rochelle, N.Y.: Caratzas, 1978), 11; Mayes, *Makarios*, 248; Harry J. Psomiades, "Greece: From the Colonels' Rule to Democracy," in *From Dictatorship to Democracy: Coping with the Legacies of Authoritarianism and Totalitarianism*, ed. John H. Herz (Westport, Conn.: Greenwood, 1982), 252–54.

60. Woodhouse, *The Rise and Fall of the Greek Colonels*, 171; Hitchens, *Cyprus*, 107, 142; Psomiades, "Greece," 256.

61. Hitchens, *Hostage to History*, 90.

62. *New York Times*, December 20, 1987.

63. *New York Times*, February 27, 1988. Christos P. Ioannides, "Changing the Demography of Cyprus," in *Cyprus: Domestic Dynamics, External Constraints*, ed. Christos P. Ioannides (New Rochelle, N.Y.: Caratzas, 1992), 20–26, 38.

64. Van Coufoudakis, "Cyprus: Domestic Politics and Recent U.N. Proposals," in Ioannides, *Cyprus*, 5.

65. Hitchens, *Hostage to History*, 107.

66. Hitchens, *Hostage to History*, 139, 179; Coufoudakis, "Cyprus," 7.

67. *New York Times*, March 30, 1988.

68. McDonald, *The Problem of Cyprus*, 50–51.

69. Ioannides, *Cyprus*, x.

70. Coufoudakis, "Cyprus," 14; Norma Salem, *Cyprus: A Regional Conflict and Its Resolution* (New York: St. Martin's, 1992), 210–18.

71. Michael R. Gordon, "Greek Cypriots to Get Missiles from Russians," *New York*

Times, April 29, 1988; Stephen Kinzer, "New Rumblings in Cyprus Raise Specter of War," *New York Times*, April 30, 1998; Chris Hedges, "With Only Hate in Common, They Share an Island," *New York Times*, May 31, 1995.

72. Hitchens, *Hostage to History*, 25.

73. *New York Times*, July 21, 1986.

N I N E

DEMOCRATIZATION AND DIVISION

Czechoslovakia, Ethiopia, the Soviet Union, and Yugoslavia were partitioned in 1991–1992. The division of these four countries resulted in the creation of twenty-four successor states, perhaps more. Unlike previous partitions, these states were divided by indigenous forces, not by outside powers. Partition in Czechoslovakia, the Soviet Union, and Yugoslavia was largely a product of democratization, a global process that began in 1974 with the fall of dictators in southern Europe.[1] During the twenty years that followed, economic and political crises combined to sweep dictators from power in countries across Latin America, East Asia, Eastern Europe, and southern Africa. In most cases, dictators peacefully surrendered power to civilian democrats, who then revised constitutions, held multiparty elections, and adopted new economic policies designed to repair the damage done by their capitalist and communist predecessors. Dictators typically transferred power to democrats in unitary states. But when power was transferred in Czechoslovakia, the Soviet Union, and Yugoslavia, it was also divided, and multiple states created. In parts of Yugoslavia and the Soviet Union, partition led to uncivil and interstate war.

In Ethiopia, by contrast, partition was primarily a product of problems dating back to postwar decolonization and dictatorship. The United Nations' 1950 decision to assign Eritrea, a former Italian colony, to Ethiopia, and Haile Selassie's 1960 decision to annex it, fueled the rise of Eritrean independence movements in the early 1960s. It would wage a thirty-year war against Ethiopian dictatorships, first against a monarchist regime backed by the United States and then, after 1974, against a Marxist dictatorship backed by the Soviet Union and assisted by Cuba and Israel. In the late 1980s, Gorbachev's decision to reduce its military support for client regimes—a consequence of democratization in the Soviet Union—triggered a fatal crisis for the Ethiopian dictatorship, leading to the partition of Ethiopia and the creation of an independent state in Eritrea.

Partition in these four countries flowed, like two rivers, from two historically different processes: democratization in Czechoslovakia, the Soviet Union, and Yugoslavia; decolonization and dictatorship in Ethiopia. These two currents converged as a result of democratization in the early 1990s, then immediately divided, their successor states, now individual streams, reaching separately across a wide delta toward the sea.

In Czechoslovakia, the Soviet Union, and Yugoslavia, democratization and division in the 1990s was the end result of economic and political problems that first emerged in the late 1960s and early 1970s. Before 1970, communist regimes in these countries, and throughout Eastern Europe, had rebuilt war-battered economies and promoted economic growth. Regimes, however, used different policies to promote reconstruction and development. The Soviet Union and most of the communist dictatorships in Eastern Europe, Czechoslovakia among them, used shared economic and military institutions to assist each other. The Council for Mutual Economic Assistance (COMECON), which was established in 1949 as a Soviet response to the U.S. Marshall Plan, organized industrial relations and promoted trade among Eastern European states.[2] The Warsaw Pact, which was created in 1955 to counter NATO, integrated the armies of member countries under a single, Soviet military command.[3] By coordinating their industries, trade, and defense, communist regimes achieved economies of scale, divisions of labor, and monetary savings that they could not have managed on their own. These collective institutions helped promote economic growth.

Yugoslavia, by contrast, did not belong to these institutions and adopted rather different economic policies. Although Josip Broz Tito had established a communist regime in Yugoslavia after the war, he broke with Stalin in 1948 and took Yugoslavia out of the newly established Soviet sphere of influence in Eastern Europe. Tito's regime was able to survive economically because the United States and its allies provided Yugoslavia with grants, loans, and military aid amounting to $2.7 billion between 1951 and 1960.[4] As U.S. aid declined in the late 1950s, the regime adopted an economic strategy based on exporting Yugoslav workers and importing Western European tourists, a policy also being used by capitalist dictatorships in Spain, Portugal, and Greece.[5] Income from the remittances of Yugoslav workers employed in Western Europe, principally

West Germany, and money from Western European workers who vacationed along the Adriatic coast, provided Tito's government with the hard currency it needed to purchase goods, develop industries, and create domestic jobs. During the 1960s, Yugoslavia had nearly one million workers employed abroad, and they returned about $1 billion in remittances annually.[6] The number of tourists visiting Yugoslavia grew from forty-one thousand in 1950 to six million in 1973, injecting $470 million into the economy.[7] Earnings from emigre workers and vacationing tourists "made it possible [for the regime] to realize . . . rapid growth without running up against the balance of payments problems that bring growth to a grinding halt in most poor countries."[8]

But policies that facilitated economic growth in the 1950s and 1960s were unable to maintain economic momentum or address problems that emerged in the early 1970s. The economies of regimes throughout Eastern Europe and the Soviet Union began stagnating in the late 1960s. Then in the early 1970s, rising oil and food prices created a serious crisis for communist governments across the region.

The regime in Czechoslovakia was one of the first to experience difficulties. After growing rapidly in the 1950s, the economy stalled in the 1960s—annual growth fell from 7 percent in 1956–1960 to only 1.8 percent in 1961–1965—largely because its trade with China collapsed, a casualty of the widening Sino-Soviet split.[9] Searching for ways to restart the economy, reformers led by Alexander Dubcek adopted an "Action Program" in 1968 that was designed to introduce some market mechanisms and submit "the economy to the pressure of the world market."[10] But Soviet leaders were determined to prevent economic and political reforms that threatened the integrity of collective institutions in their sphere. So they invaded Czechoslovakia in 1968 and reinstalled a conservative communist regime under Gustav Husak. Although Husak immediately scrapped most of the Action Plan, he adopted one part of it, which envisioned borrowing money from the West to finance economic growth.[11] This subsequently became the way that regimes throughout Eastern Europe and the Soviet Union addressed economic crisis in the 1970s.

When the 1973 Yom Kippur War erupted, the Organization of Petroleum Exporting Countries (OPEC) began restricting oil supplies, driving up oil prices around the world. While oil prices skyrocketed, Soviet grain harvests withered. Crop failures in 1972, 1974–1975, 1977, and 1979–1982 forced the Soviets to import massive quantities of grain—10.5 million metric tons in 1972, 40 million metric tons by 1981.[12] This drove food prices up to levels not seen since World War II. The combination of rising oil and food prices created serious problems for communist economies.

In the Soviet Union, rising oil prices should have increased its income from oil exports to Eastern European countries. But the Soviets continued to deliver oil at below world market prices to shelter client regimes from world market inflation. (The price benefits provided by the Soviet Union to its partners in Eastern Europe amounted to between $20 and $30 billion during the 1970s.[13]) Meanwhile, massive grain imports contributed to growing trade deficits, drained currency reserves, and forced the government to spend more on food subsidies, which were designed to prevent domestic inflation and contain the social unrest associated with price increases.[14]

For regimes in Eastern Europe, higher oil and food prices created large trade deficits. This threatened to undo economic gains of the previous decade and trigger the kind of riots against rising food prices that had erupted in Poland and forced Wladyslaw Gomulka from power in 1971.[15]

Tito's regime in Yugoslavia was not immune from these problems. Rising oil prices triggered a recession in Western Europe. Governments there responded to rising unemployment by sending emigre "guest workers" back home, which reduced remittance income and increased unemployment in Yugoslavia. Because fewer Western European workers vacationed abroad, tourist receipts fell and businesses that relied on the tourist trade suffered. Although they had adopted different economic development policies, the impact of oil embargo and Soviet crop failure on regimes throughout Eastern Europe was the same: inflation, stagnation, and looming political turmoil.

To address these problems, communist regimes seized upon a common solution. They borrowed heavily from the growing Eurodollar market. The Eurodollar market had been created in the 1950s, when the Soviet Union, China, and other private investors deposited the U.S. dollars that they had earned in trade in the European subsidiaries of U.S. banks.[16] The modest amount of money available in this Eurodollar banking pool ($10 billion in 1960) had grown to about $110 billion by 1970. It grew rapidly in the 1970s, as OPEC countries filled Eurodollar coffers with money earned from oil price increases. The money available in the Eurodollar market increased from $110 billion in 1970 to $1.525 trillion by 1980.[17] Dictatorships in Eastern Europe, and indeed throughout the world, tapped this monetary reservoir to meet their pressing financial, industrial, military, and social needs.[18]

Czechoslovakia's foreign debt grew from $608 million in 1970 to $6.8 billion in 1980; Yugoslavia's doubled from $2.7 billion to $5.8 billion between 1971 and 1975, then rocketed to $20.5 billion by 1980; and the Soviet Union's grew from $6.3 billion in 1975 to $11 billion by 1980, to $37.4 billion by 1984, and to $50.6 billion by 1989.[19]

Although debt enabled regimes to stave off economic and social ills during the 1970s, borrowed money simply deferred the underlying crisis for a decade. In 1979, U.S. officials announced that the Federal Reserve would raise interest rates to battle inflation in the United States, where prices were climbing at a 14 percent annual rate.[20] Changed U.S. monetary policy increased interest payments for debtors the world over and triggered a global recession. Regimes that had borrowed heavily saw their interest payments rise and their incomes shrink, because recession reduced the demand for their exports. The resulting debt crisis became manifest first in Eastern Europe, when Poland announced in 1981 that it could no longer repay its $27 billion debt.[21] Although Czechoslovakia, the Soviet Union, and Yugoslavia had not borrowed as much money as Poland, indebtedness joined them all in a common crisis.

In Czechoslovakia, the economy again stagnated and its position in the world economy continued to decline. Before World War II, Czechoslovakia was "one of the ten most industrialized countries in the world," with a GDP per capita comparable to that of Austria.[22] But by 1990, "Czechoslovakia's GDP per capita . . . [was] comparable to that of Venezuela and [only] one-fifth that of Austria."[23]

The debt crisis in Yugoslavia led to widespread shortages of imported goods, rising unemployment, falling real wages, and anemic rates of growth.[24] Between 1985 and 1988, per capita GDP had declined from $3,000 to $2,400, and in 1991 the World Bank predicted that Yugoslavia would not regain 1989 income levels for more than a decade.[25]

The Soviet Union experienced similar difficulties. "Between 1980 and 1985, the rate of economic growth appears to have fallen to zero," one economist observed.[26] The resulting economic stagnation, or *zastoi*, brought the economy to a grinding halt.[27]

This widespread economic crisis threatened to create a social and political crisis because governments across the region were forced to adopt austerity measures to repay debt. In Poland, rising prices and falling incomes antagonized workers and intellectuals and fueled the growth of Solidarity, which challenged Communist Party rule.[28] Although Gen. Wojciech Jaruzelski used martial law to ban Solidarity and arrest and imprison thousands of its activists, it was clear that opposition movements such as Solidarity might easily emerge in other countries where similar conditions existed.[29]

The Soviet response to the crisis proved crucial for other regimes in Eastern Europe because it organized and maintained relations among them. By the end of the 1980s, Soviet policies would lead first to democratization in Eastern Europe and then to democratization and division in Yugoslavia, Czechoslovakia, and the Soviet Union itself.

The economic turmoil in the Soviet Union was compounded in the 1980s by military and political problems. In 1979, the Soviets sponsored a pro-Soviet coup in Afghanistan and sent troops to support the government against the domestic, anti-communist opposition.[30] Although the Soviets deployed some 115,000 troops against the mujahedin guerrillas, they were unable to defeat the rebels in the field.[31] The decade-long war would result in nearly fifty thousand Soviet casualties, perhaps one million Afghan deaths, and cost about $100 billion, a sum that nearly exhausted Soviet gold and diamond reserves.[32] As Mikhail Gorbachev later admitted, these developments "have turned Afghanistan into a bleeding wound."[33]

Foreign military misadventure cost the Soviets dearly. But the deaths, in rapid succession, of Soviet leaders in the early 1980s prevented the regime from adopting a coherent response to multiple problems. The political crisis began when Leonid Brezhnev, who had been the general secretary of the Communist Party since 1964, died suddenly on November 10, 1982.[34] In the battle to choose his successor, Brezhnev's favorite Konstantin Chernenko was passed over, and Yuri Andropov was selected. But Andropov, already sixty-eight years old, suffered from poor health and he died after a long illness on February 9, 1984, only fifteen months after taking power.[35] A second battle over a successor ensued. Andropov's protege Mikhail Gorbachev was passed over and Brezhnev's old favorite Chernenko chosen instead. But Chernenko, then seventy-two, was also in poor health, and he died a year later, on March 10, 1985. Gorbachev, then fifty-four, assumed power the next day.[36]

Although Gorbachev would remain in power for six years, his selection did not end the battle for succession. Others soon contested his authority, and he would eventually surrender his power not to one but to many successors. The battle over succession, which began with Brezhnev's death in November 1982 and ended with Gorbachev's resignation in December 1991, was initially waged by factions within the Communist Party. But as the decade wore on, it was increasingly waged by communist and former communist leaders in the Soviet Union's constituent republics, a development that would contribute both to democratization and to division.

When Gorbachev took power in 1985, he confronted multiple economic, military, and political problems. "By the beginning of the 1980s, the [Soviet Union] found itself in a state of severe crisis which embraced all spheres of life," he said.[37]

To address these problems, Gorbachev advanced three sets of reforms. To revive the moribund economy and promote economic growth, Gorbachev proposed that agriculture and industry be restructured, a process he called *perestroika*. But because important sectors of the population, the party, the bureaucracy, and the military opposed substantive economic reform, Gorbachev soon realized that he needed to mobilize political support for this "titanic job."[38] So he rallied support for his reforms by promoting political "openness," or *glastnost*, and limited democratization. "We will not succeed with the tasks of perestroika if we do not firmly pursue democratization," he maintained.[39] He also recognized that the Soviets could not win the war in Afghanistan and that heavy military spending—which consumed between one-quarter and one-third of the country's GNP—was an economic burden the country could no longer support.[40] So he called for "restricting military potential within the bounds of reasonable sufficiency" and moved quickly to withdraw from Afghanistan, reduce troop levels along the frontier with China, initiate arms control treaties with the United States and its allies, reduce support for client regimes such as those in Ethiopia and Cuba, and reduce troop levels in Eastern Europe. This last decision had important consequences for client regimes throughout Eastern Europe.

Since World War II, Soviet leaders insisted that they had a right to intervene in Eastern Europe, by force if necessary, to defend their sphere of influence and protect the communist regimes they had installed. But Gorbachev argued against "any interference in the internal affairs of other states under any pretext whatsoever," asserting that "all nations had a right to 'their own roads of social development.' "[41] His decision to withdraw fifty thousand troops and five thousand tanks from Eastern Europe, announced on December 7, 1988, underscored the Soviet's new, non-interventionary foreign policy. No longer would the Soviets support client regimes in Eastern Europe. As Foreign Minister Gennady Gerasimov explained, the new policy would be called the "Sinatra Doctrine," because the American singer Frank Sinatra "had a song. 'I did it my way.' So every country decides in its own way which [economic and political] road to take."[42]

For regimes that had long relied on Soviet military power— which had been deployed to defend them in East Germany in 1953, Hungary in 1956, and Czechoslovakia in 1968—the new policy was a fatal blow. In 1989, they faced serious economic crisis and growing domestic opposition movements. In Poland, Solidarity had survived the government's ban and reemerged as the representative of an alliance between workers and intellectuals.[43] In East Germany, massive migration through Hungary brought the economy to a standstill and the government to the brink of collapse.[44] In Yugoslavia, ethnic regional movements had emerged in the country's constituent republics. Because regimes were unable to solve their economic problems, unable to contain or co-opt diverse opposition movements, and unable to call on domestic groups or foreign military intervention to defend them, they collapsed as a group in the summer and fall of 1989, only one year after Gorbachev announced that he would stop supporting Eastern European regimes. By the end of 1989, communist regimes had transferred power to civilian democrats in Poland, Hungary, East Germany, Czechoslovakia, Bulgaria, and Romania.

In the Soviet Union, meanwhile, Communist Party factions opposed to Gorbachev or his reforms continued to struggle for power, prolonging the crisis of succession. Because they were relatively weak at first and could not easily compete with Gorbachev for control of the central government, they turned to the republics, using the party structures and parliaments there as a base of operations.

Communist Party factions based in the republics emerged first in the Baltics: Estonia, Latvia, and Lithuania. Communist Party leaders there used history and the Soviet constitution to their advantage, arguing that their annexation by the Soviet Union, under secret terms of the 1939 Hitler-Stalin Pact, was illegal and that provisions in the Soviet constitution gave them the right to secede from the union in any case.[45] On August 23, 1989, the fiftieth anniversary of the Hitler-Stalin Pact, two million Balts formed a "continuous 370-mile human chain from Vilnius through Riga to Tallin to demand independence."[46] In the fall, communist parties in the Baltic republics joined with noncommunist parties—Sajudis in Lithuania and the Popular Front in Estonia and in Latvia—to declare their "sovereignty," which gave laws passed in the republics precedence over Soviet law.[47]

Although regionally based communists and their political allies were vulnerable to any reassertion of central Soviet authority, they were able to resist Soviet pressure because Gorbachev had to admit that the Soviet Union had, in fact, improperly annexed the Baltics and because they soon found supporters in some of the other, larger republics.[48] The emergence of Communist Party factions based in Ukraine and in Russia protected the small republics from direct, central government assault.

In Ukraine, historical and contemporary disasters fueled anticenter senti-ment. In 1987 and 1988, Ukrainian scholars blamed central government poli-cies for the terrible 1932–1933 famine in the Ukraine.[49] Grassroots antinuclear groups meanwhile demanded an end to Soviet nuclear policies, which they blamed for the disastrous meltdown of the Chernobyl nuclear reactor near Kiev in 1986. That accident released ninety times more radioactive material than the atomic bomb at Hiroshima.[50] Many people in the Ukraine came to agree with anticenter activists, who argued, "We have understood that the only way out of the crisis is also out of the Soviet Union."[51] Communist Party leader Leonid Kravchuk took advantage of widespread anticentral government views to argue for greater Ukrainian autonomy, particularly for the authority to deal with economic problems. By 1990, Kravchuk insisted, "Our aim is not to de-stroy the Soviet Union, but we don't want to see it once again become a formal union of 'sovereign states' where powerless [regional] governments . . . would once again be required to rubber-stamp dictates from the center."[52] As grass-roots groups joined with Communist Party elites, support for anticenter politics grew rapidly. Only 20.6 percent of the people in the Ukraine supported inde-pendence in September 1989, but 90.3 percent voted for independence two years later.[53]

The ability of Communist Party factions to struggle for power from bases in the republics was enormously strengthened by the emergence of party factions in the Russian Republic. It would be the Russian struggle against the center that proved decisive, and divisive, for all the republics.

Initially it was conservative Communists in Gorbachev's government who demanded and received approval in June 1990 to establish a Russian Commu-nist Party and Russian legislature like those that had long existed in other re-publics.[54] As John Dunlop has argued, "It should be underlined that these conservative communist attitudes to Russian autarchy were . . . primarily tactics to get themselves an independent power base from which to attack Gorba-chev."[55]

But while conservative factions lobbied for the creation of new political in-stitutions in the Russian Republic, it was Boris Yeltsin and his allies who used them effectively. After Yeltsin spoke critically of Gorbachev and his reforms in October 1987, he had been removed from his post and exiled to the margins of central power.[56] As a result, he moved to take advantage of institutions that were available to him. Yeltsin found them in the Russian Republic, where he "effectively employed a 'horizontal' strategy that [sought] ties among the re-publics to curtail the center's political and economic dominance."[57] Yeltsin was able to seek these ties in his role as chairman of the new Russian Congress. Capturing 84 percent of the vote in his district, Yeltsin maneuvered past Gorbachev's allies and conservative communist factions to become chairman on May 29, 1990. He then passed a declaration of Russian sovereignty in June 1990.[58] In June 1991, Yeltsin won Russia's first presidential election with 57.3 percent of the vote and was inaugurated in July.[59] The creation of republican institutions in Russia provided Yeltsin with a power base, and the growing strength of Yeltsin's anti-Gorbachev, pro-republican politics made it easier for factions based in other republics to make headway against the center.

Factions within the Communist Party found refuge in the republics. But they also needed to find supporters who could elect them to office in revived republican parliaments. In the Baltics, people who supported anticentrist policies were easy to find, as opposition to Soviet annexation and central Soviet authority was widespread. But in the Ukraine and Russia, Communist leaders such as Kravchuk and Yeltsin had to find allies among those who had long supported Soviet power. They found their supporters among urban workers and intellectuals who had been adversely affected by Gorbachev's reforms.

Although Gorbachev's reforms were designed to revive the economy, they undermined living standards for urban workers and intellectuals. Cuts in defense spending increased unemployment among skilled and educated workers.[60] Rising prices for food and housing, both in short supply, contributed to inflation and undermined the standard of living for urban residents.[61] For the reforms to work, the government needed to eliminate subsidies and force consumers to pay market prices for goods they purchased. As Gorbachev argued in 1990, "Without price reform, we cannot and shall not create satisfactory economic relations in the economy."[62] But the regime's repeated efforts to raise prices created widespread opposition to economic reform.

Yeltsin and other anticentrist politicians in the republics understood that opposition to economic reforms was growing. So Yeltsin appealed first to workers and intellectuals opposed to reform in Moscow, his initial constituency, and then allied himself with coal miners who had been conducting strikes across the country since July 1989. Most of the 2.5 million Soviet miners joined the strikes because rising food and housing prices had eroded real wages.[63] The government's insistence that miners pay for soap was the "symbolic last straw."[64] Yeltsin supported the miners in their battles with Gorbachev, and then workers in heavy and service sector industries, who struck and demanded higher wages.[65]

Yeltsin and other anticentrist politicians simultaneously campaigned *for* and *against* reform. They were *for* political reform, demanding that central govern-ment power be transferred to the republics, where multiparty elections would be held. For them, political reform would result in devolution and democratiza-tion. But they also fought *against* economic reform to retain the support of their new political constituency, which had been adversely affected by price hikes and declining living standards. By opposing price increases, anticentrist politicians in the republics made it impossible for Gorbachev to promote seri-ous economic reform. And they thought that an expanded policy-making role for the republics would enable them "to compete more effectively in a zero-sum struggle over diminishing resources."[66]

Opposition to economic reform and central power was not universal. People in the poorer central Asian republics generally supported Gorbachev's efforts to promote economic reform and preserve central power. They did so because they believed that the central government provided economic benefits that would not be forthcoming if the Soviet Union disappeared. They saw union as a way to preserve redistributive economic policies, which had transferred some wealth from prosperous to poor republics. The problem for the central govern-ment was that "the support for a continuation of union was greatest precisely in those areas where Gorbachev needed it the least."[67]

Faced with determined opposition from the prosperous republics, Gorba-chev suspended efforts to eliminate state subsidies and increase prices in 1991.[68] Without these measures, economic reform could not succeed, and the economic crisis deepened. Soviet trade deficits soared, the value of the ruble fell, foreign debt mounted, inflation climbed, and industrial output plum-meted.[69] By 1991, "aggregate output had dropped by 17 percent, a magnitude of decline not seen since the devastating Nazi invasion [of 1941]."[70]

It was in this context that a conservative faction of the Communist Party launched a coup on August 19–21, 1991, while Gorbachev was vacationing in the Crimea. The conservatives who led the coup—Vice President Gennadi Ya-nayev, Prime Minister Valentin Pavlov, Defense Minister Dmitrii Yazov, and KGB chairman Vladimir Kryuchov—were the heirs of the Brezhnev-Cher-nenko legacy within the party.[71] Unlike Yeltsin and Kravchuk, they had re-mained as a faction *within* the central government, opposing Gorbachev's reforms as centrist insiders rather than republican outsiders. But they finally split from Gorbachev and launched a coup to depose him because they op-posed the proposed Union Treaty, which would have devolved considerable central government authority to the republics, because they opposed economic and military reform, and because they wanted to reassert central Communist authority, which was rapidly draining away.[72] Defense Minister Yazov observed that it had become "practically impossible" to draft soldiers and objected to the demand by authorities in the republics that conscripts serve only within the republics. "The armed forces can exist only under a single command," Yazov complained. "When everybody commands them, they're not armed forces."[73] And Yanayev argued during the coup that "the situation has gone out of control in the USSR and we are facing a situation of multirule."[74]

But the coup quickly failed. The conservatives acted too late, after much of the central government's authority had already evaporated. Other factions based in the republics had grown strong in the years since Gorbachev took office. Yeltsin could now successfully appeal for political support from the populace, and his defense of the Russian White House proved a turning point. Importantly, the army refused to join the conservatives. Many officers were already supporting political leaders and planning careers in armies of the republics. As an institution, the army had been weakened by defeat in Afghanistan and by defense spending cuts. Its leaders worried too that the coup might trigger a civil war between the center and the republics, a risk they were not prepared to take.

After the coup collapsed, Gorbachev returned to office. But his long alliance with the conservatives who plotted the coup eroded his credibility. The massive exodus from the Communist Party—20 percent of the membership resigned from the party during the first six months of 1991—deprived the central government of the only reliable constituency that might defend the union.[75] Gorbachev conceded that he "had underestimated the forces of nationalism and separatism that were hidden deep within our system" and admitted that he had become "totally isolated."[76] As a result, he was quickly exiled to the margins of power during the fall of 1991.[77] Yeltsin abolished the Communist Party, declared the independence of the constituent republics, forced Gorbachev to resign, and finally dissolved the Soviet Union on December 30, 1991. In its place he established a "Commonwealth of Independent States," consisting of eleven of the Soviet Union's fifteen successor states.[78]

Starting in 1980, Yugoslavia was beset by economic problems related to the debt crisis and by political difficulties associated with Tito's death. During the next ten years, these problems combined to democratize and divide the country into five, and perhaps more, successor states.

When the United States raised interest rates in 1979, debtors had to pay more for the money they had borrowed. For Yugoslavia, which had amassed a

$20.5 billion debt in the 1970s, this meant a substantial increase in its costs. But while its costs increased, its income from workers and tourists declined. Governments in Western Europe insisted that foreign workers leave, and nearly five hundred thousand Yugoslav workers returned home by 1985, reducing the country's income from remittances and increasing domestic unemployment.[79] Because fewer Western European workers vacationed in Yugoslavia, receipts from the tourist trade fell. As a result, the government was forced to adopt austerity measures, which led to a 40 percent decline in the standard of living between 1982 and 1989.[80]

In many countries the debt crisis was a collective evil, joining disparate social groups in a common misery. But in Yugoslavia, it accentuated long-standing regional economic differences and drove people in opposite political directions.

Throughout the postwar period, Tito promised that his government would reduce economic disparities between the prosperous republics (Slovenia and Croatia) and the poorer republics (Serbia, Montenegro, Macedonia, and Bosnia-Herzegovina).[81] But the regime never managed to achieve regional equality because its adoption of a worker-export, tourist-import development policy in the 1960s favored the prosperous republics. Most of the workers who migrated to Western Europe came from Slovenia and Croatia, so the money they remitted provided hard currency and economic benefits to families and businesses in these regions.[82] As it happened, tourists vacationed in Slovenia and Croatia, along the Dalmatian coast, not in the interior, so workers and businesses servicing tourists in these regions were the principal beneficiaries of the tourist trade and the hard currency earnings associated with it. There was also a synergy between the two: worker remittances helped finance private, tourist industry businesses for households in the region.

Tito recognized that his policies contributed to uneven development. So he used a variety of mechanisms and institutions—hard currency regulations, the Fund for Development—to take some of the income and hard currency earned in prosperous republics and transfer it to the poorer republics.[83] But Tito's redistributive policies antagonized people in the prosperous republics. In 1970–1971, Croatian students demanded a greater share of the country's foreign exchange earnings, arguing that the government's hard currency policies shortchanged them and unfairly subsidized the poorer republics.[84] What's more, redistributive policies failed to close the economic gap between regions.[85] The gap between the prosperous and poor republics grew wider during the postwar period: "In 1947, the per capita social product in Slovenia was 2.4 times higher than in Kosovo, while in 1974 it was over 6 times higher."[86]

The government's response to the debt crisis generally increased regional inequality. Repeated currency devaluations were good for the prosperous republics, because devaluations promoted tourism and made it easier for them to export their goods. But they were bad for the poorer republics, which were forced to pay more for imports.[87] As the economic crisis deepened, people in different regions turned toward separate political solutions. People in the prosperous republics demanded that they be able to keep what they earned from remittances and tourism and use these scarce resources for their own benefit.[88] They resisted redistributive policies and resented the central government, which siphoned off their income to the poorer republics. Slovenians, for example, complained that they "subsidize the rest of the country with heavy taxes and provide 27 percent of the federal budget, for which they get nothing in return."[89] As one Croatian hotelier explained, "The best thing is for us to live together with the Serbs, but with separate governments and separate accounting books. If the books were kept separate, then I think we would get along."[90]

But in the poor republics, people wanted to keep redistributive policies and central government institutions intact, so they could use the resources they provided to weather the storm.[91] They saw economic advantage in central government and political union.

These two economic and political approaches became increasingly irreconcilable. The prosperous republics began refusing to share their wealth, the poor republics began insisting that it be redistributed.[92] In 1990, these differences became manifest when a trade war erupted between prosperous and poor republics. Consumers boycotted goods made in other republics, legislators in the republics withheld payment of federal taxes, and regional governments imposed punitive and retaliatory taxes on goods originating in other republics.[93] As a result, growing regional *economic* inequalities contributed to the intensification of regional *ethnic* identities.

The economic crisis that began in 1980 was joined by a political crisis that followed Tito's death in the same year.[94] As in the Soviet Union after Brezhnev's demise, Tito's death touched off a battle for succession within the Communist Party. Factions began organizing political support in the republics, which had been given significant constitutional roles. Tito had repeatedly rewritten, revised, and amended the constitution to "prevent any individual from acquiring as much power as Tito himself had and to prevent any of Yugoslavia's peoples from dominating the federation."[95] But Tito's maneuvering left the government unprepared for an orderly succession and provided the republics with the right to self-determination, "including the right to secession."[96]

During the 1980s, factions within the League of Yugoslav Communists attached themselves to regional republican institutions and rallied people around the ethnic identities associated with them.[97] By the late 1980s, leaders of some factions abandoned Communist Party affiliations, established regional "nationalist" parties in their place, and demanded democratization and devolution.[98] As the Croatian leader Franjo Tudjman argued, "The democratization of Croatia will lead neither to the breakup of Yugoslavia nor to civil war . . . [but rather] to greater autonomy."[99]

In Serbia, the largest but also one of the poorer republics, Slobodan Milosevic used regional economic and ethnic themes to bid for power within the Serbian League of Communists, one of the constituent groups of the League of Yugoslav Communists.[100] After driving his opponents from the regional party, he rallied Serbian workers against the government's austerity program and demanded a greater share of political and economic power relative to the other republics. This, of course, greatly antagonized people in the smaller and more prosperous republics.

In January 1990, Milosevic called an extraordinary congress of the League of Communists in Yugoslavia to bid for control. The congress voted to end the Communist Party's monopoly on power, paving the way for multiparty elections and democratization in the republics.[101] But delegations from the prosperous republics, Slovenia and Croatia, then walked out, leading to the dissolution of the League of Communists as a shared political institution.[102] After they returned to their respective republics, Slovene and Croatian delegates shed their communist identities and began campaigning for upcoming elections as ethnic nationalists. In Slovenia, the ex-Communist Party lost the April 1990 parliamentary elections but retained control of the presidency.[103] Elections in Macedonia produced similar results.[104] In Croatia, Tudjman, a former Communist general, took office.[105] In Bosnia, Communists joined a coalition government. And in Serbia and in Montenegro, Milosevic and other communists won decisively.[106]

The spring 1990 elections gave the constituent republics greater political autonomy. But growing political autonomy made economic cooperation more difficult, and internecine trade wars intensified.

Then in the fall of 1990, leaders of the Yugoslav army joined the fray. Although the army was itself an important faction within the Communist Party, it had stayed out of the internal battles that raged during the late 1980s. But

its leaders became alarmed at the growing autonomy of the republics, particularly with Tudjman's demand that army conscripts serve only in their republic
of origin, which echoed demands being made by republican leaders in the Soviet Union.[107] Because these developments threatened the army's role as an
institution, its leaders, many of them Serbs, forged an alliance with Milosevic
to defend and reassert central government authority.[108] But the army-Milosevic
alliance, and provocative army maneuvers in Slovenia and Croatia, antagonized
the other republics and accelerated their efforts to wrest power from the central government. The Slovenian government quickly organized a plebiscite on
independence and, "as soon at the result was official on December 26, 1990,
the Slovenian parliament declared its intent to secede from Yugoslavia in six
months time if there were no progress towards a negotiated settlement of the
country's future."[109]

Because the federal constitution provided for a rotation of power, which allowed Serb leaders to control "four of the eight seats in the federal Presidency,
including that of the President during the crucial year, 15 May 1990 to 15 May
1991," Serb officials blocked Croatian and Slovenian proposals for greater autonomy and insisted that important central government powers be preserved
in the negotiations that followed.[110] They evidently believed that their alliance
with the army gave them the political weight they needed to win concessions
from the other republics. But leaders in Slovenia and Croatia refused to concede, hoping that the rotation of a Croat into the federal presidency would
soon assist them. But when their turn to assume the presidency approached,
the Serbs blocked it, creating a constitutional impasse. "Serbia has staged a
camouflaged coup d'etat," argued Milan Kucan, the president of Slovenia.[111]
On June 26, 1991, Slovenia and Croatia withdrew from the federation and declared their independence.[112]

Central government troops then assaulted both breakaway republics, but
stiff resistance from Slovene and Croat militias forced tank columns to withdraw. Multisided uncivil war soon erupted in Croatia and then Bosnia–
Herzegovina, where residual Serb minorities in Croatian and residual Serb and
Croat minorities in Bosnia took up arms against the new republics. Serb militias in both Croatia and Bosnia were assisted by the residual central government's regular army forces. The result was civil war, the slaughter of unarmed
civilians and "ethnic cleansing," massive migrations, and the subdivision of successor states in Croatia and Bosnia.

In Yugoslavia, democratization was accompanied by partition and civil war.
The country was partitioned because factions within the Communist Party

were unable or unwilling to find solutions to their economic differences or the political problems left unresolved by Tito's death. Factions retreated to the republics, where some demanded greater autonomy and other insisted on the reassertion of central government authority. Tension between prosperous and poor republics led to economic and political conflict, both increasingly defined and expressed in regional ethnic terms.

In Czechoslovakia, democratization and division took place in stages. The collapse of the communist regime in 1989 led to the "Velvet Revolution" and democratization in a unitary state. But problems associated with democratization led, three years later, to division, a "Velvet Divorce" between Czech and Slovak republics.

In 1989, Milos Jakes's government peacefully surrendered power to dissident democrats led by Vaclav Havel, a poet who began the year in jail and ended the year as president of Czechoslovakia.[113] In elections the following year, the non-communist Civic Democratic Party came to power. Its prime minister, the free market economist Vaclav Klaus, moved quickly to address the country's serious economic problems by dismantling socialist economic policies and introducing "capitalism without adjectives."[114] In Czechoslovakia, as elsewhere in democratizing states, this meant opening the economy to foreign investment and trade, selling state assets to private entrepreneurs, and demilitarizing the economy.[115] But these policies had different regional consequences, contributing to growing economic inequality in Bohemia and Slovakia.

The Klaus government's efforts to open the economy to foreign investment and trade provided greater benefits to Bohemia than to Slovakia. Bohemia received between 80 and 95 percent of all new foreign investment, which helped create jobs in the region.[116] Successive devaluations of the crown, which fell 70 percent in 1990, had "more of a beneficial effect on Czech exports than on Slovak ones."[117] Workers from Bohemia took advantage of the new open border policies to seek employment in reunited and rebuilding Germany, providing hard currency remittances for the region. Western European tourists meanwhile flooded into Prague, assisting economic development there. Bohemia, like Slovenia and Croatia, benefited from the export of workers and the influx of tourists. But Slovakia, like poor Yugoslav republics, did not.[118]

The government's sale of state businesses and public assets also had different regional consequences. Because the government privatized twice as many businesses in Bohemia as in Slovakia, and because Czech entrepreneurs won control of the vast majority of these firms, the benefits of privatization were unevenly distributed, with Bohemia capturing the lion's share.[119]

Demilitarization produced similar results. The government's 1990 decision to end arms exports, and the general collapse of Eastern European and Soviet markets for weapons made in Czechoslovakia, devastated the important arms industry.[120] By 1991, the value of the arms trade had fallen from $8 billion to only $1 billion.[121] But because the arms industry was concentrated in Slovakia, workers there were harder hit by the collapse of trade.[122] Although the government reversed itself in 1991, its decision to renew arms sales did not greatly improve the situation because the arms that could be sold on world markets were made in Bohemia, not Slovakia.[123] Light aircraft and firearms made in Bohemia found ready markets, while heavy tanks, which comprised 99 percent of arms exports from Slovakia, found few buyers.[124]

As a result of these new economic policies, regional disparities quickly became evident. In 1990–1991, employment rates and income levels in the two regions diverged sharply. Whereas unemployment in Bohemia rose to 4.4 percent, unemployment in Slovakia climbed to 12.7 percent, a rate four times greater.[125] Although the introduction of "capitalism without adjectives" adversely affected incomes throughout the country—incomes fell 20 to 30 percent in 1990–1991—declining incomes "created greater hardship in Slovakia, where a higher proportion of [poorer] households are found."[126] As one woman complained, "There was a lot of money before [the fall of communism], but no goods. Now there is no money, but lots of goods."[127]

Diverging economic fortunes in the two regions reversed the postwar trend toward regional economic equality.[128] During the 1950s and 1960s, the communist regime in Czechoslovakia, like Tito's in Yugoslavia, used tax, price, and investment policies to transfer wealth from prosperous (Bohemia) to poor (Slovakia) republics.[129] These policies were more successful in Czechoslovakia than in Yugoslavia, increasing Slovakia's share of industrial production (from 13.1 percent of the country's total in 1946 to 25.5 percent in 1970) and raising income levels in Slovakia (from 70 percent of that of Czechs in 1948 to 92 percent in 1989). But in 1990, the government announced that it would end redistributive programs, stop Czech "subsidies" amounting to $300 million annually, and require Slovakia to live "mainly on the resources generated" in the region.[130] This decision marked the end of the central government's efforts to promote regional economic equality and threatened to accelerate growing economic inequality.

People living in the two regions experienced economic change before and after 1989 in different ways. For Czechs, the communist regime's redistributive "convergence" policies before 1989 had undermined their economic development and improved conditions in Slovakia at their expense. They viewed Klaus's introduction of capitalism after 1989 as a positive development because they expected it to improve their position and stop the drain of Czech resources to Slovakia.

For Slovaks, however, communist programs before 1989 had improved their economic circumstances, while free market policies after 1989 undermined their position and threatened to undo previous gains. Because Czechs and Slovaks drew different lessons from shared economic developments, they advanced different solutions to contemporary problems. The Czechs supported free market policies as an antidote to ruinous communist economic policies. Slovaks, by contrast, wanted to revive communist policies as a solution to problems caused by ruinous free market policies. Implicit in these solutions were different conceptions of the state. Proponents of free market policies wanted to reduce the role of government in the economy. Defenders of revised or "reform communist" policies wanted to maintain an important role for the state. These diverging views quickly became evident in the two regions. Public opinion polls identified a strong constituency for market policies and a reduced role for the state in Bohemia, a strong constituency for reform communism and an important role for the state in Slovakia.[131]

As economic developments pushed people in Bohemia and Slovakia in opposite political directions, the unitary state came under attack first from former communists based in Slovakia, and then from free market democrats based in Bohemia. As in Yugoslavia, economic differences quickly assumed ethnic characteristics.

In Slovakia, former communists led by Vladimir Meciar organized the Movement for Democratic Slovakia (MDS) to defend Slovakia against the Klaus government's free market policies. Meciar used residual institutions such as the Slovak National Council and Slovak assembly, which had earlier been established by the communist regime, as a political base, largely because former communists could not compete effectively in countrywide elections against popular dissident Czech politicians such as Havel and Klaus. These republican institutions helped Slovak politicians establish a regional political base, much as they had for Kravchuk and Yeltsin in the Soviet Union and Tudjman and Milosevic in Yugoslavia.

Meciar appealed to Slovak ethnic identity, arguing that Slovaks shared a common history, which included a brief period of "independence" during

World War II, and now faced common problems resulting from Czech free market policies and their status as a minority in the unitary state.[132] Ethnic appeals enabled Meciar to construct a multiclass coalition that could contest for power, at least in Slovakia, and the MDS became the region's dominant political party.[133] Based on his regional strength, Meciar demanded that free market reforms be slowed, that former communists be readmitted to the civil service and the legislature (they had been barred by a "lustration" law), and that Slovakia be given greater autonomy, which he said would create "two internationally recognized entities" and separate memberships in the United Nations.[134]

But while Meciar had a strong regional base, he was not strong enough to insist on the division of the state, largely because a majority of people in Slovakia rejected the idea of separation, though they were nonetheless to lend their support to Meciar's party.[135] As it happened, Slovak nationalists would not have to act alone. As one politician in the party led by Alexander Dubcek, the reformer who had been ousted by Soviet invasion in 1968, warned, "We're not afraid of separatists in Slovakia, but of separatists in Bohemia. Klaus is willing to work only with those who fully support his economic program. If everyone doesn't support it, he'll divide the republics."[136] This turned out to be prescient. Slovak nationalists were joined by Czech nationalists in 1992, when Klaus decided that Czech economic interests were best served by dividing the country and pursuing free market reforms in a separate state.[137]

In the June 1992 elections, Klaus's CDP won one-third of the votes, enough to outdistance all other parties, including Meciar's, but not enough to form a government on its own. In an effort to form a government, Klaus began negotiating with Meciar, who had placed a distant second, with only half as many votes. But in the talks, Klaus insisted that he would not consider modifying his economic policies to mollify Slovaks. "We know that it's impossible to decelerate the pace of economic reform," he said, and he maintained that economic issues were "nonnegotiable."[138] Meciar responded by saying, "We have economic interests in Slovakia which have been at odds with Czech interests for a long time. The situation would be worsened if the common state was maintained."[139]

When negotiations stalled, Klaus announced that "the federation is lost . . . and the common state as well."[140] Klaus and Meciar then agree to divide the country into two parts. President Havel objected, demanding that a referendum be held. "A referendum is the only constitutional and moral way" to avoid a "wild divorce," Havel argued.[141] He also pointed to opinion polls showing that only 16 percent of the people in Slovakia supported independence. But while partition was not supported by a majority in either republic, Klaus brushed aside Havel's demands for a referendum, saying "a referendum is not impossible, but also not obligatory."[142]

Havel could not insist on a referendum or resist Klaus and Meciar's decision to partition Czechoslovakia without putting it to an electoral test, for two reasons. First, although Havel was an extremely popular president, he could not rally an organized political constituency or party to the defense of union. Before 1989, Havel had helped organize Charter 77 and then Civic Forum, dissident movements opposed to communist rule. But Charter 77 possessed an ideology that eschewed mass politics, insisting that it was "not an organization, has no rules, permanent bodies or formal membership" and did "not aim to set out its own programmes of political or social reforms or changes."[143] Many of the dissidents who participated in Charter 77's "antipolitics" during the communist era later joined Civic Forum, then served in Havel's government after 1989, and had few ties with groups outside student-intellectual circles or outside Prague, where they were based. Given their narrow social constituency, limited geographic base, and self-effacing politics, it is not surprising that they did poorly in the 1990 elections, almost disappearing as a political entity in the crucial 1992 elections. Because the dissident movement had evaporated, Havel had no organized constituency that could support his calls for a referendum or continued union.

Second, legislators from Slovakia blocked Havel's reelection as president in July 1992.[144] This created a constitutional impasse, limiting the effectiveness of the chief executive at a crucial time, much as it had in Yugoslavia, where Serb leaders prevented a Croat from rotating into the presidency. Although Havel remained president as caretaker and was later reelected as president of the Czech Republic in 1993, his political effectiveness was crippled despite widespread personal popularity.

During the summer of 1992, Klaus and Meciar pressed ahead with partition. Although Meciar had raised political demands, including the threat of secession, to wrest economic concessions from Klaus, he overplayed his hand. Klaus essentially called Meciar's bluff. Partition became the common solution for both leaders. For Klaus, partition meant he could pursue capitalist policies without obstruction from the Slovak minority. For Meciar, partition meant he could assume power on his own terms. The two parties thus agreed to a "Velvet Divorce," and Czechoslovakia was divided into two states on New Year's Eve 1992.

Ethiopia was divided in 1991, and successor states established in Ethiopia and Eritrea two years later. But partition there was the result of problems associated with decolonization in Eritrea and dictatorship in Ethiopia, dating back to the 1950s and 1960s.

The Italians colonized Eritrea in 1890.[145] They then invaded Ethiopia in 1896 but failed miserably. A second assault by Mussolini's forces in 1935 succeeded in driving Haile Selassie from his throne in Addis Ababa.[146] When World War II broke out, the British army defeated Italian forces and occupied both Ethiopia and Eritrea in 1941.[147]

During the war, British authorities differed with U.S. officials about the future of Eritrea. British officials argued that "the best solution for Eritrea would be its partition between Ethiopia and the Sudan in such as way as to allow the Eritrean Abyssinians [Christians] to join their kinsmen in Ethiopia and the Moslem tribes of western Eritrea to be incorporated into the Sudan."[148]

Roosevelt, however, told Churchill in 1944 that Eritrea should be handed over to Ethiopia, a position enthusiastically received by Selassie.[149] But because the two great powers could not agree, the matter was turned over to the United Nations in 1948. Two years later, the UN General Assembly adopted a resolution that Eritrea should "constitute an autonomous unit federated with Ethiopia under the sovereignty of the Ethiopian Crown" and provided Eritrea with "legislative, executive, and judicial powers in the field of domestic affairs."[150]

Initially, decolonization in Eritrea resulted in its assignment to Ethiopia, neither independent nor incorporated. But Selassie was not content to possess Eritrea partially. So during the next ten years, he banned political parties and unions in Eritrea, cracked down on dissidents, imposed Amharic as the official language, installed Ethiopians in government posts, suspended the Eritrean constitution, forcibly persuaded the assembly to change the name of the government from the "Eritrean Government" to the "Eritrean Administration" in 1960, and finally, in 1962, formally annexed Eritrea as a province of Ethiopia.[151] Whereas decolonization in some countries led to partition in this period, decolonization and dictatorship led in this instance to Eritrea's incorporation by Ethiopia.

Ethiopia's slow-moving *anschluss* was driven by the expansionary character of the Ethiopian monarchy, which had built an empire outside its highland base during the previous century and now wanted access to the Red Sea through ports in Eritrea.[152] Selassie argued that Eritrea "is not economically a self-contained state . . . [but] part of a larger picture, which is Abyssinia plus Eritrea," and he maintained that the populations of southern Eritrea and northern Ethiopia "are as similar as the people of Nebraska and Kansas."[153]

The dictatorship was able to achieve its goals in Eritrea because it found support for its policies among some groups in Eritrea and, more important, from the United States.

During the 1940s, different movements emerged in Eritrea. The Muslim League and other smaller Islamic parties demanded an independent state, while the Unionist Party, representing Christian groups, demanded union with Ethiopia, much like supporters of *enosis* in Cyprus sought union with Greece.[154] Their disagreements made it difficult for the United Nations to grant either independence or union, so the United Nations split the difference, making it an "autonomous unit federated with Ethiopia." In the 1952 elections, the Unionists won thirty-two of the sixty-eight seats in the assembly.[155] During his decade-long campaign to incorporate Eritrea, Selassie used the Unionist Party's popularity to argue that Eritreans had given annexation a political mandate.[156] Selassie was able to outmaneuver Eritrean parties, which were divided along confessional and political lines, and wrest autonomous government from them.[157]

The dictatorship evaded UN condemnation and possible intervention on Eritrea's behalf because U.S. officials supported Selassie's annexationist policies. During the 1940s, U.S. officials backed the idea of assigning Eritrea to Ethiopia after the British occupation expired, largely because they worried that an independent Eritrea would be a "weak state exposed to Soviet aggression" and because they wanted its Red Sea frontage in secure, allied hands.[158] But U.S. officials left the decolonization of Eritrea to the United Nations. The outbreak of the Korean War in 1950, and the need for air bases and communications facilities along the Red Sea coast, persuaded U.S. officials to support Selassie's annexationist aspirations. Secretary of State John Foster Dulles told the United Nations in 1952, "From the point of view of justice, the opinions of the Eritrean people must receive consideration. Nevertheless the strategic interests of the United States in the Red Sea basin . . . make it necessary that the country *has* to be linked with our ally, Ethiopia [emphasis added]."[159]

The following year, Ethiopia agreed to a twenty-five-year lease for U.S. military bases in Eritrea. In return, the United States provided Selassie with economic and military aid and defended his policies in Eritrea.[160]

Of course, decolonization and dictatorship angered independence-minded Eritreans, particularly the Moslem population, and many came to view Ethiopian rule as "a form of colonial subjugation no different from that of Italian or British colonialism."[161] Although the independence movement had been weak and divided in the 1940s and 1950s, a decade of tightening Ethiopian rule led to the organization of Marxist "national liberation" movements—the Eritrean Liberation Movement in 1958 and the Eritrean Liberation Front in 1960—that took up arms against the monarchist regime to secure Eritrean independence.[162] Fighting began in 1961 and would continue for thirty more years. Eritrean movements generally cooperated during the 1960s, but fought each other in 1972–1974, and then they cooperated during the 1970s and 1980s, though organizational splits in 1970 and 1976 complicated relations and made military coordination difficult.[163] Although Eritrean movements received some financial aid from Sudan, Syria, and Saudi Arabia, their efforts were largely self-sufficient. They received no assistance from either superpower and no legal support or recognition from international groups such as the United Nations or Organization of African Unity.[164] In addition, they faced a formidable set of opponents: monarchist and then communist dictatorships in Ethiopia, supported in turn by the United States and the Soviet Union, and assisted in the field by Cuban and Israeli forces.

Ethiopia is a poor country, one of the poorest in the world. Selassie's regime was able to survive economically in the 1950s and 1960s because U.S. military aid furnished it with weapons to keep Eritrean insurgents at bay, while U.S. economic aid covered the country's perennial trade deficits.[165] Selassie survived politically because he managed to defeat a 1960 military coup and successfully divided and isolated potential challengers in his government.[166] But in 1973, the regime was beset by multiple crises. First, a drought led to famine, which killed more than two hundred thousand people.[167] The government's ungainly efforts to cover up the disaster and its refusal to accept food relief triggered widespread outrage and dismay. Second, the OPEC oil embargo raised oil prices and threw the fragile economy into disarray.[168] These developments, and the growing perception that the aging Selassie could not cope with mounting problems, prompted a successful military coup in September 1974.[169] Monarchist dictatorship was replaced by a communist regime organized by the Coordinating Committee of the Armed Forces, which became known as the Dergue (Amharinya for "Committee").[170]

After taking power, the Dergue faced problems associated with famine and poverty. They were also confronted by three political challenges.[171] In the capital, civilian Marxists agitated against the government, demanding power on behalf of the country's workers and peasants. Some took up arms and attempted to assassinate Dergue leaders.[172] The regime also antagonized other ethnic groups, particularly the Omoro and people in Tigre province, and Marxist opponents of the regime in that region took up arms against it in 1976.[173] In Eritrea, the regime faced insurgents who had resolved their factional disputes and began to cooperate in the field. Although the Dergue initially tried to negotiate a settlement with Eritrean forces, it soon adopted Selassie's policy of using force to crush the rebellion.[174] It tried to mobilize a peasant army to march against Eritrean forces in 1976, a "kind of Christian holy war against [Moslem] Eritreans."[175] But this ill-conceived venture ended in disaster, as Eritrean forces mauled the unprepared peasant army and then took to the offensive, securing important gains in 1977–1978.[176] Meanwhile, neighboring Somalia, governed since 1969 by a communist military regime backed by the Soviet Union, renewed its claims to Ethiopian lands in the Ogaden Desert.[177] Guerrilla incursions and then a full-scale invasion by Siad Barre's army in 1977–1978 drove Ethiopian forces from much of the disputed region.

In addition to these troubles, the Dergue was consumed by internal fighting—many of its leaders were killed in a bloody shoot-out in 1977—and was being abandoned by the United States.[178] U.S. officials began cutting aid and withdrawing support for the regime, partly to express U.S displeasure with its increasingly communist orientation and its brutality toward domestic opponents, but primarily because they no longer needed U.S. military bases in Eritrea, which had been made obsolete by new satellite technology.[179] The approaching expiration of the lease for the bases gave U.S. officials the opportunity to withdraw and abandon the regime to its many Marxist opponents, foreign and domestic.

To survive, Mengistu Haile Miriam, who became head of the Dergue as a result of the shoot-out, asked the Soviet Union for assistance. The Soviets responded enthusiastically in 1977 because they, like the United States previously, wanted an ally on the Red Sea.[180] To secure this alliance and defend the regime, Soviet leaders abandoned Somalia, a longtime client, airlifted seventeen thousand Cuban troops to fight for the Ethiopians in the Ogaden, and provided the regime with arms and aid, amounting to perhaps $11 billion over the next thirteen years.[181] To counter the Soviets, U.S. officials then began supporting the communist government in Somalia, a decision that would later lead to U.S. intervention there.

By 1978, massive Soviet aid and Cuban arms drove back the Somali invaders, helped the Ethiopian army to contain and reverse Eritrean gains, and gave Mengistu the means to crush civilian Marxist opponents. Some three thousand to ten thousand people died at the hands of the regime in 1977 and 1978.[182] Having escaped this crisis, the regime then survived in the 1980s because it received important help from other unlikely sources.

In the early 1980s, famine struck Ethiopia again, with even greater severity than it had in 1973–1974, and nearly one-third of its population faced starvation.[183] But whereas famine in the 1970s had crippled Selassie's government, famine in the 1980s assisted Mengistu's regime.[184] Famine undermined Selassie's rule because the government tried to cover it up and refused international food aid. But Mengistu appealed for relief, the international community responded with more than $2 billion in aid, and "the large influx of famine relief aid in 1984 and 1986 served almost as a blessing in disguise for the Dergue."[185]

The Dergue also found Israel to be an important source of military and financial support. During the late 1970s, Israeli pilots had flown combat missions for the government because they wanted to assist Ethiopia against Moslem opponents in Eritrea and Somalia.[186] Then in the 1980s, Israeli officials developed an interest in Ethiopian Jews, or "Falashas," who had lived in Ethiopia since biblical times. In 1984, the Israelis airlifted several hundred Falashas, who had taken refuge from famine in Sudan, to Israel.[187] But thousands more remained in Ethiopia. Then in the late 1980s, Mengistu agreed to let some Falashas emigrate to Israel in return for Israeli arms and aid.[188] As the Dergue weakened, it demanded more arms and aid from Israel; Israel insisted on more rapid emigration.[189] They came to terms in 1991, and Israel airlifted 14,200 Falashas from Ethiopia to Israel in thirty-four hours.[190]

Foreign aid from diverse sources helped the regime survive the 1980s. But when Gorbachev cut Soviet aid to communist regimes around the world in the late 1980s and began withdrawing Cuban troops from Ethiopia, the regime began to unravel.[191] Ethiopia had amassed a $3 billion debt, a huge amount given the size of its economy, and had become *the* poorest country in the world.[192] In 1988, insurgent forces in Eritrea and Tigre had become strong enough to mount a new offensive, killing or capturing eighteen thousand Ethiopian troops.[193] And in 1991, Eritrean forces besieged Asmara and Massawa and began pushing, with anti-Mengistu Marxist rebels from Tigre, toward the Ethiopian capital of Addis Ababa. As the military situation deteriorated, Mengistu fled by plane to Kenya on May 21, the besieged armies in Asmara and Massawa surrendered, and the capital fell to insurgent armies one week later.[194]

In July 1991, Ethiopian rebels who had seized the capital agreed that Eritrea had a right to secede from Ethiopia and that a 1993 referendum would decide whether Eritrea would become an independent state. Two years later, on April 27, 1993, Eritreans voted overwhelmingly for independence, and Ethiopia was formally divided.[195]

In Ethiopia, partition *un*did the decolonization and annexation of an earlier era. To some extent, Eritrean separation was similar to the departure of the Baltic states from the Soviet Union. The success of the Eritrean independence movements is remarkable, given the political forces arrayed against it. It is notable too because, after 1974, all of its opponents, save Israel, were communists. To a large extent, the struggle in Ethiopia was a battle among different communist factions, much as it was in the Soviet Union and Yugoslavia. One might have expected communists to get along with one another. But they did not. The battles among them left a bitter legacy. Internecine civil war claimed 400,000 civilian lives in Eritrea and Ethiopia, some 600,000 Ethiopian soldiers were killed or reported as missing inaction between 1974 and 1991, 625,000 Eritrean refugees fled into Sudan, and 3,000 to 10,000 Ethiopian civilians were killed by the regime in 1977–1978.[196] These grim statistics do not include the hundreds of thousands who died from famine, which was caused in part by heavy military spending in a country that could ill afford it.

Democratization did not typically lead to partition. Of the thirty countries that democratized around the world between 1974 and 1994, only three were divided. Even in Eastern Europe, most of the communist regimes transferred power to civilians in unitary states. So why did democratization lead to partition only in Yugoslavia, the Soviet Union, and Czechoslovakia?

In all three states, uneven economic development and regional inequality created different economic interests that drove people in opposite political directions. People in the more prosperous republics supported greater political autonomy and an end to the redistributive policies of the central government. People in the poorer regions generally supported central government and the benefits provided by redistributive programs. Separate economic interests laid the groundwork for partition as a political solution.

Partition was also legitimized by constitutional provisions that had been adopted by communist parties. Yugoslavia and Czechoslovakia used the Soviet constitution as the model for theirs. These constitutions created federal states with constituent republics, each with rudimentary political institutions for party officials and government functionaries, and each republic was defined, more or less, in ethnic terms. These constitutions all guaranteed constituent republics the right of self-determination, including the right to secession, a legacy of early Leninist thinking. Of course, communist regimes for many years permitted constituent republics very little real power, prevented ethnic identity from assuming any serious political expression, treated constitutional rights as being rhetorical rather than substantive, and never imagined that ethnic groups in the republics might actually try to exercise their constitutional prerogatives. But when crisis emerged, central governments could not easily prevent communist party factions from reviving moribund institutions, mobilizing ethnic identities, and demanding constitutional rights. To a large extent, the road to partition was paved in advance by communist constitutions.

Communist party factions were able to create ethnic political movements in the constituent republics because each had histories of independence or oppression that could be used to forge "national" identities. By recalling a time when their country was independent, they could imagine a future when it might be sovereign again.

Of course, federal governments typically oppose the devolution of central power, constitutional provisions notwithstanding. But in all of these states, central government authority had been decisively weakened by ongoing economic crisis and persistent political factionalism. The inability of presidents to mobilize constituencies outside the government in defense of union critically weakened central government authority. Without political allies, they could not easily resist devolutionary pressures and centrifugal forces.

Partition in these three countries, and also in Ethiopia, had familiar consequences for the two dozen successor states that emerged. Generally speaking, partition contributed to problems associated with cross-border migrations, discrimination against residual minority populations, and conflicts over the sovereign rights of successor states, though the scale and intensity of these problems varied widely.

In Czechoslovakia, cross-border migrations were small, while in Yugoslavia hundreds of thousands crossed frontiers to escape the fighting. Migration in the post-Soviet republics is difficult to establish, but it was considerable. Given the fact that more than twenty-five million ethnic Russians reside outside Russia, and every republic has large residential minorities, the potential for further migration is vast.[197] The same is true in Ethiopia, where a quarter million Eritreans reside.[198] The more immediate problem in Ethiopia and Eritrea is how to demobilize tens of thousands of soldiers, repatriate hundreds of thousands of refugees living in Eritrea, Ethiopia, and Sudan, and accommodate the return of eighty thousand political exiles from countries around the world.[199]

Although partition triggered cross-border migrations, many people stayed put. Unfortunately, many successor states took steps to discriminate against residual minority populations. Discrimination has taken myriad forms, and it would be difficult to describe them all in detail. A few examples will suffice. Some states refused to grant citizenship automatically to some ethnic residents, insisting that they first meet stringent residency requirements or pass difficult language tests, while at the same time they awarded citizenship to people with ethnic affinities who were already citizens of other states, practices common in the Baltic republics.[200] In the Czech Republic, the government granted citizenship to 360,000 Slovaks between 1993 and 1995, easing relations between the two major ethnic groups, but it routinely denied citizenship to Gypsies.[201] In Slovakia, the government declared that it would be a nation for Slovaks, despite the fact that one-fifth of the population claims Hungarian, Gypsy, and Ruthen identities.[202] In the post-Soviet republics, the adoption of official languages has handicapped residents who speak other languages, preventing them from accessing government services, running for office, or attending universities. Naturally, these developments have antagonized minority groups, persuading some to migrate and others to protest government policies.

What's more, many of the successor states have not really democratized. In Slovakia, in some republics in Yugoslavia, and in many of the post-Soviet states, power was transferred to former communists who quickly established authoritarian regimes. These dictatorships have adopted policies that discriminate against public participation by minority and majority groups alike. This has led to further struggles for democratization in many successor states.

Partition has also led to disputes over the sovereignty of successor states. In Yugoslavia, residual minorities and newly established governments contested the borders between successor states. Post-Soviet republics argued not only about their territorial boundaries but also the division of nuclear arms, military assets, and national debts. Some successor states were given diplomatic recognition, given aid, and admitted to the United Nations or NATO. But others were not. Macedonia was for many years denied international recognition as a sovereign state because Greece objected to its use of the name "Macedonia." Many successor states argue that preferential treatment for some states is a form of diplomatic discrimination.

While some of these disputes are symbolic, they are important because governments use symbols to assert their identity as sovereign states. When Croatia introduced a new currency called the "Kuna," neighboring states and indigenous minorities objected because the Kuna was the currency used by the fascist government in Croatia during World War II, a regime that massacred Serbs and Jews.[203]

Symbolic disputes can also lead to real conflicts. In 1998, governments in Ethiopia and Eritrea, which had been allies in the war against the Mengistu regime, made territorial claims on a small chunk of land along their common border, a dispute described by one observer as akin to two bald men fighting over a comb. The Eritrean regime's decision to close its Red Sea ports to Ethiopian access reignited war between the successor states, and battles raged along the frontier.[204]

Partition in the 1990s contributed to problems associated with migration, citizenship, and sovereignty within and between many of the successor states. But problems have not necessarily led to conflict and war, as it did so often in states divided by great, superpower, and regional powers in earlier years. Of course, partition led immediately to war among successor states in Yugoslavia. But relations between Czech and Slovak republics have been amicable. And partition in the Soviet Union resulted in conflict between some, but not all, of the successor states.

Why did partition ignite war in Yugoslavia but not in Czechoslovakia? And why did war erupt in some but not all parts of the Soviet Union? The answer, I think, has a lot to do with the historical experiences and policies of central governments prior to partition in each of these states.

In Yugoslavia, partition led to war because Tito's celebration of civil war in the 1940s helped legitimize renewed civil war in the 1990s, because his military policies prepared citizens to wage partisan war, and because leaders of central government institutions were determined not to redistribute power after Tito died.

It is often said that war contributes to state building. This was certainly true of Yugoslavia. The Communist Party's successful partisan war against Axis invaders and its civil war against domestic fascist and royalist forces during World War II enabled Tito to assume power and then build a socialist state.[205] Because force of arms enabled Tito to defeat foreign and domestic opponents during the war, and then deter Soviet intervention after it, the regime celebrated civil war and memorialized its violence in schools and in the media as a heroic, purposeful activity throughout the postwar period.[206] But by celebrating civil war, the regime helped sanction violence and legitimize future civil war.

In a landmark global study of the relation between war and homicide, sociologists Dane Archer and Rosemary Gartner found that homicide rates increased in states that went to war, particularly in states that were *victorious* in battle.[207] They explained this phenomenon by arguing "that wars do tend to legitimate the general use of violence in domestic society" because they teach the unmistakable moral lesson that homicide is an acceptable, even praiseworthy, means to certain ends . . . [a] lesson [that] will not be lost on at least some of the citizens in a warring nation."[208] They noted that murder rates were less likely to rise in countries defeated in war, arguing that because citizens in these countries viewed war as sense*less*, public defeat effectively discouraged private acts of violence.[209] By analogy, Tito's decades-long celebration of brutal civil war, his insistence that it was purposeful and helped build socialism in Yugoslavia, may have helped convince many citizens that civil war was a legitimate way to settle disputes in the 1990s.

Of course, many governments memorialize interstate war. Relatively few, however, celebrate civil war, because it antagonizes defeated coresidential groups. Tito's regime not only memorialized civil war, it also adopted policies that prepared people to *wage* civil war.

In the late 1950s, the government adopted "General People's Defense" as a central part of its military doctrine.[210] It then conscripted, trained, and armed citizens to serve in territorial defense forces and militias based in the republics. These units were expected to wage a guerrilla war against any invader, much as communist partisans had done during World War II. The regime adopted partisan war as a military doctrine because it had been effective during World War II, because Soviet invasions (of Hungary and later Czechoslovakia and Afghanistan) reinforced the regime's fear of invasion, and because military leaders thought that an armed-nation approach to defense (like that deployed in Switzerland and Israel) was sound military policy.[211] So the government distributed advanced military weapons and communications equipment among its citizens, who were versed in the martial arts.[212]

The problem with this doctrine was that the armed citizenry might turn their guns on their neighbors, not foreign invaders. As Adam Roberts, a prescient military analyst, observed in 1986, "The Yugoslav defense system rests on fragile social and political foundations. If those foundations fail, the idea of General People's Defense might be quickly forgotten; or worse, it might be perversely misused for civil war."[213]

As it happened, the regime's military policy organized and prepared a heavily armed populace to wage war on their own initiative. If military arms and radios had not been stockpiled and widely distributed around the country in the years before partition, it would have been difficult for militias in the republics to resist the army's initial advance or then to initiate and coordinate violence along postpartition frontiers.

Of course, Titoist policies are not wholly responsible for the outbreak of war. Communist Party factions could not agree on a process to devolve or redistribute power after Tito's death. Still, the political impasse of the early 1990s need not have led to war if the Yugoslav army had retired after its initial incursions were rebuffed by militias in Croatia and Slovenia, and the central government had surrendered its authority without complaint. But military and political leaders in Serbia and Montenegro were determined to reassert central government authority and assist Serb minorities living in the breakaway republics. When Serbs organized militias to assert their sovereignty over territories in Croatia and Bosnia, civil war erupted. They were then assisted by remnants of the Yugoslav army and the residual central government in Belgrade.

Central government authorities were able to help Serb militias and wage war against the armies of breakaway republics because the military and bureaucracy were relatively popular political institutions, at least among Serbs, the largest ethnic group in Yugoslavia. Central government institutions were popular because they represented a regime (dating back to World War II) that had defeated foreign invaders and domestic adversaries, resisted incorporation into the Soviet sphere of influence, developed an independent foreign policy, and promoted economic development, at least for a time. When crisis struck, Tito's successors in Belgrade could call on a considerable reservoir of domestic political support. Because Milosevic's regime was seen by many Serbs as Tito's legitimate heir, and because the army could claim that it was defending Serb minorities outside the boundaries of the residual Yugoslav state, the central government could use force to contest partition.[214] Their determination to resist partition led to widespread violence and multisided civil war, first in Croatia, then in Bosnia, and more recently in Kosovo, a province of Serbia.

Partition had very different consequences in Czechoslovakia, largely because the institutions of the unitary state were extremely weak. In this setting, central government weakness made it possible for partition to have a peaceful outcome.

Historical developments and contemporary events combined to weaken the unitary state in Czechoslovakia. As an institution, the state had been repeatedly compromised by foreign powers and domestic elites. At Munich in 1938, the great powers abrogated the state's sovereign authority, allowing Germany to annex Czechoslovakia and then divide it. At Yalta in 1945, the superpowers assigned Czechoslovakia to the Soviet sphere of influence, allowing the Soviet Union and its domestic allies in Czechoslovakia to dissolve the elected government and establish a communist regime in 1948. In 1968, the Soviet Union and its allies invaded Czechoslovakia, overthrew Dubcek's reform government, and reorganized the regime under new leaders. And in 1989, Gorbachev's decision to withdraw Soviet military guarantees for the regime it had installed in 1968 dealt communist rule a fatal blow. Successive interventions had crippled, compromised, and constrained the state in Czechoslovakia, making it difficult for central government officials to exercise or enjoy any real sovereignty.

Domestic political elites also undermined the strength of state institutions by conceding power without a fight in 1938, 1948, 1968, and 1989. Because state officials did not resist foreign intervention or, in 1989, domestic protest, central government institutions were not tested or tempered as organizations, so they were unable to make a concerted effort to defend the state. What's more, political elites had long recognized rights and provided institutions for Slovaks, as distinct from Czechs, in the unitary state.[215] Although these constitutional provisions were frequently ignored, neglected, or abrogated, they legitimated demands for greater Slovak autonomy and thereby undermined the constitutional authority of the unitary state, much as the Soviet and Yugoslav constitutions provided a legal basis for self-determination and secession in the constituent republics.[216]

As demands for Slovak autonomy and then independence grew after 1989, central government authority was severely tested. But the institutions that might have been expected to defend the union were unable or unwilling to do so.

The bureaucracy did not rally to defend the unitary state because democratization and the passage of the lustration law, which barred former Communists from public office, forced many bureaucrats from the government. They were replaced by public servants with little experience, and many of them had obtained their jobs as a result of political appointments. Because they owed their allegiance to political parties, not the civil service as an institution, and because many of them agreed with Klaus that the state's role should be extremely limited, they were reluctant to defend the unitary state. So when the two leading parties decided to divide the state between them, this inexperienced and timid bureaucracy followed their lead.

Much the same is true of the army. In most countries, the army is organized and prepared to defend the state against foreign invasion and domestic insurgency. In Yugoslavia and the Soviet Union, the army intervened forcefully to prevent the dissolution of the state and the division of the country. So why didn't the Czechoslovak army attempt to do the same? It did not because several developments had weakened it as an institution. First, the army had no combat experience, in either foreign or domestic wars. The army had only fought once, briefly, at the end of World War II, and then only under Soviet direction. When invasion or uprising threatened in 1938, 1948, 1968, and 1989, state officials had asked the army *not* to fight, even though the state was in mortal jeopardy, and the army complied.[217]

Second, the Soviets had insisted that the army be purged of politically "unreliable" officers in 1948 and again in 1968. Successive purges and defections crippled the army as an effective military organization.[218] Indeed, Soviet policy so weakened the army that they could not rely on it to fulfill its treaty commitments or assist its allies. For example, the Soviet Union did not even ask the Czechoslovak army to help train third world allies, much less participate as combat troops in places such as Ethiopia.[219] The Soviets invited Cuban troops to campaign in Africa, but not forces from Czechoslovakia. Third, after 1989, the army was reduced in size and many troops demobilized, leading to widespread demoralization in the ranks and declining public confidence in it as an institution.[220] Given these developments, it is not surprising that military leaders were unwilling to defend the unitary state or risk war on its behalf.

As partition approached, the only institution willing to defend the state was the executive. President Havel argued that the state should not be divided. But as noted previously, he had few constitutional powers to prevent it and no mass-based political party that could be rallied to defend it.

Because the institutions that might, in other countries, defend the state were weak in Czechoslovakia, the unitary state fell when Czech and Slovak politicians combined against it. Elites representing the two largest regional parties simply negotiated a division of state power. The fact that President Havel was unable to put the constitutional questions associated with partition to an electoral test—this *despite* widespread public support for a unitary state in both regions—demonstrates the fundamental weakness of the state.[221]

In contrast to events in Yugoslavia, partition in Czechoslovakia was peacefully accomplished. But this was due primarily to the fact that the two parties *agreed* that partition was in their mutual interest and the fact that the state was too *weak* to resist. If Klaus and Meciar had disagreed about the division and devolution of power, or if the unitary state had been stronger and willing to resist partition, events could well have taken a different, perhaps violent turn. Ironically, the weakness of the state made it possible for partition to proceed without violence. But where these conditions do not obtain, where people disagree and central government is strong, a peaceful result is much less likely.

In the Soviet Union, political disagreements were sharper and the central government was stronger than they were in Czechoslovakia; political differences were less acute and the central government was weaker than then they were in Yugoslavia. Political differences among Gorbachev and other factions based in the republics were fairly acrimonious, but Gorbachev was not as stubborn as Milosevic. It was difficult for him to preserve central government authority because faction fighting had eroded its political authority and deepening economic crisis had undermined its economic credibility. Under these conditions, Gorbachev was willing to devolve considerable central government authority to the republics under the revised Union Treaty. Unlike Havel, he was nonetheless strong enough to insist that devolution be put to an electoral test. Of course, some members of his government were determined to defend central government authority and mounted a coup. But the mass-based Communist Party, which they expected to rally in defense of the unitary state, had been weakened by defections to new parties based in the republics. Moreover, the army had been demoralized by defeat in Afghanistan, by the demobilizations associated with Gorbachev's military reforms, and by the defection of officers to armies in the republics. The central government's political and military institutions were unwilling to save the unitary state, and the bureaucrats could not defend it alone. So the coup collapsed with a minimum of violence, and the devolution of central government power accelerated. Partition was accomplished with minimal violence because most factions agreed that the dissolution of central power was in their mutual interest and because the institutions of the unitary state were too weak to resist violently.

Of course, once the Soviet Union was partitioned, leaders of the new republics were determined to create strong states and defend them against neighboring states or domestic opponents. And this has led to conflict within and between states in some parts of the former Soviet Union, particularly in the Caucasus. But partition in the Soviet Union has led both to war and peace. For the Soviet Union, the Caucasus is its Yugoslavia, the Baltics its Czechoslovakia.

NOTES

1. See Robert K. Schaeffer, *Power to the People: Democratization around the World* (Boulder, Colo.: Westview, 1997).

2. Richard Sakwa, *Gorbachev and His Reforms, 1985–1990* (Upper Saddle River, N.J.: Prentice Hall, 1990), 282–83.

3. Walter LaFeber, *America, Russia and the Cold War, 1945–85* (New York: Knopf, 1985), 70.

4. William Zimmerman, *Open Borders, Nonalignment, and the Political Evolution of Yugoslavia* (Princeton, N.J.: Princeton University Press, 1987), 18, 22–23; Duncan Wilson, *Tito's Yugoslavia* (Cambridge: Cambridge University Press, 1979), 68, 75; Di-

jana Plestina, "From 'Democratic Centralism' to Decentralized Democracy? Trials and Tribulations of Yugoslavia's Development," in *Yugoslavia in Transition: Choices and Constraints*, ed. John B. Allcock, John L. Horton, and Marko Milivojevic (New York: Berg, 1992), 132–33.

    5. Schaeffer, *Power to the People*, 65–69.

    6. Jasminka Udovicki, "Nationalism, Ethnic Conflict and Self-Determination in the Former Yugoslavia," in *The National Question: Nationalism, Ethnic Conflict and Self-Determination in the 20th Century*, ed. Berge Berberoglu (Philadelphia: Temple University Press, 1995), 292; Milan Mesic, "External Migration in the Context of the Post-War Development of Yugoslavia," in Allcock, Horton, and Milivojevic, *Yugoslavia in Transition*, 180; Carl-Ulrik Shierup, *Migration, Socialism and the International Division of Labor: The Yugoslav Experience* (Aldershot, England: Avebury, 1990), 18, 77.

    7. Wilson, *Tito's Yugoslavia*, 156, 232, 238–39.

    8. Caglar Keyder, "The American Recovery of Southern Europe: Aid and Hegemony," in *Semiperipheral Development: The Role of Southern Europe in the 20th Century*, ed. Giovanni Arrighi (Beverly Hills, Calif.: Sage, 1985), 135, 145.

    9. J. N. Stevens, *Czechoslovakia at the Crossroads: The Economic Dilemmas of Communism in Postwar Czechoslovakia* (New York: Columbia University Press, 1985), 45; R. Shen, *Economic Reform in Poland and Czechoslovakia: Lessons in Systemic Transformation* (Westport, Conn.: Praeger, 1993), 52–53, 61, 72–73; J. Batt, *East-Central Europe: From Reform to Transformation* (London: Pinter, 1988), 92.

    10. G. Golan, *Reform Rule in Czechoslovakia: The Dubcek Era 1968–1969* (Cambridge: Cambridge University Press, 1973), 35, 37.

    11. Golan, *Reform Rule in Czechoslovakia*, 39–40.

    12. Daniel Yergin, *The Prize: The Epic Quest for Oil, Money and Power* (New York: Simon & Schuster, 1991), 625; Ernst J. Oliveri, *Latin American Debt and the Politics of International Finance* (Westport, Conn.: Praeger, 1992), 11; Nick Butler, *The International Grain Trade* (New York: St. Martin's, 1986), 55; Robert K. Schaeffer, *Understanding Globalization: The Social Consequences of Political, Economic, and Environmental Change* (Latham, Md.: Rowman & Littlefield, 1997), 147–48.

    13. Adam Zwass, *From Failed Communism to Underdeveloped Capitalism: The Transformation of Eastern Europe, the Post-Soviet Union and China* (Armonk, N.Y.: Sharpe, 1995), 147; Thomas W. Simons, Jr., *Eastern Europe in the Postwar World* (New York: St. Martin's, 1991), 160.

    14. David A. Dyker, *Restructuring the Soviet Economy* (London: Routledge, 1992), 103; Silviu Brucan, *The Post-Brezhnev Era: An Insider's View* (New York: Praeger, 1983), 83; Marshall I. Goldman, *Gorbachev's Challenge: Economic Reform in the Age of High Technology* (New York: Norton, 1987), 77; John Sallnow, *Reform in the Soviet Union: Glastnost and the Future* (New York: St. Martin's, 1989), 19; John Walton and David Seddon, *Free Markets and Food Riots: The Politics of Global Adjustment* (Oxford: Blackwell, 1994), 295; Edward C. Cook, "Agriculture's Role in the Soviet Economic

Crisis," in *The Disintegration of the Soviet Economic System*, ed. Michael Ellman and Vladimir Kontorovich (London: Routledge, 1992), 203.

15. Michael Bernhard, *The Origins of Democratization in Poland: Workers, Intellectuals, and Oppositional Politics, 1976–1980* (New York: Columbia University Press, 1993), 39, 41; Robin Alison Remington, "Polish Soldiers in Politics: The Party in Uniform?" in *The Decline of Military Regimes: The Civilian Influence*, ed. Constantine P. Danopoulos (Boulder, Colo.: Westview, 1988), 84; Walton and Seddon, *Free Markets and Food Riots*, 292; Simons, *Eastern Europe in the Postwar World*, 156.

16. Michael Moffitt, *The World's Money: International Banking from Bretton Woods to the Brink of Insolvency* (New York: Simon & Schuster, 1983), 46. "The term 'Eurodollar' can be misleading, for it is often used to describe any currency holding outside the issuing country. Thus a Japanese yen deposit in the Panamanian international banking center can sometimes be included, as can U.S. dollar deposits in a London financial institution." Victor Blumer-Thomas, *The Economic History of Latin America since Independence* (Cambridge: Cambridge University Press, 1994), 360.

17. Sue Brnaford and Bernardo Kucinski, *The Debt Squads: The U.S., the Banks and Latin America* (London: Zed, 1988), 58.

18. Schaeffer, *Power to the People*, 176–77.

19. Marshall I. Goldman, *U.S.S.R. in Crisis: The Failure of an Economic System* (New York: Norton, 1983), 137; Sakwa, *Gorbachev and His Reforms*, 284; Michael Kaser and Michael Maltby, "Foreign Trade," in *Gorbachev and Perestroika*, ed. Martin McCauley (New York: St. Martin's, 1990), 97; Anders Aslund, *Gorbachev's Struggle for Economic Reform* (Ithaca, N.Y.: Cornell University Press, 1991), 197; Alan Smith, *Russia and the World Economy: Problems of Integration* (London: Routledge, 1993), 121, 158; J. Prusl, J. Carter, A. Cheasty, D. V. Christensen, I. Hansen, N. U. Haque, and T. van der Willigen, *The Czech and Slovak Federal Republic: An Economy in Transition*, (Washington, D.C.: International Monetary Fund, 1990), 22; Christopher Bennett, *Yugoslavia's Bloody Collapse: Causes, Course and Consequences* (New York: New York University Press, 1995), 69; Ljubomir Madzar, "The Economy of Yugoslavia: Structure, Growth Record and Institutional Framework," in Allcock, Horton, and Milivojevic, *Yugoslavia in Transition*, 84.

20. Hugh Kay, *Salazar and Modern Portugal* (New York: Hawthorn, 1970), 68–69, 88, 157, 158–60.

21. Constantine Tsoucalas, *The Greek Tragedy* (Harmondsworth, U.K.: Penguin, 1969), 123; Robert P. Clark, *The Basques: The Franco Years and Beyond* (Reno: University of Nevada Press, 1979), 94.

22. I. Sunjain and M. Sujanova, "The Macroeconomic Situation in the Czech Republic," in *The Czech Republic and Economic Transition in Eastern Europe*. ed. J. Svejnar (San Diego, Calif.: Academic Press, 1995), 120.

23. K. Dyhba and J. Svejnar, "A Comparative View of Economic Developments in the Czech Republic," in Svejnar, *The Czech Republic*, 22.

24. David A. Dyker, *Yugoslavia: Socialism, Development and Debt* (London: Routledge, 1990), 131–32; Susan L. Woodward, *Balkan Tragedy: Chaos and Dissolution After the Cold War* (Washington, D.C.: Brookings Institution, 1995), 52, 55, 82, 96; Walton and Seddon, *Free Markets and Food Riots*, 298–99.

25. Walton and Seddon, *Free Markets and Foods Riots*, 321; Plestina, "From 'Democratic Centralism' to Decentralized Democracy?" 152.

26. Sakwa, *Gorbachev and His Reforms*, 22.

27. Sallnow, *Reform in the Soviet Union*, 11–13; Zwass, *From Failed Communism to Underdeveloped Capitalism*, 62.

28. Remington, "Polish Soldiers in Politics," 86–87; Zwass, *From Failed Communism to Underdeveloped Capitalism*, 143.

29. Gales Stokes, *From Stalinism to Pluralism: A Documentary History of Eastern Europe since 1945* (New York: Oxford University Press, 1991), 214–15.

30. Stephen White, *After Gorbachev* (Cambridge: Cambridge University Press, 1993), 211.

31. Barnett R. Rubin, *The Search for Peace in Afghanistan: From Buffer State to Failed State* (New Haven, Conn.: Yale University Press, 1995), 29, 63; Peter W. Rodman, *More Precious Than Peace: The Cold War and the Struggle for the Third World* (New York: Scribner's, 1994), 206.

32. Rubin, *The Search for Peace in Afghanistan*, 63; Rodman, *More Precious Than Peace*, 315; White, *After Gorbachev*, 212.

33. Rodman, *More Precious Than Peace*, 327–28.

34. White, *After Gorbachev*, 4.

35. White, *After Gorbachev*, 5.

36. White, *After Gorbachev*, 7–8.

37. Marshall I. Goldman, "The Future of Soviet Economic Reform," *Current History* (October 1989): 329.

38. Aslund, *Gorbachev's Struggle*, 28.

39. Aslund, *Gorbachev's Struggle*, 34.

40. Ruth Sivard, *World Military and Social Expenditures, 1987–88* (Washington, D.C.: World Priorities, 1988), 5, 54–55; Somnath Sen, "The Economics of Conversion: Transforming Swords into Plowshares," in *Economic Reform in Eastern Europe*, ed. Braham Bird (Brookfield, Vt.: Elgar, 1992), 26; Sallnow, *Reform in the Soviet Union*, 85; Sakwa, *Gorbachev and His Reforms*, 335; Henry S. Rowen and Charles Wolf, eds., *The Impoverished Superpower: Perestroika and the Soviet Military Burden* (San Francisco: Institute for Contemporary Studies Press, 1990), 7.

41. Walton and Seddon, *Free Markets and Food Riots*, 301; Sakwa, *Gorbachev and His Reforms*, 326.

42. "Sinatra's song was actually a sad little piece about an old man's 'final curtain' when 'the end is near,' but never mind," wrote Ralf Dahrendorf. Ralf Dahrendorf, *Reflections on the Revolution in Europe* (New York: Times Books, 1990), 16; Karen Dawi-

sha, *Eastern Europe, Gorbachev and Reform: The Great Challenge* (Cambridge: Cambridge University Press, 1990), 220.

43. Schaeffer, *Power to the People*, 178–79.

44. Schaeffer, *Power to the People*, 182–85.

45. Anatol Lieven, *The Baltic Revolution: Estonia, Latvia, Lithuania and the Path to Independence* (New Haven, Conn.: Yale University Press, 1993), 225, 227; Mark R. Beissinger, "Demise of an Empire State: Identity, Legitimacy, and the Deconstruction of Soviet Politics," in *The Rising Tide of Cultural Pluralism: The Nation-State at Bay*, ed. Crawford Young (Madison: University of Wisconsin Press, 1993), 108.

46. Lieven, *The Baltic Revolution*, 219.

47. Lieven, *The Baltic Revolution*, 228; Jonathan Steele, *Eternal Russia: Yeltsin, Gorbachev and the Mirage of Democracy* (Cambridge, Mass.: Harvard University Press, 1994), 306.

48. Lieven, *The Baltic Revolution*, 223.

49. Peter J. S. Duncan, "Ukrainians," in *The Nationalities Question in the Soviet Union*, ed. Graham Smith (London: Longman, 1990), 102–03.

50. Jane I. Dawson, *Eco-Nationalism: Anti-Nuclear Activism and National Identity in Russia, Lithuania, and Ukraine* (Durham, N.C.: Duke University Press, 1996), 4; Steele, *Eternal Russia*, 13; David R. Marples, *Ukraine under Perestroika: Ecology, Economics and the Worker's Revolt* (New York: St. Martin's, 1991), 26.

51. Taras Kuzio and Andrew Wilson, *Ukraine: Perestroika to Independence* (London: Macmillan, 1994), 143.

52. Kuzio and Wilson, *Ukraine*, 160–62.

53. Beissinger, "Demise of an Empire-State," 106.

54. John Dunlop, *The Rise of Russia and the Fall of the Soviet Empire* (Princeton, N.J.: Princeton University Press, 1993), 21–22.

55. Dunlop, *The Rise of Russia*, 18.

56. Dunlop, *The Rise of Russia*, 21–22.

57. Dunlop, *The Rise of Russia*, 59.

58. Dunlop, *The Rise of Russia*, 23–27.

59. Dunlop, *The Rise of Russia*, 35.

60. William Moskoff, *Hard Times: Impoverishment and Protest in the Perestroika Years: The Soviet Union 1985–1991* (Armonk, N.Y.: Sharpe, 1993), 133.

61. Seweryn Bialer, "The Yeltsin Affair: The Dilemma of the Left in Gorbachev's Revolution," in *Politics, Society, and Nationality Inside Gorbachev's Russia*, ed. Seweryn Bialer (Boulder, Colo.: Westview, 1989), 98.

62. Sakwa, *Gorbachev and His Reforms*, 276.

63. Moskoff, *Hard Times*, 183.

64. Moskoff, *Hard Times*, 190.

65. Moskoff, *Hard Times*, 211.

66. Kuzio and Wilson, *Ukraine*, 164; Gail Lapidus, Victor Zaslavsky, and Philip Gold-

man, "Introduction: Soviet Federalism—Its Origins, Evolution and Demise," in *From Union to Commonwealth: Nationalism and Separation in the Soviet Republics*, ed. Gail Lapidas, Victor Zaslavsky, and Philip Goldman (Cambridge: Cambridge University Press, 1992), 6.

67. Lapidus, Zaslavaky, and Goldman, "Introduction," 14.

68. Moskoff, *Hard Times*, 94; Zwass, *From Failed Communism to Underdeveloped Capitalism*, 68.

69. Zwass, *From Failed Communism to Underdeveloped Capitalism*, 22; Aslund, *Gorbachev's Struggle*, 184; Melvin Gurtov, *Global Politics in the Human Interest* (Boulder, Colo.: Rienner, 1994), 162; White, *After Gorbachev*, 272.

70. Moskoff, *Hard Times*, 15. Steven Greenhouse, "U.N. Calls East's Slide at Depression Point," *New York Times*, December 3, 1991.

71. Zwass, *From Failed Communism to Underdeveloped Capitalism*, 20.

72. Rasma Karklins, *Ethnopolitics and Transition to Democracy: The Collapse of the USSR and Latvia* (Baltimore, Md.: Johns Hopkins University Press, 1994), 30.

73. Serge Schmemann, "Soviet Rightists See a Nation Run Amok," *New York Times*, June 28, 1991.

74. "Excerpts from the New Leader's Remarks: 'Law and Order,' " *New York Times*, August 20, 1991.

75. Karklins, *Ethnopolitics and Transition*, 31.

76. Ronald Suny, "State, Civil Society, and Ethnic Cultural Consolidation in the USSR—Roots of the National Question," in Lapidas, Zaslavaky, and Goldman, *From Union to Commonwealth*, 35; New York Times, "The Gorbachev Account: A Coup 'against the People, against Democracy,' " *New York Times*, August 23, 1991.

77. *New York Times*, "The Gorbachev Account."

78. Francis X. Clines, "Former Soviet States Form Commonwealth Without Clearly Defining Its Powers," *New York Times*, December 22, 1991.

79. Bennett, *Yugoslavia's Bloody Collapse*, 68.

80. Bennett, *Yugoslavia's Bloody Collapse*, 69.

81. Dijana Plestina, *Regional Development in Communist Yugoslavia: Success, Failure, and Consequences* (Boulder, Colo.: Westview, 1992), 141–42.

82. Mesic, "External Migration," 185; Chris Martin and Laura D'Andrea Tyson, "Can Titoism Survive Tito? Economic Problems and Policy Choices Confronting Tito's Successors," in *Nationalism and Federalism in Yugoslavia, 1963–1983*, ed. Pedro Ramet (Bloomington: Indiana University Press, 1984), 197; Plestina, "From 'Democratic Centralism' to Decentralized Democracy?" 140.

83. Plestina, "From 'Democratic Centralism' to Decentralized Democracy?" 140, 144; Pedro Ramet, "Apocalypse Culture and Social Change in Yugoslavia," in Ramet, *Nationalism and Federalism in Yugoslavia*, 140; Plestina, *Regional Development in Communist Yugoslavia*, 161.

84. Plestina, *Regional Development in Communist Yugoslavia*, 168; T. V. Sathyamar-

thy, *Nationalism in the Contemporary World: Political and Sociological Perspectives* (London: Pinter, 1983), 94.

85. Plestina, *Regional Development in Communist Yugoslavia*, 172.

86. Plestina, "From 'Democratic Centralism' to Decentralized Democracy?" 133–34; Schierup, *Migration, Socialism and the International Division of Labor*, 166, 168; John Breuilly, *Nationalism and the State* (New York: St. Martin's, 1982), 179–82.

87. Martin and Tyson, "Can Titoism Survive Tito?" 189; Dyker, *Yugoslavia*, 101; Laura D'Andrea Tyson, *The Yugoslav Economic System and Its Performance in the 1970s* (Berkeley, Calif.: Institute of International Studies, 1980), 76.

88. Plestina, *Regional Development in Communist Yugoslavia*, 169; Sathyamurty, *Nationalism in the Contemporary World*, 95.

89. Marlise Simons, "In Slovakia, Link to Rest of Nation Weakens," *New York Times*, July 13, 1990.

90. Blaine Harden, "A Body Blow to Croatia's Tourist Industry," *San Francisco Chronicle*, June 17, 1991.

91. Susan Bridge, "Some Causes of Political Change in Yugoslavia," in *Ethnic Conflict in the Western World*, ed. Milton Esman (Ithaca, N.Y.: Cornell University Press, 1975), 355.

92. Woodward, *Balkan Tragedy*, 69, 74, 115, 130.

93. Marlise Simons, "A Sign of Bad Times in Yugoslavia, Trade War between Two Republics," *New York Times*, January 28, 1990; Stephen Engelberg, "Feuds Crippling Yugoslav Economy," *New York Times*, April 19, 1991.

94. Sabrina Ramet, *Balkan Babel: The Disintegration of Yugoslavia from the Death of Tito to Ethnic War* (Boulder, Colo.: Westview, 1996), 39.

95. Bennett, *Yugoslavia's Bloody Collapse*, 70; Robert Howse, "A Horizon Beyond Hatred?" in *Yugoslavia the Former and Future*, Payam Akhavan and Robert Howse (Washington, D.C.: Brookings Institution, 1995), 4.

96. Vojin Dimitrijevic, "The 1974 Constitution and Constitutional Process as a Factor in the Collapse of Yugoslavia," in Akhavan and Howse, *Yugoslavia*, 58.

97. J. F. Brown, *Surge to Freedom: The End of Communist Rule in Eastern Europe* (Durham, N.C.: Duke University Press, 1991), 234.

98. Brown, *Surge to Freedom*, 236.

99. Franjo Tudjman, "All We Croatians Want is Democracy," *New York Times*, June 30, 1990.

100. Bennett, *Yugoslavia's Bloody Collapse*, 94–96; Plestina, *Regional Development in Communist Yugoslavia*, 174.

101. Marlise Simons, "Yugoslav Communists Vote to End Party's Monopoly," *New York Times*, January 23, 1990.

102. Bennett, *Yugoslavia's Bloody Collapse*, 110–11.

103. Bennett, *Yugoslavia's Bloody Collapse*, 119.

104. Bennett, *Yugoslavia's Bloody Collapse*, 120.

105. Geoffrey Pridham and Tatu Vanhanen, *Democratization in Eastern Europe: Domestic and International Perspectives* (London: Routledge, 1994), 128–29; Bennett, *Yugoslavia's Bloody Collapse*, 119.

106. Bennett, *Yugoslavia's Bloody Collapse*, 121.

107. Blaine Harden, "Croatian President-Elect Plans Sovereign State," *Washington Post*, April 30, 1991.

108. Bennett, *Yugoslavia's Bloody Collapse*, 133; John Zametica, *The Yugoslav Conflict* (London: Brassey's, 1992), 42.

109. Bennett, *Yugoslavia's Bloody Collapse*, 137.

110. Bennett, *Yugoslavia's Bloody Collapse*, 137–38.

111. Celestine Bohlen, "New Crisis Grips Yugoslavia Over Rotation of Leadership," *New York Times*, May 16, 1991.

112. Chuck Sudetic, "2 Yugoslav States Decide to Secede if Terms Go Unmet," *New York Times*, June 26, 1991.

113. Sharon L. Wolchik, "Czechoslovakia," in *The Columbia History of Eastern Europe in the Twentieth Century*, ed. Joseph Held (New York: Columbia University Press, 1992), 145, 150–51; Christine Sadowski, "Autonomous Groups as Agents of Democratic Change in Communist and Post-Communist Eastern Europe," in *Political Culture and Democracy in Developing Countries*, ed. Larry Diamond (Boulder, Colo.: Rienner, 1993), 188; Dawisha, *Eastern Europe, Gorbachev and Reform*, 287.

114. Milan Svec, "Czechoslovakia's Velvet Divorce," *Current History* (November 1992): 377–78.

115. Schaeffer, *Power to the People*, 226–38.

116. William E. Schmidt, "Election in Czechoslovakia Will Be a Test of Tension," *New York Times*, June 3, 1992; J. C. Brada, "Breaking Up is Hard to Do: The Economics of Creating Independent Czech and Slovak Republics," in *Current Economics and Politics of (ex-)Czechoslovakia*, ed. J. Krovak (Commack, N.Y.: Nova Science, 1994), 21.

117. Shen, *Economic Reform*, 117, 171.

118. J. Urban, "The Czech and Slovak Republics: Security Consequences of the Breakup of the CSFR," in *Central and Eastern Europe: The Challenge of Transition*, ed. R. C. Carp (Oxford: Stockholm International Peace Research Institute, Oxford University Press, 1993), 113.

119. Shen, *Economic Reform*, 187.

120. A. A. Michta, *East Central Europe After the Warsaw Pact: Security Dilemmas in the 1990s* (New York: Greenwood, 1992), 128.

121. C. S. Leff, *The Czech and Slovak Republics: Nation versus State* (Boulder, Colo.: Westview, 1997), 229.

122. Leff, *The Czech and Slovak Republics*, 229.

123. Michta, *East Central Europe*, 127.

124. Urban, "The Czech and Slovak Republics," 117.

125. J. Svejnar, K. Terrel, and D. Munich, "Unemployment in the Czech and Slovak

Republics," in *The Czech Republic and Economic Transition in Eastern Europe*, ed. J. Svejnar (San Diego, Calif.: Academic Press, 1995), 286.

126. M. Vavrejnova and I. Moravcikova, "The Czech Household Sector in Transition," in Svejnar, *The Czech Republic*, 319.

127. Tom Burkett, "Gritty Towns Spawn Leftist Mood," *Prognosis: The English Language Newspaper of Czechoslovakia*, June 12–15, 1992, 5.

128. M. Kucera and Z. Pavlik, "Czech and Slovak Demography," in *The End of Czechoslovakia*, ed. J. Musil (Budapest: Central European University Press, 1995), 36.

129. Sujan and Sujanova, "The Macroeconomic Situation in Czechoslovakia," 126.

130. Leff, *The Czech and Slovak Republics*, 185; Peter Passel, "An Economic Wedge Divides Czechoslovakia," *New York Times*, April 19, 1992; New York Times, "Czech Republic Hints at Independence," *New York Times*, July 14, 1992.

131. J. R. Millar and S. L. Wolchik, "Introduction: The Social Legacies and the Aftermath of Communism," in J. R. Millar and S. L. Wolchik, eds., *The Social Legacy of Communism* (Cambridge: Woodrow Wilson Center Press and Cambridge University Press, 1994), 7–15; S. L. Wolchik, "The Politics of Ethnicity and the Breakup of the Czechoslovak Federation," in *Ethnic Conflict in the Post-Soviet World: Case Studies and Analysis*, ed. L. Drobizheva, R. Gottemoeller, C. M. Kelleher, and L. Walker (Armonk, N.Y.: Sharpe, 1996), 76.

132. T. R. Judt, "Metamorphosis: The Democratic Revolution in Czechoslovakia," in *Eastern Europe in Revolution*, ed. I. Banac (Ithaca, N.Y.: Cornell University Press, 1992), 104.

133. Batt, *East-Central Europe*, 98.

134. New York Times, "Czechs and Slovaks Edging Toward a Separation," *New York Times*, June 17, 1992.

135. Leff, *The Czech and Slovak Republics*, 137–38.

136. Ken Layne, "The End of Federation Likely," *Prognosis*, June 12–25, 1992, 4.

137. J. F. Brown, *Hopes and Shadows: Eastern Europe after Communism* (Durham, N.C.: Duke University Press, 1994), 60–62; Leff, *The Czech and Slovak Republics*, 131.

138. Layne, "The End of Federation Likely," 4.

139. Layne, "The End of Federation Likely," 4.

140. Layne, "The End of Federation Likely," 3.

141. Charles T. Powers, " 'Velvet Divorce' Partners May Yet Remarry," *San Francisco Chronicle*, June 22, 1992.

142. "Czechoslovakia Will Become Two Nations, Its Leaders Agree," *San Francisco Chronicle*, June 20, 1992.

143. E. Bosak, "Slovaks and Czechs: An Uneasy Coexistence," in *Czechoslovakia: 1918–88: Seventy Years from Independence*, ed. H. G. Skilling (Oxford: Macmillan, 1991), 133–34.

144. Stephen Engelberg, "Slovak Deputies Block Reelection of Vaclav Havel," *New York Times*, July 4, 1992.

145. Basil Davidson, "A Historical Note," in *Behind the War in Eritrea*, ed. Basil Davidson, Lionel Cliffe, and Bereket Habte Selassie (Nottingham: Spokesman, 1980), 11–12.

146. Davidson, "A Historical Note," 12–13.

147. Harold G. Marcus, *Ethiopia, Great Britain, and the United States, 1941–1974: The Politics of Empire* (Berkeley: University of California Press, 1983), 9.

148. Richard Sherman, *Eritrea: The Unfinished Revolution* (Westport, Conn.: Praeger, 1980), 18–19.

149. Marcus, *Ethiopia*, 39.

150. Sherman, *Eritrea*, 23; Richard Greenfield, "Pre-Colonial and Colonial History," in Davidson, Cliffe, and Selassie, *Behind the War in Eritrea*, 30–31.

151. Mortin H. Halperin, David J. Scheffer, and Patricia L. Small, *Self-Determination in the New World Order* (Washington, D.C.: Carnegie Endowment for International Peace, 1992), 125–26; Alexis Heraclides, *The Self-Determination of Minorities in International Politics* (London: Cass, 1991), 181; Edmond J. Keller, *Revolutionary Ethiopia: From Empire to People's Republic* (Bloomington: Indiana University Press, 1988), 153.

152. Sherman, *Eritrea*, 30; Marcus, *Ethiopia*, 51, 79.

153. Marcus, *Ethiopia*, 20–21.

154. Keller, *Revolutionary Ethiopia*, 152; Marcus, *Ethiopia*, 81.

155. Keller, *Revolutionary Ethiopia*, 152.

156. Sherman, *Eritrea*, 31.

157. Sherman, *Eritrea*, 27; John Markakis and Nega Ayele, *Class and Revolution in Ethiopia* (Nottingham: Spokesman, 1978), 63.

158. Marcus, *Ethiopia*, 83.

159. Bereket Habte Sellassie, "From British Rule to Federation and Annexation," in Davidson, Cliffe, and Selassie, *Behind the War in Eritrea*, 39.

160. Marcus, *Ethiopia*, 84–85, 89.

161. Sherman, *Eritrea*, 36.

162. Fred Halliday and Maxine Molyneux, *The Ethiopian Revolution* (London: New Left Books, 1981), 182, 187; David Pool, "Eritrean Nationalism," in *Nationalism and Self-Determination in the Horn of Africa*, ed. I. M. Lewis (Cambridge: Cambridge University Press, 1983), 184.

163. Halliday and Molyneux, *The Ethiopian Revolution*, 182; Sherman, *Eritrea*, 81–82.

164. Sherman, *Eritrea*, 74; Heraclides, *The Self-Determination of Minorities*, 190, 192.

165. Sherman, *Eritrea*, 55–56; Keller, *Revolutionary Ethiopia*, 120; Marcus, *Ethiopia*, 177; Marina Ottaway, *Soviet and American Influence in the Horn of Africa* (Westport, Conn.: Praeger, 1982), 49.

166. Marcus, *Ethiopia*, 116–17.

167. Ottaway, *Soviet and American Influence*, 91.

168. Keller, *Revolutionary Ethiopia*, 171.

169. Keller, *Revolutionary Ethiopia*, 202.

170. Markakis and Ayele, *Class and Revolution*, 105.

171. Steven R. David, *Choosing Sides: Alignment and Realignment in the Third World* (Baltimore, Md.: Johns Hopkins University Press, 1991), 106.

172. David, *Choosing Sides*, 111–12.

173. John Markakis, *National and Class Conflict in the Horn of Africa* (Cambridge: Cambridge University Press, 1987), 253; Marcus, *Ethiopia*, 99.

174. Ottaway, *Soviet and American Influence*, 98; Keller, *Revolutionary Ethiopia*, 202.

175. Sherman, *Eritrea*, 86.

176. Gerard Chaliand, "The Guerrilla Struggle," in Davidson, Cliffe, and Selassie, *Behind the War in Eritrea*, 52; Halliday and Molyneus, *The Ethiopian Revolution*, 173.

177. David, *Choosing Sides*, 100.

178. David, *Choosing Sides*, 122.

179. Mark Duffield, "Famine, Conflict, and the Internationalization of Public Welfare," in *Beyond Conflict in the Horn*, ed. Martin Doornboos, Lionel Cliffe, Abdel Ghaffas M. Ahmed, and John Markakis (London: Currey, 1992), 69.

180. Ottaway, *Soviet and American Influence*, 114.

181. Colin Legum and Bill Lee, *The Horn of Africa in Continuing Crisis* (New York: Africana, 1979), 142; Lars Bondestam, "External Involvement in Ethiopia and Eritrea," in Davidson, Cliffe, and Selassie, *Behind the War in Eritrea*, 68–70; Keller, *Revolutionary Ethiopia*, 267; David, *Choosing Sides*, 134–35; Jane Perlez, "On the Ethiopian Front, Rebel Confidence Rises," *New York Times*, February 7, 1990.

182. Ottaway, *Soviet and American Influence*, 136; Keller, *Revolutionary Ethiopia*, 206–7; Halliday and Molyneux, *The Ethiopian Revolution*, 173.

183. Markakis, *National and Class Conflict*, 268.

184. Markakis, *National and Class Conflict*, 268.

185. Keller, *Revolutionary Ethiopia*, 224–25; Markakis, *National and Class Conflict*, 268–69; Paul Henze, "Ethiopia and Eritrea: The Defeat of the Derge and the Establishment of New Governments," in *Making War and Waging Peace: Foreign Intervention in Africa*, ed. David R. Smock (Washington, D.C.: U.S. Institute of Peace Press, 1993), 72–73.

186. Sherman, *Eritrea*, 91.

187. Henze, "Ethiopia and Eritrea," 67.

188. Henze, "Ethiopia and Eritrea," 68.

189. Jane Perlez, "Israelis Widening Role in Ethiopia," *New York Times*, February 7, 1990; Clifford Krauss, "Ethiopian Said to Cut Off Flight of Jews in Effort to Gain Israeli Arms," *New York Times*, July 12, 1990.

190. Clifford Krauss, "Israelis Begin Airlift of Ethiopia's Jews," *New York Times*, May 25, 1991; Jill Hamburg, "Problems for Israel's Latest Immigrants," *San Francisco Chronicle*, July 24, 1991.

191. Mary Battiata, "Ethiopia Seeks Thaw in Frosty Relations with US," *Washington Post*, April 30, 1989.

192. Bona Malwal, "Prospects for Peace, Recovery, and Development in the Horn of Africa," in Doornbos, Cliffe, Ahmed, and Markakis, *Beyond Conflict*, 14; John W. Harbeson, *The Ethiopian Transformation: The Quest for the Post-Imperial State* (Boulder, Colo.: Westview, 1988), 207, 211.

193. Keller, *Revolutionary Ethiopia*, 179.

194. Henze, "Ethiopia and Eritrea," 63; Clifford Krauss, "Ethiopia's Leader Agrees to Give Up Capital to Rebels," *New York Times*, May 28, 1991.

195. "Eritrea Declares Independence from Ethiopia After Landslide Vote," *San Francisco Chronicle*, May 3, 1993.

196. Neil Henry, "Tigre Province: A Land of Night," *Washington Post*, May 16, 1990; New York Times, "Flight and Futility Are Routine in the Horn of Africa," *New York Times*, September 10, 1989; Kinfe Abraham, *Ethiopia: From Bullets to the Ballot Box* (Lawrenceville, N.J.: Red Sea, 1994), 9; Jane Perlez, "Prisoner No. 14279: Forlorn Pawn in Ethiopia's Long and Ruinous Civil War," *New York Times*, February 19, 1990.

197. Dan Suther, "What Eritrean Secession Will Mean for Ethiopia," *San Francisco Chronicle*, May 3, 1993.

198. Suther, "What Eritrean Secession Will Mean."

199. Jill Hamburg, "Eritrea Showing Lots of Promise," *San Francisco Chronicle*, April 9, 1992; Roy Pateman, "Eritrea Takes the World Stage," *Current History* (May 1994): 229–30; Donatella Lorch, "Ethiopians Return, Glad to Help Build a New Land," *New York Times*, May 13, 1993.

200. Alex Grigorievs, "The Baltic Predicament," in Richard Caplan and John Feffer, eds., *Europe's New Nationalism: States and Minorities in Conflict* (Oxford: Oxford University Press, 1996), 124–36.

201. Jane Perlez, "Czechs Use Laws to Exclude Gypsies," *New York Times*, December 27, 1995.

202. George Schopflin, "Nationalism and Ethnic Minorities in Post-Communist Europe," in Caplan and Feffer, *Europe's New Nationalism*, 154–55.

203. Roger Cohen, "Croatia's Currency's Name Protested," *New York Times*, May 27, 1995.

204. "Eritrea Blocking a Port in Dispute With Neighbor," *New York Times*, May 24, 1998; James C. McKinley Jr., "Ethiopia and Eritrea Seem Ready to Do Battle," *New York Times* May 21, 1998; James C. McKinley Jr., "Border Dispute in Horn of Africa Threatens War," *New York Times*, June 1, 1998; James C. McKinley Jr., "Ethiopians and Eritreans Resume Battle Along Border," *New York Times*, June 4, 1998.

205. Aleksa Djilas, *The Contested Country: Yugoslav Unity and Communist Revolution, 1919–1953* (Cambridge, Mass.: Harvard University Press, 1991), 88.

206. Duncan Wilson, *Tito's Yugoslavia* (Cambridge: Cambridge University Press, 1979), 39; Robert Adams, *Nations in Arms: The Theory and Practice of Territorial Defense* (Houndmills, England: Macmillan, 1986), 140, 142; Ramet, *Balkan Babel*, 40–41.

207. Dan Archer and Rosemary Gartner, *Violence and Crime in Cross-National Perspective* (New Haven, Conn.: Yale University Press, 1984), 79, 86.

208. Archer and Gartner, *Violence and Crime*, 65–66, 76, 92, 94–95.

209. Archer and Gartner, *Violence and Crime*, 86.

210. Adams, *Nation in Arms* 137, 154–55, 172–73; James Gow, *Legitimacy and the Military: The Yugoslav Crisis* (London: Pinter, 1992), 44–46; Woodward, *Balkan Tragedy*, 26.

211. Adams, *Nation in Arms*, 159, 161, 163–64; Zimmerman, *Open Borders*, 30.

212. Adams, *Nation in Arms*, 180–81, 215–16.

213. Adams, *Nation in Arms*, 217.

214. Robin Alison Remington, "Political-Military Relations in Post-Tito Yugoslavia," in Ramet, *Nationalism and Federalism in Yugoslavia*, 57; Adams, *Nation in Arms*, 202.

215. R. W. Dean, *Nationalism and Political Change in Eastern Europ: The Slovak Question and the Czech Reform Movement* (Denver: University of Denver Press, 1973), 5–6; J. Bugajski, *Nations in Turmoil: Conflict and Cooperation in Eastern Europe* (Boulder, Colo.: Westview, 1995), 67–68.

216. J. F. N. Bradley, *Politics in Czechoslovakia, 1945–1990* (New York: Columbia University Press, 1991), 78.

217. Leff, *The Czech and Slovak Republics*, 61; C. S. Leff, "Czech and Slovak Nationalism in the Twentieth Century," in *European Nationalism in the Twentieth Century*, ed. P. F. Sugar (Washington, D.C.: American University Press, 1995), 139; C. Rice, *The Soviet Army and the Czechoslovak Army, 1948–1983: Uncertain Alliance* (Princeton, N.J.: Princeton University Press, 1984), 3–4.

218. Rice, *The Soviet Army and the Czechoslovak Army*, 59, 62, 168.

219. Rice, *The Soviet Army and the Czechoslovak Army*, 84, 91.

220. Millar and Wolchik, "Introduction," 20.

221. Bugajski, *Nations in Turmoil*, 304.

T E N

ALTERNATIVE STATES

Ethnic movements around the world are clamoring for states of their own. Although they are motivated to do so for different reasons, many see state power as a way to solve problems and redeem the promise of self-determination.[1]

Some movements have organized to protest the invasion and annexation of their country by neighboring states: Kashmir by India in 1947; Tibet by China in 1959; East Timor by Indonesia in 1975. Although these incorporations took place at separate times and for different reasons—partition and the consolidation of state power in India; revolution and consolidation in China; and democratization in Portugal, decolonization in East Timor, and acquisitive dictatorship in Indonesia—movements in each demanded independence, much like their counterparts in the Baltics and Eritrea.[2]

In other countries, ethnic movements emerged in response to discrimination and assault by indigenous government. The Karen in Burma, Basques in Spain, Kurds resident in Iraq, Iran, Syria, and Turkey all organized to defend themselves against dictatorships that persecuted, imprisoned, and attacked them.[3] Elsewhere, Tamils in Sri Lanka, Sikhs in India, Quebecois in Canada, Catholics in Northern Ireland, Maori in New Zealand, and Corsicans and Bretons in France have objected to discrimination by democratic states governed by different ethnic majorities.[4] Although conflict is perhaps more intense in states where ethnic minorities confront dictatorships, democracies are not immune from inter-ethnic violence.

Only a handful of states are ethnically homogeneous "in the sense that minorities account for less than 5 percent of the population."[5] Even relatively homogeneous countries such as Japan have ethnic minorities, like the Ainus, who want lands of their own.[6] This suggests that ethnic minorities might be per-suaded to seek states of their own wherever discrimination exists.

There are also ethnic groups with substantial political power, groups who may even be part of ruling majorities, such as the Czechs in Czechoslovakia, who see partition as a way to rid themselves of burdensome ethnic minorities. In Italy, Roberto Ronchi, a League of the North official, argued that a state of Padania should be established in the northern part of the country because "[w]e're tired of paying all the taxes to support lazy southerners and corrupt officials in Rome."[7] And the separatist movement demanding a "Republic of the Pampas" in southern Brazil, which draws its support from Brazilians of Eu-ropean descent, a privileged social group, makes the same case, arguing that their taxes support indigent non-Europeans in the Amazon.[8]

Although ethnic movements have different reasons for acquiring states, they all believe that state power will provide tangible benefits. With state power they could levy taxes, raise armies, vote in the United Nations, borrow money from the World Bank, and field athletes at the Olympic Games. With state power they could redeem the promise of self-determination.

In recent years, ethnic movements have emerged in rich and poor countries, dictatorships and democracies around the world. The only notable exception has been in Latin America. There, ethnic independence movements are rare because different ethnic groups speak common languages (Spanish or Portu-guese), confess in the same faith (Catholicism), share a common colonial past (with Spain or Portugal), and experience a common contemporary reality (debt crisis and democratization). These affinities generally outweigh ethnic differ-ences in most Latin American settings, though rebellion in Chiapas suggests some caution in excepting Latin America from the general trend.

How widespread are ethnic independence movements? It is hard to say with precision, but the number is large and growing. In 1993, Ted Robert Gurr re-ported that there were 233 "politically active communal groups," which num-bered "some 900 million people, about one-sixth of the world's population."[9] Of these, about 120 are engaged in conflict with the governments of states where they reside.[10] Since then, their number has grown, drawing support from the five thousand ethnic "nations" around the world.[11]

Of course, because states already claim sovereignty over the world's territory and its inhabitants, any decision to provide states to ethnic movements would result in the partition of existing states. And there are several problems with partition as a political practice. It should be clear by now that partition has *not* been the solution to problems that its proponents and practitioners imagined.

It was initially advanced by great and superpower states to avoid conflict between competing independence movements. But instead of promoting peaceful self-determination in separate states, partition routinely led to large-scale migrations, discrimination against ethnic and secular minorities, internecine conflict, interstate war, and the proliferation of nuclear weapons. Of course, partition has not always and everywhere resulted in conflict. In Czechoslovakia, for instance, partition was peacefully accomplished. But partition there should be seen less as a model and more as an exception to the general rule.

Even if partition were widely recognized as an ineffective solution, many movements would still try to secure states of their own. But they may find that this is an elusive goal. Where states are strong, where ethnic minorities are relatively small or dispersed, and where great powers and international institutions are indifferent to their fate, it may be extremely difficult for ethnic movements to win their independence. Recall that Eritrean movements fought for thirty years before achieving their independence. The Karen in Burma, Kurds in Turkey and Iraq, Kashmiris and Sikhs in India, and Tamils in Sri Lanka have fought for years, sometimes decades, without appreciable success. If bureaucracies and armies are willing to defend the unitary state, if movements are unable to attract international sympathy or receive money and material support from emigre communities, great powers, or the United Nations, then revolt may only produce unending civil war. Dramatic developments can sometimes alter the balance of forces—the Persian Gulf War revived international interest in the plight of the Kurds, for instance. But the success of armed rebellion in Eritrea has to be set against its numerous failures elsewhere.

A more general problem is that partition contributes to the proliferation of states in the interstate system. The interstate system that emerged after World War II was designed by its superpower architects to promote the proliferation of independent nation-states. Decolonization was the principal way that U.S. and Soviet leaders promoted the growth of the new system, though partition also played an important role. But the proliferation of states—the number of constituent states has nearly quadrupled from fifty in 1945 to almost two hundred in 1998—has been a tumultuous process.[12] Decolonization and partition often assigned people to states they did not meaningfully choose. This was particularly evident with decolonization in Africa. But it was also apparent with partition in Czechoslovakia, where citizens were denied the opportunity to ratify or reject their leader's decision to divide the country. What's more, the creation of independent states around the world did not necessarily promote either democratization or economic development. Instead, it frequently contributed to dictatorship and poverty. The economic gap between rich and poor countries has widened during the postwar period, despite or perhaps even because of decolonization and partition. These problems may have been due in part to the fact that decolonization and partition were largely unregulated.[13] There were few guidelines, policies, or institutions to direct the process or address the problems that accompanied them. Decolonization and partition were handled by great powers and the United Nations on an individual, ad hoc basis. In retrospect, it was hubris to imagine that a single, uniform political institution—the nation-state republic—could address the diverse social, economic, and political needs of people around the world. Perhaps it is time to rethink the assumption that homogeneous political institutions and the unregulated proliferation of states in the interstate system is sound political practice. Recently, some people have begun to question postwar assumptions. "If we don't find some way that the different ethnic groups can live together in a country, how many countries will we have?" Secretary of State Warren Christopher asked. "We'll have 5,000 countries rather than the hundred plus we have now."[14] And UN secretary-general Boutros Boutros-Ghali warned that "the new danger which will appear in the next ten years is more fragmentation. Rather than 100 or 200 countries, you may have at the end of the century 400 countries, and we will not be able to achieve any kind of economic development, not to mention more disputes on boundaries."[15]

Of course, any effort to review assumptions about the structure of the interstate system and proliferation of states would require a rethinking of its commitment to the principle of self-determination. Partition was supposed to promote self-determination by providing different ethnic or ideological groups with states of their own. By creating relatively homogeneous nation-states, one might have expected that self-determination and democracy would be more fully realized in divided states than in multiethnic states. But this has not occurred, largely because partition established the right to rule without regard for minorities who were not part of the "nation." Officials of divided states did not generally protect the civil rights of minority populations because they believed that minorities could find protection in neighboring states, which had been expressly created for them, and because they wanted to exercise their own self-determination without restraint. So instead of protecting the rights of all resident groups, they advanced the rights of only some groups. Partition then presented minorities with a choice. They could either migrate to the state where their compatriots had assumed power and exercise their self-determination *there*, or seek state power on their own terms, in their own land. Some chose the first and migrated; others demanded the right to secede and create new states of their own. The problem is that partition has progressively narrowed the meaning of self-determination and democracy and promoted self-interest instead.

People and movements have choices. They need not see partition as the only solution to their problems. They might instead consider three political alternatives: reunification, shared sovereignty, or democratization. Each of these has been adopted as solutions in some settings, each has the potential for wider application, and each may avoid problems associated with partition.

REUNIFICATION

Two divided states have been reunited: Vietnam by force; Germany by choice. Vietnam was reunited by North Vietnam in 1975, after its armies defeated South Vietnamese forces and captured Saigon. Germany was reunited in 1990, after voters in East and West Germany elected representatives who secured superpower permission to reunify the country and then negotiated the merger of the two states.[16]

Reunification brought an end to the decades-long war in Vietnam and to cold war confrontation in Germany, where crises in Berlin had brought the superpowers to the brink of world war. But although reunion eliminated the source of conflict, it nonetheless generated problems of its own. Ironically, the difficulties associated with reunification were remarkably similar to the problems produced by partition: disruptive migrations, discrimination, and disputes with neighboring states.

In Vietnam, 1.5 million "boat people" from the South fled the country between 1975 and 1985, many traveling to the United States. One million more applied for legal permission to emigrate, and fifty thousand signed up for "guest worker" programs in East Germany.[17] Large-scale, cross-border migrations also preceded and accompanied reunification in Germany.[18] When Hungary opened its border with Austria in 1989, East Germans rushed into the breach, and 343,854 East Germans fled through Hungary to Austria and then West Germany during the next six months.[19] This "disorganized" social movement crippled the East German economy, forced the regime to resign, and paved the way for reunification. Although West German officials expected reunification to stem the westward migration, it nonetheless continued, as unemployed workers from the East sought jobs in the West, and ethnic Germans living in Eastern European countries and the former Soviet Union returned to their "homeland."[20] Reunification also brought an end to guest workers programs in the East, and foreign workers, which included migrants from Vietnam, were persuaded or forced to leave.[21]

In both Vietnam and Germany, discrimination also emerged as a problem after reunification. The communist government in Vietnam discriminated against people who had worked for or "collaborated" with the South Vietnamese government, barring them from public service and sending many to prison or "reeducation camps."[22] The capitalist government in Germany barred communist officials from public service, while private businesses and West Germans discriminated against "Ossies" from the East. In the East, discrimination against "foreigners" became widespread, and violence was directed at residual guest workers from Turkey and Vietnam.[23]

Sovereignty was also an issue for Vietnam and Germany. Vietnam invaded Cambodia in 1978 to overthrow Pol Pot's murderous regime. It then fought a brief border war with China in 1979. But Vietnam's withdrawal from Cambodia in 1989 greatly reduced tensions with its neighbors.[24] The German government called into question Poland's possession of former German lands along its border and complained about the expulsion of ethnic Germans from Czechoslovakia after World War II.

The fact that partition and reunification were both accompanied by similar problems suggests that any fundamental change—the breakup or makeup of states—can have disruptive social consequences. The difference is that problems associated with unification brought an end to war and conflict, whereas partition had contributed to it.

In Vietnam and Germany, officials expected reunification to provide substantial economic benefits. Reintegration, they thought, would lead to economic renewal. But this did not occur in Vietnam. The legacy of war and ruinous economic policies contributed to economic decline, falling incomes, and widespread hunger in the first decade after reunification.[25] By 1986, Gen. Vo Nguyen Giap admitted, "My generation washed away the shame of losing our country's independence and now it is your [generation's] turn to wash away the shame of a poor and backward country."[26] Economic reform in the 1990s helped revive the economy, but progress has been slow and costly.[27]

Reunification has also been extremely costly for Germany. The government has spent more than $500 billion in the East to rebuild railroads, upgrade phone service, furnish housing, compensate domestic banks, privatize businesses, and pay for the withdrawal of Soviet troops.[28] But while reunification has been burdensome—increasing taxes in the West and unemployment in the East—massive government spending has raised living standards in the East and laid the groundwork for the further expansion of the economy, already one of the strongest in the world.

Is reunification an alternative to conflict between other divided states? It is a serious possibility for states in China and Korea. Government officials on both sides of the divide have long agreed that reunification is a policy objective. But they disagree vehemently about the terms, conditions, and meaning of reunification, and they have failed to agree on a process that might facilitate negotiations on these issues. In the late 1980s, officials from China and Taiwan made some progress in reunifications talks, but negotiations have since stalled for three reasons. First, the Chinese government's 1989 massacre of dissidents in Tiananmen Square led to a break in relations between the two countries. Second, democratization in Taiwan during the 1990s increased the political distance between the two governments, which until then had both been ruled by one-party dictatorships.[29] The subsequent election of a president born in Taiwan and growing sentiment against reunification on the island has alienated the Chinese leadership.[30] Third, the cost of German reunification had a big impact on people in Taiwan. Support for reunification there has waned because many on the island now believe that its economic costs would outweigh any benefits. "When people [in Taiwan] think about unification, they think: 'What's in it for us?' [Do we] want to equalize incomes with the mainland?'" one business leader asked.[31] Or as one judge in Taipei explained:

> The average annual income of the people on the mainland is only about $250, but that of the Taiwan people is about $5,000. . . . What is Taiwan's annual income going to be if it is unified by China? If you think it is a good thing to reduce our annual income [down to the level of that in China] you must have some serious mental problem.[32]

Still, representatives of the two Chinas met in 1998 to discuss possible reunification.[33] The two countries are increasingly joined economically by Taiwanese investment in China, and as China embraces capitalism they are becoming *more* alike in economic terms, though *less* alike in political terms. Reunification prospects depend, in large part, on how China manages its reunification with Hong Kong and how Taiwan manages indigenous demands for independence. If Hong Kong's reunification goes smoothly, if China does not redistribute the wealth of its inhabitants, then resistance to reunification in Taiwan may wane. But if Hong Kong's residents are adversely affected by reunification, support for independence in Taiwan may grow, and China may use force to accomplish what it cannot achieve through negotiations.[34] The problem for China and Taiwan is whether unification, if it moves ahead, is achieved by force (as it was in Vietnam) or by choice (as it was in Germany).

Governments of the two Koreas have also said they wanted reunification, albeit on their own terms. But support for reunification has cooled during the 1990s. Democratization in South Korea during the late 1980s and early 1990s has increased the political distance between the two countries, which until then had both been ruled by one-party dictatorships. Various developments in the 1990s also increased their economic distance. The ruinous economic policies of North Korean dictator Kim Il Sung and, after he died in 1994, his son Kim Jong Il led to economic decline, widespread hunger, and famine. North Korea's economic collapse contrasted sharply with the South, where economic fortunes had improved. As the cost of German reunification became apparent, South Koreans began to worry that reunification with the North, increasingly in dire straits, would be extremely costly. One government agency in South Korea estimated that unification would cost $980 billion.[35] While partition had long been regarded as a political evil, it increasingly came to be seen as an economic good. The election of longtime dissident Kim Dae Jung as president of South Korea in 1998 may lead to new negotiations, but it is difficult to tell whether growing political and economic differences will diminish the prospects for unification (as it has in Taiwan) or contribute to democratization and unification (as it did in Germany).

Whatever the actual prospects for reunification in China and Korea, it remains a serious possibility, largely because populations in each pair share a common language, ethnic identity, and history. Many people have relatives living across the divide, and they yearn to be reunited with family and friends. It is more difficult, however, to imagine reunification as a political possibility in divided states where these social conditions do not exist. In states partitioned along ethnic-religious lines, the prospects for reunification are remote. Reunification has occurred and is still possible in states divided along secular ideological lines (capitalist/communist), but not in states partitioned along ethnic-religious lines. This suggests that partition based on ethnic identity may be more durable than division based on secular identity. If this is true, it may be necessary to consider other political alternatives in places where ethnicity marks political divides.

SHARED SOVEREIGNTY

For states divided along ethnic lines, reunification is a remote possibility. More likely is subdivision, as occurred in Pakistan. Recently, however, an alternative to partition and subdivision has emerged in some of the states where ethnic identities are strong and conflict between resident groups is sharp. In Northern Ireland, Israel and the occupied territories, and in Bosnia, indigenous ethnic groups have struggled to find alternatives to ethnic conflict. They have negotiated peace processes that may create shared political institutions for resident ethnicities.

On May 22, 1998, a majority of voters in Northern Ireland and in the Irish Republic ratified a new power-sharing agreement designed to end Catholic-Protestant violence, which has resulted in 3,200 deaths since 1969.[36] The agreement, which was the product of intense negotiations between political parties in Northern Ireland and government officials from the United Kingdom, Ireland, and the United States, created a new set of political institutions. It reestablished a regional assembly in the North that would permit Protestant and Catholic parties to legislate domestic policy (the provincial legislature had been abandoned in 1972 after the British government assumed direct authority over affairs in Northern Ireland), provided a council of ministers from Ireland, Britain, and Northern Ireland to "consult, cooperate and take decisions on matters of mutual interest" such as tourism and fishing, and created an intergovernmental body that would meet in biannual summits to address general issues associated with the peace process.

The creation of shared political institutions with overlapping rights and responsibilities was made possible by agreements reached between governments and among contending ethnic groups. The Irish government agreed to drop its constitutional claim to Northern Ireland; British officials agreed that it would renounce its claim on the North and allow Northern Ireland to rejoin Ireland *if* a majority in the North agreed.[37] Most Catholic and Protestant militias agreed to renounce violence and participate in elections for the new assembly. Governments and ethnic groups made concessions because they were weary of war and because they hoped that new political arrangements would promote economic development in the region, which had fallen behind its neighbors in the United Kingdom and Ireland.[38]

A peace process is also under way in Israel and the occupied territories. On September 13, 1993, Israeli prime minister Yitzhak Rabin and Palestine Liberation Organization Chairman Yasser Arafat met at the White House and signed an agreement designed to end Arab-Israeli conflict in Israel's occupied territories. Since 1987, an Arab Palestinian uprising, or *intifada*, in the West Bank and Gaza Strip had resulted in the deaths of about 200 Israelis and about 1,800 Palestinians.[39] The agreement reached by Rabin and Arafat, the "Declaration of Principles on Interim Self-Governing Arrangements for Palestinians in the Gaza Strip and Jericho (DOP)," is more commonly known as the Oslo Agreement because it was secretly negotiated in Norway.[40] It created Palestinian institutions that would be given limited authority over some territories in the West Bank and Gaza Strip, provided for the withdrawal of Israeli troops from some areas, and created joint political and economic institutions to address problems and settle disputes while negotiations on the "permanent status" of Israeli and Palestinian relations were concluded.[41] Rabin's assassination on November 4, 1995, by an Israeli, the subsequent election of Benjamin Netanyahu as prime minister, and continuing violence between Arabs and Jews has delayed implementation of the Oslo Agreement and slowed permanent-status negotiations. Still, Israeli authorities and Palestinian officials have jointly addressed common problems for the first time, trying to figure out how they might share police duties, customs controls, water resources, air waves, agricultural markets, and labor forces.[42]

In Bosnia-Herzegovina, one of Yugoslavia's successor states, representatives of the great powers persuaded ethnic groups in 1995 to sign the Dayton Accords, which were designed to end the bitter civil war that had claimed thousands of lives and created nearly seven hundred thousand refugees since 1992.[43] The Dayton agreement created a single state with two constituent parts: a Federation of Bosnia and Herzegovina, and a Serb Republic.[44] These entities would have a central government responsible for foreign policy, trade, the economy, and immigration policy, while governments in the two parts could legislate on other, domestic policies. They could not, however, control or restrict the movement of goods or people across their common borders. The enforcement of rights for resident civilians and refugee populations would be protected, initially, by sixty thousand NATO troops, and disputes arbitrated by an international "High Representative," who has the authority to implement policy throughout the country.[45]

The agreements reached in Northern Ireland, Israel and the occupied territories, and Bosnia all created shared political institutions with overlapping rights and responsibilities. In Northern Ireland and Bosnia, outside governments played important roles. Because different ethnic groups share some rights and responsibilities and participate in some common institutions, the peace process has resulted in what some political scientists have called a "consociational alternative" but what might be more easily described as "shared sovereignty."[46]

Several things might be said about shared sovereignty as a political alternative to partition and conflict. First, the agreements reached in Belfast, Oslo, and Dayton were chosen, not imposed. No doubt arms were twisted and deals made. But their sponsors invited participation by all of the contending groups, which had not previously met or negotiated face to face, and the results were subjected to approval by indigenous political parties and electorates. That has greatly enhanced their legitimacy and improved their ability to reduce violence and promote peace. This process stands in sharp contrast to partition, which has never, anywhere been subjected to a meaningful, indigenous electoral test.

One problem, however, is whether the relations and institutions provided for in these agreements are "permanent" or only "temporary," whether they are durable or simply way stations to something else. In Northern Ireland, many Protestants fear that the agreement will lead eventually to reunification and, "at the end of the day, our Protestant identity and culture would be submerged in the Catholic South."[47] In Israel, many Jews worry that the Oslo accords will set the stage for a second partition (the first partition of Palestine was approved by the United Nations in 1948 but never implemented) and the creation of a sovereign Palestinian state.[48] In 1994, 74 percent of Israelis believed that such a state would eventually be established.[49] Palestinians, meanwhile, worried that the "interim" agreement would become a "permanent" state of affairs, frustrating their desire for independence.[50] And in Bosnia, Serb leaders, and many international observers, believe that the Dayton agreement will not survive the eventual withdrawal of UN troops, that it is simply a prelude to partition and the creation of fully sovereign successor states.[51] By contrast, a majority of the Moslem population told pollsters in 1997 that the accords would make it possible for all three major ethnic groups to live together peacefully and thought the agreement would facilitate interethnic cooperation.[52]

It is difficult at present to determine whether shared sovereignty is a durable political alternative. There is considerable international pressure on states to conform with political norms, and institutions such as the United Nations find it difficult to recognize shared sovereignty as a viable or legitimate political form. Some indigenous groups want to undo these arrangements and force them to a "conclusion," either reunification (in Ireland) or repartition (in Israel and Bosnia). But there is also some chance that shared and autonomous institutions may survive. Evidence indicates that these kinds of arrangements may have application in other settings.

Ethnic movements in other states have promoted political alternatives that may provide a way for them to divide and share political power with other ethnic groups.[53] In Puerto Rico, "Commonwealth" is used to describe a shared set of relations between Spanish-speaking islanders and the United States, whereas "sovereignty-association" is used by native Hawaiians and by French-speaking Quebecois in Canada to describe the kind of relations they would like to establish with English-speaking majorities.

In Puerto Rico, the electorate voted in 1993 and 1998 referendums to retain the island's commonwealth status, rejecting proposals to apply for statehood in the United States by narrow margins and proposals for independence by large margins.[54] Commonwealth was initially established by the United States in 1952 as a way to transfer some political power to the inhabitants. But Puerto Ricans have supported commonwealth in successive elections (1967, 1993, and 1998) because they evidently believe it best suits their century-long relation with the United States. In practical terms, it provides hybrid forms of sovereignty and citizenship. The island's legislature possesses some powers that U.S. states do not have: for example, Puerto Rico enjoys UN recognition as an "autonomous political entity," which enables it to participate in the Olympic Games under its own flag and enter it own contestant in Miss Universe pageants, rights that the electorate values highly.[55] But security, trade, and law enforcement policies are all controlled by the U.S. Congress, which admits only a nonvoting delegate from Puerto Rico. Residents also possess a hybrid form of citizenship. Islanders are subject to the draft and serve in the U.S. army but pay no federal income tax, while receiving social security and welfare benefits. They may migrate freely to the United States, as more than two million have done, but they cannot vote in Puerto Rico for president, and their rights as citizens could be revoked by Congress.[56]

While shared sovereignty is a reality in Puerto Rico, it is only a prospect in Hawaii. There, movements of ethnic Hawaiians, the *Kanaka Maoli*, have argued that political solutions to the problems created by U.S. conquest in 1893 and admission as a state in 1960 be developed with this history and contemporary realities in mind. "Every Hawaiian in his heart would like to be independent," argues Mililani Trask, a leader of *Kalahui Hawaii* (Hawaiian Nation). "But we owe it to ourselves to be realistic. There is no mechanism for seceding from the Union. Secession doesn't do anything for the native people."[57]

As an alternative, some Hawaiian groups have proposed "sovereignty-associ-ation," though they debate its meaning.[58] In a special 1996 plebiscite, native Hawaiians agreed that they should "elect delegates to propose a Native Hawai-ian government" by a three-to-one margin.[59] For many, sovereignty-association might restore the Hawaiian monarchy and also create secular, representative political institutions for the indigenous minority. These institutions would ac-quire and share specified power with the state and federal governments.[60]

In Canada, French-speaking Quebecois have also said they seek "sover-eignty-association," though unlike the Hawaiians they do not attach any royalist meaning to the term. For the Quebecois, sovereignty-association would allow the government of Quebec to protect the linguistic and cultural identity of Quebecois, while retaining existing economic relations with Canada and trade relations with the United States. But some critics argue that the movement's commitment to shared sovereignty is more rhetorical than real. Many Canadi-ans think it is a prelude to independence in a sovereign state, not a permanent set of relations. A Quebecois proposal for change was narrowly defeated in a 1995 referendum, but movement leaders have vowed to revisit the issue of sov-ereignty-association in the future.[61]

Although hybrid political arrangements such as commonwealth and sover-eignty-association may provide an alternative to secession and sovereignty, they are not without difficulty. One problem is that it is difficult to determine who can participate in constitutional referendums and plebiscites. Political parties debated whether Puerto Ricans living in the United States could vote in the 1993 referendum and decided they could not, despite their obvious stake in the outcome. In Hawaii, nonnative residents sued to void the 1996 plebiscite because it barred them from voting.[62] In Canada, the government asked the Supreme Court to determine whether Quebec may secede and, if it can, how such a decision would be reached and by whom.[63]

A second problem is that decisions about constitutional issues may not be regarded as final. In Puerto Rico and Canada, the losers vowed to try again, demanding that referendums be held in the future. Presumably they will keep revisiting the question until they win.[64] Under these circumstances, it is diffi-cult to develop permanent institutions or durable relations. Still, to the extent that hybrid political forms such as commonwealth and sovereignty-association are freely chosen, establish equitable relations between minority and majority, or find ways to accommodate the needs of different ethnic groups, they may provide an alternative to ethnic conflict and partition. If they are adopted and survive, they may also make the interstate system more heterogeneous and less dependent on the sovereign nation-state as the standard political institution around the world.[65]

DEMOCRATIZATION

In some places, democratization can solve some of the problems that ethnic groups experience in republican states. The democratization of the Philippines in 1986 eventually made it possible in 1996 for the government to reach an accommodation with the Moros, a Moslem minority that had fought a twenty-six-year war for independence on Mindanao, a conflict that took 150,000 lives.[66] The fall of dictators might likewise improve relations between governments and ethnic minorities, such as the East Timorese in Indonesia and the Karen in Burma.

But democratization is not always a panacea, as we have seen in Czechoslovakia, Yugoslavia, and the Soviet Union, where it exacerbated ethnic differences. In some democratic states, ethnic minorities—Tamils in Sri Lanka, Kashmiris and Sikhs in India—experience discrimination at the hands of elected governments supported by ethnic majorities. What might ethnic minorities do in democratic states where majorities are determined to exercise power with little regard for resident minorities?

One possibility is for ethnic minorities to demand constitutional restraints on majority rule and greater protection for minority rights. In some settings, proportional representation, redistricting, and weighted voting systems can provide minorities with the kind of political voice they need to prevent or moderate discrimination.[67] Constitutional amendments and bills of rights can be adopted to protect minority rights against derogation by elected majorities. This is what the government in Canada has tried to do. The 1981 Ottawa Conference, 1987 Meech Lake Accord, and 1992 Charlottetown Accord were constitutional reforms designed to address issues raised by the Quebecois.[68] The problem with electoral and constitutional reform is that they must be approved by majorities, who may not be inclined to surrender power or accommodate minorities. Constitutional reform in Canada, for example, has been a difficult and relatively unsuccessful process because majorities and minorities could not agree on the rights and responsibilities of each.

Under these circumstances, movements might try to change the "ethnic identities" of majority and minority alike, a strategy adopted in the United States by Dr. Martin Luther King, Jr.

During the 1950s and 1960s, King and the civil rights movement tried to persuade government officials and the white majority to rescind the pernicious aspects of majority rule, particularly in the American South, and demanded that they observe and extend the civil rights of the disenfranchised minority. Because southern whites and government officials were unwilling or reluctant to do so, the movement waged a protracted nonviolent campaign to enhance the meaning of democracy in America.

But one of the problems King encountered was that political, economic, and social roles in the United States had become closely associated with ethnic identities. So long as political power, economic divisions of labor, and legal rights were closely linked to ethnic identity, it would be extremely difficult for a minority movement to challenge majority rule. King defended majority rule but insisted that the social composition of the majority must periodically change. In this he followed Abraham Lincoln, who argued that a "majority held in restraint by constitutional checks and limitations, and *always changing easily with deliberate changes of popular opinion and sentiment, is the only true sovereign of a free people.*"[69]

The problem for King was how to challenge a majority that had become defined in ethnic terms. He decided to try and change the ethnic identities on which majority and minority were based. By encouraging blacks to abandon their given identity as "Negroes" and develop a "new sense of 'somebodyness' and self-respect," King hoped to create a wider identity that could find common ground with other social groups. But for this to happen, the movement needed to change not only the identity of "Negroes" but also of "whites." So King reached out to whites and asked them to change how they saw themselves. "Having faith that the white majority is not an undifferentiated whole, Negro leaders have welcomed a moral appeal which can reach the emotions and intellects of significant white groups," he argued.[70] The effort to change the identities of minority and majority alike lay at the center of his organizing strategy. As King argued:

> In a multiracial society no one group can make it alone. To succeed in a pluralistic society, and an often hostile one at that, the Negro obviously needs organized strength, but that strength will only be effective when it is consolidated through constructive alliances with the majority group. . . . There is no separate black path to power and fulfillment that does not intersect white paths, and there is no separate white path to power and fulfillment, short of social disaster, that does not share that power with black aspirations for freedom and human dignity. We are bound together in a single garment of destiny.[71]

The transformation of ethnic identities and social roles also lay at the heart of his philosophy, a view best expressed in his speech at the Lincoln Memorial in 1963: "I have a dream that one day on the red hills of Georgia, sons of former slaves and sons of former slave-owners will sit down together at the table of brotherhood."[72] This would only be possible if each abandoned their given identities and adopted new ones.

King's efforts to alter ethnic identities as a way to change political, economic, and social roles were an ambitious but not impossible dream. Religious, linguistic, economic, and cultural identities are not as fixed as many people imagine. They change all the time. Migration and marriage change ethnic identities, scientific developments alter religious ones, technological innovations transform economic ones, media and education shape linguistic and cultural ones, and social movements change political ones. As Massimo d'Azeglio famously observed after the unification of Italy in 1860, "We have made Italy, now we must make Italians."[73] He did not take Italian identity as a given but something to be made, a difficult project given the fact that "only two and one-half percent of the population then used [Italian] for everyday purposes."[74]

Although King's assassination in 1968 weakened support for a politics based on changing social identities, and many in the civil rights movement retreated to a politics based on *given* social identities, his ideas still have contemporary application for people and movements around the world.

Unless social movements and governments find a way to promote democracy in heterogeneous states, to deconstruct social identities defined by historical animosities and shaped by contemporary problems, and to find peaceful alternatives to conflict within and between states, the divisions created by partition will deepen and the walls dividing people will continue to rise.

NOTES

1. See Robert K. Schaeffer, "Separatism: Rationality and Irony," in *Separatism: Democracy and Disintegration*, ed. Metta Spencer (Lanham, Md.: Rowman & Littlefield, 1998).

2. Benedict R. O. Anderson, "The State and Minorities in Indonesia," in *Southeast Asian Tribal Groups and Ethnic Minorities: Prospects for the Eighties and Beyond*, ed. Cultural Survival (Cambridge, Mass.: Cultural Survival, 1987), 78.

3. Edith Mirante, "Ethnic Minorities of the Burma Frontiers and Their Resistance Groups," in Cultural Survival, *Southeast Asian Tribal Groups and Ethnic Minorities*, 60–61; Ananda Rajah, "Ethnicity, Nationalism and the Nation-State: The Karen in

Burma and Thailand," in Gehan Wijeyewardene, *Ethnic Groups across National Boundaries in Mainland Southeast Asia* (Singapore: Institute of Southeast Asian Studies, 1990), 110–12.

4. David B. Knight, "Geographical Perspectives on Self-Determination," in *Political Geography: Recent Advances and Future Directions*, ed. Peter Taylor and John House (London: Croom Helm, 1984), 180; Colin H. Williams, *National Separatism* (Vancouver: University of British Columbia Press, 1982), 5.

5. Michael E. Brown, "Causes and Implications of Ethnic Conflict," in *Ethnic Conflict and International Security*, ed. Michael E. Brown (Princeton, N.J.: Princeton University Press, 1993), 6; Anthony D. Smith, *The Ethnic Revival* (Cambridge: Cambridge University Press, 1981), 9–10.

6. James Sterngold, "This Man Has a Dream. It's Most Un-Japanese," *New York Times*, August 19, 1994.

7. Celestine Bohlen, "Secession for Northern Italy Goes Forward, Symbolically," *New York Times*, August 22, 1996; Personal interview, June 10, 1992.

8. James Brooke, "White Flight in Brazil? Secession Caldron Boils," *New York Times*, May 12, 1993.

9. Ted Robert Gurr, *Minorities at Risk: A Global View of Ethnopolitical Conflicts* (Washington, D.C.: U.S. Institute of Peace Press, 1993), 3.

10. Nancie L. Gonzalez, "Conflict, Migration, and the Expression of Ethnicity: Introduction," in Nancie L. Gonzalez and Carolyn S. McCommon, *Conflict, Migration and the Expression of Identity* (Boulder, Colo.: Westview, 1989), 6; David Binder and Barbara Crossette, "As Ethnic Wars Multiply, U.S. Strives for a Policy," *New York Times*, February 7, 1993.

11. Gurr, *Minorities at Risk*, 5.

12. Kamal S. Shehadi, *Ethnic Self-Determination and the Break-up of States* (London: Brasseys, 1993), 12.

13. Shehadi, *Ethnic Self-Determination*, 22.

14. Shehadi, *Ethnic Self-Determination*, 3; Hurst Hannum, *Autonomy, Sovereignty, and Self-Determination: The Accomodation of Conflicting Rights* (Philadelphia: University of Pennsylvania Press, 1990), 454–55.

15. Shehadi, *Ethnic Self-Determination*, 9, 59.

16. Robert K. Schaeffer, *Power to the People: Democratization around the World* (Boulder, Colo.: Westview, 1997), 182–85.

17. Robert Kaylor, "Hanoi Still Aches A Decade After Victory," in *Vietnam Ten Years After*, ed. Robert Emmet Long (New York: Wilson, 1986), 9, 11; John Tagliabue, "Foreign Workers Leaving Eastern Germany," *New York Times*, October 11, 1991.

18. Schaeffer, *Power to the People*, 182–85.

19. Konrad H. Jarausch, *The Rush to German Unity* (Oxford: Oxford University Press, 1994), 24; Thomas W. Simons Jr., *Eastern Europe in the Postwar World* (New York: St. Martin's, 1991), 209.

20. David B. Walker, "Germany: Confronting the Aftermath of Reunification," *Current History* (November 1992): 359; John Tagliabue, "Bonn Wants Russia to Restore Republic for Ethnic Germans," *New York Times*, January 11, 1992.

21. John Tagliabue, "Foreign Workers Leaving Eastern Germany," *New York Times*, October 11, 1992.

22. Nicholas Eberstadt, *Korea Approaches Reunification* (Armonk, N.Y.: Sharpe, 1995), 2.

23. Stephen Kinzer, "With Unity's Euphoria Gone, Germans in East Feel Scorned," *New York Times*, April 18, 1992; Craig R. Whitney, "Germans, 5 Years Later: Bitter and Still Divided," *New York Times*, January 24, 1995; Stephen Kinzer, "A Wall of Resentment Now Divides Germany," *New York Times*, October 14, 1994; Craig R. Whitney, "Germans Find Unity May Mean Long-Term Change and Sacrifices," *New York Times*, December 26, 1993.

24. T. Louise Brown, *War and Aftermath in Vietnam* (London: Routledge, 1991), 268–69; James W. Morley, "Politics in Transition," in *Vietnam Joins the World*, ed. James W. Morley and Masashi Nisihara (Armonk, N.Y.: Sharpe, 1997), 25.

25. Schaeffer, *Power to the People*, 156–57.

26. David W. P. Elliott, "Vietnam Faces the Future," *Current History* (December 1995): 414.

27. Schaeffer, *Power to the People*, 157.

28. Walker, "Germany: Confronting the Aftermath of Reunification," 360–61.

29. Schaeffer, *Power to the People*, 132–49.

30. Sheryl WuDunn, "Taiwan Proposes to Drop a Convenient Fiction, Risking the Wrath of China," *New York Times*, July 4, 1997.

31. Nicholas D. Kristof, "Adrift, Taiwan Loses Urge for Firmer Footing," *New York Times*, December 25, 1992; Nicholas D. Kristof, "Taiwan's Desire for Mainland is Dwindling," *New York Times*, February 5, 1989.

32. Jaushieh Joseph Wu, *Taiwan's Democratization: Forces behind the New Momentum* (Hong Kong: Oxford University Press, 1995), 150.

33. Edward A. Gargan, "China Breaks the Ice to Offer Political Talks With Taiwan," *New York Times*, February 25, 1998.

34. Patrick E. Tyler, "Macao and Taiwan Next, Says China Chief," *New York Times*, July 2, 1997.

35. Ian Jeffries, *Socialist Economies and the Transition to the Market: A Guide* (London: Routledge, 1993), 205; Schaeffer, *Power to the People*, 156.

36. Warren Hoge, "Irish Island Unites in Commerce, Even before an Accord," *New York Times*, May 7, 1998; James F. Clarity, "New Political Structure for Northern Ireland Emerging at Talks," *New York Times*, February 9, 1998; Warren Hoge, "Irish Talks Produce an Accord to Stop Decades of Bloodshed With Sharing of Ulster Power," *New York Times*, April 11, 1998.

37. Warren Hoge, "Irish Votes, North and South, Give Rousing 'Yes' to Peace," *New York Times*, May 24, 1998.

38. Hoge, "Irish Island Unites in Commerce"; Maura Sheehan, Hamilton Douglas, and Ronnie Munck, "Political Conflict, Partition, and the Underdevelopment of the Irish Economy," in *Political Violence in Northern Ireland: Conflict and Conflict Resolution*, ed. Alan O'Day (Westport, Conn.: Praeger, 1997), 127; Warren Hoge, "For Britain and Ireland, One Goal: Peace in Ulster Now, Imposed If Necessary," *New York Times*, March 15, 1998.

39. Robert Bowker, *Beyond Peace: The Search for Security in the Middle East* (Boulder, Colo.: Rienner, 1996), 68, 75; Yezid Sayigh, "The Armed Struggle and Palestinian Nationalism," in *The PLO and Israel: From Armed Conflict to Political Solution, 1964–1994*, ed. Avraham Sela and Moshe Ma'oz (New York: St. Martin's, 1997), 32.

40. Connie Bruck, "The Wounds of Peace," *The New Yorker*, October 14, 1996, 72.

41. Michael C. Hudson, "The Clinton Administration and the Middle East: Squandering the Inheritance?" *Current History* (February 1994): 55; Bruck, "The Wounds of Peace," 72–73; Don Peretz, *The Arab-Israeli Dispute* (New York: Facts on File, 1996), 101–02.

42. Thomas L. Friedman, "Dividing a Homeland," *New York Times*, September 15, 1993; Alan Cowell, "Hurdle to Peace: Parting the Mideast's Waters," *New York Times*, October 10, 1993.

43. Lenard J. Cohen, "Bosnia and Herzegovina: Fragile Peace in a Fragmented State," *Current History* (March 1996); 107, 112; Lenard J. Cohen, "Whose Bosnia? The Politics of Nation-Building," *Current History* (March 1998): 103.

44. Mihailo Crnobrnja, *The Yugoslav Drama* (Montreal: McGill-Queen's University Press, 1996), 275–76; Cohen, "Bosnia and Herzegovina," 108.

45. Cohen, "Whose Bosnia?" 109–10; Cohen, "Bosnia and Herzegovina," 110.

46. Karl E. Meyer, "Some Divided Nations Do Find a Way to Stand," *New York Times*, May 23, 1998.

47. William E. Schmidt, "Peace is Topic, But Doubts Are the Issue in Ulster," *New York Times*, December 5, 1993.

48. Mark A. Heller, "The Israeli-Palestinian Accord: An Israeli View," *Current History* (February 1994): 56; Peretz, *The Arab-Israeli Dispute*, 106.

49. Bowker, *Beyond Peace*, 75.

50. Bruck, "The Wounds of Peace," 74; Susan Hattis Rolef, "Israel's Policy toward the PLO: From Rejection to Recognition," in Sela and Ma'oz, *The PLO and Israel*, 256.

51. David Binder, "U.S. Policymakers on Bosnia Admit Errors in Opposing Partition in 1992," *New York Times*, August 29, 1993.

52. Cohen, "Whose Bosnia?" 104.

53. Shehadi, *Ethnic Self-Determination*, 51.

54. Larry Rohter, "Puerto Rico Votes to Retain Status as Commonwealth," *New York Times*, November 13, 1993.

55. In 1993, more than 66 percent of Puerto Ricans believed that the Olympic team and Miss Universe contestant were "not negotiable" for statehood and that their elimi-

nation was "too high a price" to pay for admission to the union. Juan M. Garcia Passalac-qua, "The Puerto Rico Question Revisited," *Current History* (February 1998): 86.

56. Robert Reinhold, "A Century After Queen's Overthrow, Talk of Sovereignty Shakes Hawaii," *New York Times*, November 8, 1992.

57. Reinhold, "A Century after Queen's Overthrow."

58. Annie Nakao, "Sovereign Sisters," *San Francisco Chronicle-Examiner, Image Magazine*, June 20, 1993, 17.

59. New York Times, "Native Hawaiian Vote Favors Sovereignty," *New York Times*, September 14, 1996.

60. "The proposed Hawaiian government could ultimately mean something like se-cession, something more like an American Indian reservation or simply more native Hawaiian control," observed *New York Times* reporter Carey Goldberg. "Native Hawai-ians Vote in Ethnic Referendum," *New York Times*, July 23, 1996.

61. Anthony DePalma, "Canada Seeks Legal Advice on the Status of Quebec," *New York Times*, February 17, 1998.

62. "Native Hawaiian Vote Favors Sovereignty."

63. DePalma, "Canada Seeks Legal Advice on the Status of Quebec."

64. Lizette Alvarez, "Senate Is Lukewarm, But Some Seek Vote on Puerto Rico," *New York Times*, March 6, 1998; "Native Hawaiian Vote Favors Sovereignty."

65. Robert H. Jackson, *Quasi-States: Sovereignty, International Relations, and the Third World* (Cambridge: Cambridge University Press, 1990), 97–98.

66. Edward A. Gargan, "Filipina Foes Meet to End Muslim Revolt," *New York Times*, August 20, 1996; Schaeffer, *Power to the People*, 112–15.

67. See Lani Guinier, *The Tyranny of the Majority: Fundamental Fairness in Repre-sentative Democracy* (New York: Free Press, 1994).

68. David J. Bercuson, "Why Quebec and Canada Must Part," *Current History* (March 1995): 123.

69. Carl Sandburg, *Abraham Lincoln: The War Years* (New York: Harcourt, Brace, 1939), vol. 1, 131–32.

70. Martin Luther King Jr., *A Testament of Hope: The Essential Writings of Martin Luther King, Jr.*, ed. James M. Washington (San Francisco: Harper & Row, 1986), 97.

71. King, *A Testament of Hope*, 582–83, 586–88.

72. King, *A Testament of Hope*, 219–20.

73. David Welsh, "Domestic Politics and Ethnic Conflict," in Brown, *Ethnic Conflict and International Security*, 44.

74. Eric J. Hobsbawm, *Nations and Nationalism since 1780: Programme, Myth, Real-ity* (Cambridge: Cambridge University Press, 1990), 60–61.

INDEX

ABOUT THE AUTHOR

Robert Schaeffer is a professor of global sociology at San Jose State University. He is the editor of *War in the World-System* (1990) and author of *Warpaths: The Politics of Partition* (1990), *Understanding Globalization: The Social Consequences of Political, Economic, and Environmental Change* (1997), and *Power to the People: Democratization Around the World* (1997). With co-author Torry Dickinson, he is currently writing a book about global changes that affect work around the world.